NEW PERSPECTIVES
ON
INDIAN ENGLISH WRITINGS

NEW PERSPECTIVES
ON
INDIAN ENGLISH WRITINGS

Edited by
Malti Agarwal

ATLANTIC
PUBLISHERS & DISTRIBUTORS (P) LTD

Published by

ATLANTIC

PUBLISHERS & DISTRIBUTORS (P) LTD

B-2, Vishal Enclave, Opp. Rajouri Garden,
New Delhi-110027
Phones : 25413460, 25429987, 25466842

Sales Office
7/22, Ansari Road, Darya Ganj,
New Delhi-110002
Phones : 23273880, 23275880, 23280451
Fax : 91-11-23285873
web : www.atlanticbooks.com
e-mail : info@atlanticbooks.com

ISBN 81-269-0689-8

Printed in India
at Nice Printing Press, Delhi

Editorial

The world is today progressing by leaps and bounds. It has opened up new vistas of knowledge for modern man. But at the same time, the modern man is passing through terrible ordeal. The contemporary literature written the world over reflects the agony, despair and traumatic experiences of this suffering young generation. The creative artists—male as well as female—give voice to the plight of the average man who is fighting boldly at every front. Indian writers writing in English throw prismatic light on the dilemmas, faced by the average modern man.

Indian writing in English initially emerged as an offshoot of English literature but soon it established itself as different from all other literatures. It, gradually, became a powerful medium of expression in the hands of the Indian writers to relate their native feelings in alien medium. Today it holds a place of its own in World Literatures and appears perfectly as indigenous literature.

Indian writers writing in English have attempted all major literary genres—fiction and poetry being in the forefront since the novel and poetry suit the Indian temper the most. The Indian English Literature with a history of almost a century is richly dipped in the hues of native cultural ethos. The works of writers like Mulk Raj Anand, Raja Rao, R.K. Narayan, Nirad Chaudhary, Manohar Malgonkar etc. are acclaimed as masterpieces. Most of these Indian writers are bilinguals and are sometimes nostalgic for their mother tongue. The literary gamut of these veteran writers is the most impressive, outstanding and enduring contribution in Indianizing the

English language. These writers have at times used native idioms and also words from their own vernacular to capture the true picture of the Indian society, rocked by various fundamental issues such as social dichotomy, cultural hegemony, clash between ethnic groups, clash between eastern and western ideologies etc.

In the modern literary ambit writers like Arun Joshi, Vikram Seth, Salman Rushdie, Amitav Ghosh, Khushwant Singh, Chaman Nahal and others hold the centre place. Among women fictionists, Kamala Markandaya, Anita Desai, Shashi Deshpande, Nayantara Sahgal, Kamala Das, Shobha De, Arundhati Roy, Manju Kapur, Gita Mehta and many others have made notable contribution and have won international acclaim. Among the twentieth century Indian English poets, there are poets like Arun Kolatkar (who died recently), Ramanujan, R. Parthasarthy, Jayant Mahapatra, Shiv. K. Kumar, Nissim Ezekiel and Kamala Das who write in English but are conscious of their Indianness. In the wake of globalization, the western culture imported to India, corrodes the indigenous values. The Indian writers, through their creations, protect the native culture from this invasion. This is the quintessence of the whole Indian Literature in English.

The present anthology consists of thirty-eight critical papers which discuss in detail the major themes in Indian English writings. The first paper by Maha Nand Sharma highlights the worth of the traditional poetry whereas the second essay by S.K. Sharma serves as an introduction to modern Indian poetry in English. Next three essays deal with the Pulitzer Prize winner Jhumpa Lahiri's literary acumen as manifested in her works—*Interpreter of Maladies* and *The Namesake*.

Indian women writers writing in English have raised their voice against gender bias and male chauvinism in the patriarchal Indian society. Sudarshan Sharma and Anuradha Verma in their papers dwell on this theme as reflected in Manju Kapur's novels. A bulk of papers in the book discuss Shashi Deshpande's women protagonists, as portrayed by her in her novels and short stories as oppressed and marginalized in many domestic and social matters. My own article sketches the Indian woman's journey from self-effacement to selfhood with a particular reference to Kamala Markandaya's Rukmani and Shashi Deshpande's Sarita. V.K. Singhal, Sharda Jain and Alka Rani in their papers discuss various issues related to Kamala Markandaya's novels. The next three research papers study in depth the poetry of Kamala Das who is chiefly known for raising a voice of protest against exploitation of women. The volume includes an article on Arundhati Roy's *The God of Small Things* that has added a new feather to the cap of Indian English writings.

Nowadays efforts are being made to analyse the creative works in the light of Indian aesthetic theories. Articles contributed by Ajai Sharma, Kshama Gupta and Mamta Sharma are attempts done in this direction. Besides, there are articles on Bhabani Bhattacharya, Arun Joshi and Manohar Malgonkar, highlighting various features of their writings. The most creditable thing for the Indian English Literature is the emergence of new talent. The present volume includes papers on emerging literary figures, namely Gita Mehta, Indira Ganesan, Bharati Mukherjee, Krishna Srinivas and Leila Seth. Papers on Girish Karnad, Ruth Prawer Jhabvala, Nissim Ezekiel and Nayantara Sahgal are other attractions of the present book.

It is hoped that this volume will be of great help to researchers, students and teachers of English Literature in developing a proper understanding of these authors and their works.

MALTI AGARWAL

Contents

1 Revolution Through Traditional Poetry

Maha Nand Sharma

The idea of revolution through traditional poetry may seem to be utopian to modern society sunk deep in the mire of materialism and inured to Quixotic experiments with free verse. Since nothing but actuality alone appeals to the modern temper, the example of *Rama Charit Manas* by Tulsi Das, so close to Indian consciousness, must convince the people of the revolutionising power of traditional poetry. *Rama Charit Manas* which popularised the spiritual values of self-sacrifice made by the members of Lord Rama's family, left upon Indian society a revolutionary impact which harmoniously united the joint families in the villages for four hundred years till the dawn of freedom in 1947. After 1947, the whirlwind of global materialism, brought about by industrial and technological advance, began to destroy the whole fabric of our civilization and culture. To the counter-action against materialism by Tulsi Das, the poets of English, Tamil, Hindi and other Indian languages—Aurobindo, Tagore, Sarojini Naidu, Subramanyam Bharti, Maithili Sharan Gupt, Ayodhya Singh Upadhyaya and Jaya Shankar Prasad—also lent their force during the British period. In England also, Milton, Wordsworth and Tennyson continued persistently to stem the tide of materialism through their traditional poetry. Why did their poetry succeed in at least impeding the tide? Why is the current poetry of post-colonialism in India failing totally to halt this tide which has changed our country into a jungle of violence, cut-throat competition and ruinous ostentation? These are the questions I propose to answer in this article.

The first cause of the failure of the present poetry to reform society is the paucity, if not the total absence, of spiritual content in it. Like the novel, the current poetry is existentialist in its content. It deals with what exists in the present, and not with what should ideally exist. Even when it hints at what should ideally exist, its ideal is materialistic, not spiritual. It refuses to receive inspiration from the past. Hence its failure to elevate the individual and the society which is made up of individuals.

It may be argued that poetry has to move with the times. No! Poetry has a higher goal of elevating the people from what they are. With this object, it has to swim against the current of the times since human nature in all times is more inclined to materialism than spirituality.

The aim of poetry to elevate the people spiritually can be achieved by metre which is the backbone of traditional poetry. The present-day poetry, mostly in free verse, fails to elevate the readers permanently and thus mould their character because it totally lacks the permanently elevating or character-moulding quality which metrical poetry has. The system of stressed and unstressed syllables in feet and enjambment and caesura lends the lines an in-built music. The lines sing themselves. Their inherent music helps the reader retain them in his memory and enjoy singing them very often in his idle moments—in the bathroom and while lying in bed 'in vacant or in pensive mood.' As a result, the lines, full of spiritual ideas, sink deep into his consciousness permanently. They become an enduring part of his personality and uplift his character. This is the process by which metrical poetry shapes and elevates the character of individuals and brings about a spiritual revolution.

Poetry, couched in free verse, cannot serve this purpose. It may appeal to the ear when the poet himself recites it according to his own system. But since it has no regular and universally accepted system of stress, fall etc., it does not sing itself. It loses all its music and reads almost like prose when it is read by the reader. Even when it expresses an elevating idea, it does not endure in the reader's memory for lack of in-built music. Needless to point out that the common ground, shared by the reader with the traditional poet in scores of rhetorical and other devices evolved over hundreds of years, helps the reader understand and appreciate the beauty of traditional poetry far more than that of free verse poetry which is as free as the wind and knows no rules. All these are the reasons why the writers of free verse have not been so enduring and popular as those of metrical verse such as those recounted in the first paragraph of this article.

It is often argued that the constraints of metre and rhyme obstruct the direct expression of the idea to be conveyed in poetry. If direct expression alone—and not the clear expression coupled with beauty—is the aim of the art if that is poetry, why not use prose? If directness of expression is to be achieved in poetry at the cost of music and other ingredients of beauty, poetry will lose its appeal and enduring quality. The words in prose or free verse do not stick to our mind permanently.

It is not merely a chance that no epic has been written in free verse. There is a convincing explanation for this limitation of free verse. In an epic there are occasions when bare facts with no emotional or philosophical tinge have to be presented. On such occasions the music of metre sustains the interest of the readers.

Tagore with his free verse in *Gitanjali* may be cited as an example to deny the importance of metrical poetry. Tagore is, no doubt, a great poet who sustains the interest of the readers by his images drawn from nature. But there are portions in *Gitanjali* which read like prose and in which the interest of the reader flags. In fact, in the oft-quoted pieces such as "Where knowledge is free..." the rhythm, a crucial element of the metre, prevents them from monotony. Great as Tagore is despite the absence of prosody, he would have been greater still and equalled Aurobindo, Milton and Wordsworth if he had acquired metrical skill.

The opponents of traditional poetry hold that the required recurrence of the same type of foot imparts monotony to metrical verse. It is not so. All that the rules of prosody demand is the predominance, not the omnipresence of base foot. The rules allow considerable scope for variations. With such variations and the selection of appropriate metre, a poet can project through his poems the atmosphere he wants to create. Tennyson's *Charge of the Light Brigade* and Fitzgerald's translation of Rubayyat of Omar Khayyam illustrate the point. In *Charge of the Light Brigade*, Tennyson conveys the atmosphere of fighting admirably by varying the syllabic length of lines and the kinds of feet in them. On the other hand, Fitzgerald, in his translation, presents suitably the atmosphere of love, drinking and indolence and the eat-drink-and-be-merry philosophy underlying it, through the slowly and smoothly moving iambic pentametric lines with few variations of feet.

It is worth noting that traditional or metrical verse lingers in our mind longer and in larger portions when it is written or printed and read aloud than when it is heard. When heard, it passes through one's ear and goes out through the other's, the listener's mind retaining only its short snatches here and there. As against this, more mental, visual, vocal and aural effort is involved in reading and singing aloud the metrical verse. Hence the mind retains the lines longer and in larger proportions. Also, since the written or printed lines of verse are at our disposal as long as, or whenever, we like, we can 'chew and digest' them. Their assimilation also helps us retain them longer.

It is now clear that the written or printed traditional or metrical verse is more enduring than free verse or music in our memory and even throughout the centuries in the memory of mankind. It has far greater capacity for uplifting human character and bringing about spiritual revolution in society.

Aristotle classifies arts into five categories—(i) Poetry; (ii) Music; (iii) Painting; (iv) Sculpture and (v) Architecture. Poetry is superior to the remaining four because it includes within itself the picturesqueness of the last three graphic arts and the musicality of the fine art of music also. Free verse deprives poetry largely of the essential trait of music which metrical verse invariably has. It has been elaborated how the in-built musicality of traditional or metrical verse plays revolutionary role in the character-building of the individual and the society.

Needless to say that character-building should begin at the formative stages of childhood and boyhood. This necessitates the introduction of metre as early as possible in the career of students of Higher Secondary stage which is the best stage for the teaching of English metre. Both the teaching and the learning of metre will be more effective if the teachers at all stages, particularly at this and the earlier stages, are well trained in phonetics. The habit of pronouncing the syllables with suitable stress on the right ones will be imbibed by the students also and will help them follow the metre at the Higher Secondary stage with keen interest.

To sum up, the spiritual revolution in the Indian rural families, brought about by the divine, traditional or metrical poetry of Tulsi Das in *Rama Charit Manas,* continued for about four hundred years till 1947. During the British period, the spiritual poets of English, Tamil, Hindi and other Indian languages—poets predominantly metrical—lent their force to this revolution. Great poets in English also tried to halt the advance of materialism through their spiritual and traditional or metrical poetry. The two questions answered in this paper are: (i) Why could their poetry elevate the people spiritually and impede this advance? (ii) Why has the current post-colonial poetry in India failed? The first cause of the failure is lack of spiritual content and refusal to receive inspiration from the past. The present-day poetry does not swim against the materialistic current of the modern age. It does not elevate people from the mire of materialism. The in-built music in metrical lines imbeds them in our memory with the result that we sing them again and again in our moments of leisure. As a result, the lines and their spiritual content become an inalienable part of our consciousness or inner personality, and uplift our character. By elevating the character of individuals and of society through them, traditional or metrical poetry brings about a spiritual revolution in society. Free verse which is not in itself musical cannot achieve this end. Needless to say that the rhetorical devices which the reader shares with the traditional poet enable him to understand and appreciate the traditional poetry still better. The aim of poetry as art is not only direct expression but beauty also. Mere direct expression which the supporters of free verse find lacking in traditional poetry is the aim of prose. Epics have been written in traditional or metrical verse only, not in free verse. Tagore who uses free verse in *Gitanjali* would have been as great as Aurobindo if he had used traditional verse. Traditional verse allows variations enough to prevent monotony. Through variations, it can create the atmosphere to be conveyed. Written traditional verse lingers in our mind longer and in larger proportions than the one merely heard. It is because more effort is required in reading and singing aloud the written or printed metrical verse. It can be easily chewed and digested because it is at our disposal whenever, and as long as, we like. Its assimilation also helps us retain it longer. Since metrical verse is more enduring, metre should be introduced at the Higher Secondary stage, along with elementary phonetics in the earlier classes.

2 Modern Indian Poetry in English: A Note

Shrawan K. Sharma

There is no permanent aesthetics, poetics or standard of literature in general and poetry in particular. Similarly there is no permanent account of great pieces of literature or poetry. It is so due to the fluctuating process of creativity. There are five aspects—creation (*srashti*), preservation (*stithi*), transformation (*samhar*), diffusion (*tirobhava*) and grace (*anugraha*)—involved in the composition of a poem. Here creation is aesthetic intuition that charges the poet, preservation denotes objects of inspiration which captivate the mind of the poet, transformation is indication of expression which is the depth of the poet, diffusion is resulting stimulation which diffuses illusion and finally grace which recognizes the universal rhythm (Parivrajak, 65). Obviously, all these aspects are not found in every poem. It is important to take into account the fact that a poem which has these aspects offers truth, meaning and knowledge; a poem lacking them is not a poem but merely a verse. The ability of recognizing the universal rhythm takes place in a particular state of mind of the poet. There are five states of the mind and the mind changes over from one state to another at a fast speed. Sometimes it is sensitive and agitative (*kshipt*), sometimes insensitive and dull (*moodh*), sometimes interruptive and disturbed (*vikshipt*), sometimes concentrative and pointed (*ekagra*) and sometimes meditative (*niruddha*), *i.e.* a state of total stillness. Of the five, meditative state is the highest. It can further be divided into two sub-states: conscious (*samprajnata*) and trans-conscious (*asamprajnata*). The first is the state of the poet as he is able to concentrate his mind on gross as well as the subtle elements of nature (earth, water, light, etc.). He can know the real nature and character of various objects and materials of nature and achieve his purpose for himself and society, and the second is of the yogi. As far as the second state is concerned, it is the final state of yogis. In this state a yogi becomes thoughtless. It is so due to the changing tastes and the challenges of new writings against the status of the old. It is artists who generally form cultural taste which is passed on or transferred through new ideas to critics and these critics finally prepare and advocate for what is worth accepting. As far as the literary standards, theories and principles of poets are concerned, they are the reflections of their views and aesthetics which are modified and promoted by editors, anthologists and other such promoters according to their own tastes.

Indian verse in English did not seriously exist before independence. The simple reason of this indictment is that it was untouched by the reality within and without. The poets fail to touch the erosion of faith and the disintegration of the modern consciousness. Not only this, they also fail to express the social and political reality around them, drought, famine, plague and colonial exploitation. The Indian poet in English feels alienated by his language from the environment and from a living idiom. One may ask, what do we mean by modern poetry in India? Is it an echo of poetry written in the India of Pre-Independence, England and America? The English poetry in India is a branch of poetry written in the India of Pre-Independence, England and America. Is this branch, however, merely a development of the parent trunk, or it is unique and original in itself? The comparison shows that there is no significant identity between the major poets either on thematic or on formal grounds. We do not find that Nissim Ezekiel, Ramanujan, R. Parthasarthy and others are concerned with the romantic flights of the Indian English poets. They are not concerned also with religion and modern man in the way that

Eliot is, or with Art and Culture in the manner of Pound or with the norms of nature as in Frost, or with the Romantic conception of poetry as in Yeats. The real relevance of the modern poetry in English must be found in its relation to Indian experience and history. In relation to modern or say contemporary Indian English poetry scene, it is important to note that the editors, anthologists and promoters involved in publication are the poets themselves and hence there are bleak chances of modification by others. They have reflected their views on contemporary poetry in their reviews, introductions, editorials and articles. These personalities are the poets, critics and editors. The representative figures who have played an important role in preparing the canon of contemporary Indian English poetry are Nissim Ezekiel, Saleem Peeradina, P. Lal, V.K. Gokak, Gouri Deshpande, Pritish Nandy, Shiv K. Kumar, Daruwalla, Jussawalla and Parthasarthy.

Among these new crusaders struggling for this disillusioned affirmation and fresh poetic sensibilities, Nissim Ezekiel is one of the most important names. He inaugurated a new era of Indian English poetry by writing of the demands of the present-day world, bringing into play a modern sensibility confronting the confusion, bewilderment and disillusion of the time, while using a modern idiom without the archaism and jangling rhyme scheme of the earlier poets. Ezekiel believes that poetry contributes to man's knowledge of himself. He holds that a poem must strive to fuse thought and emotion into images that have moral and philosophical implications [King 78]. As a result, these images make poetry a 'precise and exact' form of discourse. He continues that a poem which does not have truth, meaning and knowledge is an exercise in fiasco. Such a poem has no worth. To speak of truth, meaning and knowledge in poetry does not return to versified feeling and ideas but does mean that it will be more immediately, concretely related to society and situations, and more moral and spiritual in its tendency than art which aims at purity or non-poetic statements about itself and the nature of imagination. Ezekiel requires that:

> Poetry be grounded in reality, reflection, experience and have a logical discursive form. Poetry is seen as a different more concentrated, economical, precise kind of communication about a person's felt and considered experience of life. Poetry is not just formalized, ornamented, rhetorical expression; it results from a fusion of thought and feeling into precise images which give expression to the contemporary mind as experienced and reflected upon by the poet. This requires the discipline to create new forms of precise articulation and as far as possible the modern poet should have an intellectual framework which integrates his or her work [Sharma 101].

It is interesting to note that on the one hand Ezekiel wants the economy and precision, aesthetic distance and unified vision of the major early-twentieth century poets while on the other hand he wants poetry invested with moral awareness, truth, self-knowledge and mature experience. He holds:

"Redeemed with prayer
The aspiration
Found again
I start again
With secret faults concealed no more.

For hours and days the singing voice
To utter praise
A bit of land
A woman too
Grapes or figs
And metaphors
Insight illumination
Secret faults concealed no more."

Although Ezekiel's view of poetry is influenced by his own spiritual yearning and intellectual awareness, it was extended by other poets to further areas of social, political and cultural concern. Parthasarthy in particular seems to extend the range of Ezekiel's criticism into other areas. Parthasarthy's poetry has an unusually dense compression, economy and reliance on imagery drawn from his environment which is used symbolically. The poetry reflects personal self-knowledge, emotion reflected upon, and aims at maturity of vision; experience is placed within a dominant intellectual framework. Parthasarthy sees poetry arising from personal experience which is reflected upon; thought and feelings are fused into concise, precise images which are used to communicate knowledge (King, 80).

Parthasarthy sees his approach to the national concern about recovering a traditional culture as essential to overcome a sense of alienation from his environment, past and culture. Contemporary Indian English literature must show an awareness of the physical and human landscape of India and be involved in the local life. It should find a language, form and attitudes which express contemporary life. Ramanujan's repossession, through his poetry, of the past of his family, and of his sense of himself as a distillation of past is a possible model for how to use one's own voice. Daruwalla's sensibility is acutely aware of and committed to present -day socio-politico-cultural reality. He is conscious of his Indianness, which reflects a crisis of identity. Whereas early poets were interested in Indian legend, the contemporary poets arc concerned with finding a personal language. They, like Ramanujan, have 'turned language into an artifact' and like Kolatkar, Mehrotra and Kumar, used images as 'the kernel' of the poem. Parthasarthy's *Rough Passage* fuses personal crisis and cultural crisis into a series of linked, precise, compressed images which offer truth, meaning and knowledge. He claims that since 1971 his poems are close in style, content and irony to Tamil verse. He seeks in tradition a means of overcoming the effects of a western education which disrupted his roots in a tradition. This is a sophisticated, nuanced, complex version of regional nationalism in which the individual is to find his or her identity in terms of a specific culture. Now poetry has become conspicuous by being increasingly concise as it is progressing towards metaphor:

> "Daruwalla is said to pare language to the bone: 'images are concrete and exact'. Ezekiel's poems show a 'keen, analytical mind trying to explore and communicate on a personal level feelings of loss and deprivation'. In Kolatkar's 'the boat ride' imagination and reality are 'fused'. Kumar is praised for 'ironic humour' and his imagery and nostalgia

are mentioned. In Mahapatra's poems 'the economy of the phrasing and startling images' recall classical Sanskrit. Mehrotra piles images 'one on top on another'" (Nayak & Narayan, 1).

Critics are of the opinion that these views, to some extent, echo the views of New Critics and fail to make a new advancement about the nature of poetry. This seems to be a misleading opinion. In fact, the views of contemporary Indian English poetry seem to formulate specific goals unlike those of the New Critics who prefer form and purity to meaning. It is remarkable to note that contemporary Indian English poetry echoes the characteristics of poetry as defined by the Sanskrit acharyas. These acharyas mention certain features of poetry which lead to offer meaning. They preferred meaning to any other aspect of poetry. According to Bharat, the phrasal organization of poetry should be delightful, easily comprehensible for the better understanding of knowledge. Vedavyasa in the *Agnipurana* defines poetry as the combination of phrases coupled with *alamkaras* and informed with *gunas*, conveys the desired meaning in brief. Bhamah defines poetry as the togetherness of both word and meaning *shabdarthau sahitau kavyam*. Dandi, borrowing the phrase from Vyasa, has described the phrasal organization, conveying the desired meaning, as the body of poetry. The credit for more identification of the character of poetry attaches to Vaman who in the Vrittis states the word *kavya* as suggestive of that union of word and meaning which is cultured with *gunas* and *alamkaras*. Anandvardhana, the renowned exponent of the *Dhvani Siddhanta* aims at offering the meaning by complete transformation of the word, partial transformation of the word, suggestiveness of subject, suggestiveness of *rasa* and suggestiveness of *alamkara*. Kuntaka, the propounder of *Vakrokti Siddhanta,* following the line of Bhamah, holds that *kavya* is *Vakrokti* which consists in the delightful union of both word and meaning which depends upon the poetic function of a poet. It is also recognized as an embellishment, the physical constituents of poetry. Thereafter appears on the literary scene the great Mammat who has synthesized, in his own way, the enunciation of the previous canonists saying *tadadoshau shabdarthau sagunavanalankkritih punah kwapi* that is, *kavya* is the union of word and meaning which is devoid of *doshas*, is charged with *gunas* and may be somewhere bereft of *alamkara*. Lastly, we arrive at Panditaraja Jagannatha's definition, *ramaniyartha-pratipadakah shabdah kavyam*. That is, poetry is word, enunciative of charming meaning.

Contemporary Indian English poetry has developed along two main lines. There is the verse of social consciousness in which the poet is trying to make some adjustment to difficult political and economic conditions. Then there is the verse that seems to derive its inspiration from the modernist British and American poets. Generally this verse is cryptic and difficult in its rebellion against the subject matter and form of the immediate past. But it has variety, with its subject drawn not only from the contemporary social world but also from the mental and emotional life of the individual.

I must, however, point out that this revolt against the style and the subject matter of the past has not been an exercise in egoistic aggrandizement. It has actually been compelled, subconsciously and imperceptibly perhaps by the irresistible pressures of the spirit of the age. Such rejections and quests have been everywhere, by all the western writers. The loss of faith, the failure of the conventional ideas and the bleakness of future that haunted the western writer after First World War and even for the later decades, became a subject of concern later. Despair is universal over the question who everyone is. It is necessary to know. We have got ourselves into a position where perhaps this is possible. Disillusion is irreducible; the inherited past is totally questioned. Now something is happening. So radically protests have been lodged that the negotiations are proving no longer sufficient. We are in the midst or at the beginning of the re-creation. The dialogue of the contemporary Indian English poetry is of the greatest interest. The post-independence poets write poetry dealing with time. Time is the central feature in the post-independence Indian English poetry. These poets categorically identify Arnoldian past and present and transmit the manifestations of time. Arnold identified past, present and future as forest glade, burning plain and wide glimmering sea. Here past is associated with values, present is associated with disillusionment and future is associated with the hope of better future. Accordingly the post-independence poetry can be classified as (i) the poetry of past oriented vision, (ii) the poetry of present oriented vision and (iii) the poetry of fashion. Let me accept at this moment that this classification is not a water-tight compartment. On different grounds, their place can be shifted from one category to another (Gupta). However, for the sake of convenience this classification has been made.

The poets of the first category transmit 'cultural pessimism' and are interested in their roots and feel like returning to their own linguistic tradition to write poetry. They seem to say that an Indian who is alienated from his own roots, culture and linguistic and literary tradition has lesser possibilities of writing poetry of much significance. A.K. Ramanujan, Parthasarthy and Kamala Das fall in this category. Ramanujan in his poem, *Conventions of Despair,* holds: "I must seek and will find/my particular hell only in my Hindu mind." Parthasarthy, advocating for the cultural past in *Rough Passage,* says: "How long can foreign poets/Provide the staple of your lines?/Turn inward. Scrape the bottom of your past." As far as Kamala Das is concerned, she gives bold treatment of sexual relations which is an offshoot of her Nayar background. B.K. Das appropriately concludes the approach of these poets: "while Ramanujan's mind seems to be perpetually busy probing the areas of strength and weakness of his Hindu heritage, Kamala Das highlights with boldness the sexual permissiveness and uninhibition rooted in her native culture.... Parthasarthy is caught in the dilemma of revealing his identity exposed to two cultures—the Indian and the Western" (95).

The second category includes Nissim Ezekiel, Jayanta Mahapatra, Kamala Das, Keki N. Daruwala, Arvind K. Mehrotra, Gauri Deshpande, Shiv K. Kumar, O.P. Bhatnagar and others. They express the present attitude. They, turning themselves from the indigenous tradition, make thought-provoking observation on reality around them responsibly. A number of social issues like rituals, love, marriage, family affairs, communal riots, corruption, black marketing, political acrobatics etc. have been dealt within their poetry. In their poetry there is the truth of acknowledging what is felt and experienced in its complexity, contradictions, pleasures, fears and disillusions without preconceived ideas of what poetry should say about the life and the poet.

The third category has versifiers rather than poets. They, in fact, lack poetic talent. Unlike the poets of the above two categories, they not only fail to create an awareness among the readers but also lack the capacity to sensitize them about the contemporary social issues. In a word, they are insensitive even to what they write and to the world around them. They fail to respond to the heat and famine-stricken hunger and thirst. They do not see the bloodshed of and injustice to the human race. They do not have a heart to weep for human cause in their so-called poems. Their poetry, a product of their own enthusiasm, is hardly of any worth. They are recognized as poets merely for the fact that they somehow or the other manage to get their poetry published. There is a crowd of such poets and their number is increasing day by day for obvious reasons, it would not be in the fitness of things to name them here. It is really an arduous task to find an English knowing person or say a teacher of English, who is not enjoying the luxury of being called a poet. Alas! It could be really so.

WORKS CITED

Das, B.K. *Modern Indo-English Poetry*. Bareilly: Prakash Book Depot, 1968.

Gupta, G. Balaram. "Contemporary Indian English Poetry." *International Journal of Aesthetics*.

King, Bruce. *Modern Indian Poetry in English*. New Delhi: Oxford University Press, 1987.

Nayak, M.K. and Shyamala Narayan. *Indian English Literature 1980-2000*. Delhi: Pencraft International, 2001.

Parivrajak, Swami Satypati. *Simplified Yoga for God Realization*, trans. Tulsiram. New Delhi, 1997.

Sharma, T.R. (ed.), *Nissim Ezekiel*. Meerut: Shalabh Publications, 1990.

3 Comic Touches in Jhumpa Lahiri's *Interpreter of Maladies: Stories of Bengal, Boston and Beyond*

Ramesh K. Srivastava

Jhumpa Lahiri's *Interpreter of Maladies: Stories of Bengal, Boston and Beyond* (1999) consists of a number of delightful stories of immigrant or expatriate Indians who have been on the move from India to U.K. and to the U.S.A. or are on a short visit to their native country, either way confronting surprising, even baffling cultural differences. Jhumpa Lahiri was born of Bengali parents in London, grew up in Rhodes Island, U.S.A., studied at Boston University, and as such must have had direct experience of these continents. It is quite natural that in her stories the two worlds of the East and the West have been brought together, as if in a simile—or even in a metaphysical conceit—which tease and please the reader. Whether they are set in Bengal or Boston, "these sublimely understated stories, spiced with humour and subtle detail, speak with universal eloquence to anyone who has ever fell the yearnings of exile or the emotional confusion of the outsider" (1999: *Blurb*).

The collection consists of nine short stories which begin in a journalistic manner, giving photographic details but mixed occasionally with Indian spices, and thereby converting the bland, seemingly-insignificant incidents into quite a palatable short story to the reader. By the time a reader has gone through each of the spell-binding stories, some common details become significant and are well-placed in their assigned slots, so that the entire story becomes an organic whole. Any one who has been abroad with open eyes and has minutely observed men and manners in U.K. and U.S.A. would find himself with Jhumpa Lahiri in a familiar territory but with a sense of regret that though he too had observed the described things, he could not write so well about them. The situations appear so familiar—and stripped of the particular names of individuals and locations, they appear so universal that such things could take place at anytime in any part of the world. If one were to attempt a one-line summary of some of these stories, it would appear no different from common news items in a vernacular newspaper some of which appear everyday. Shoba, married to Shukumar, has an illicit relationship with Gillian, and their marriage turns out to be, what the title of the story is—*A Temporary Matter*. Mr. Pirzada of East Pakistan remains perpetually worried about his seven daughters in the strife-torn Dacca in the early 1970's. Mr. Kapasi in *Interpreter of Maladies* begins to suffer from the malady of illusory romantic association with Mrs. Das—a tourist's wife—but which fizzles out within a few hours. Boori Ma's unreal yet romantic tales of her past end up in a personal loss and the theft of a wash basin necessitating the search for *A Real Durwan*. Whereas all attempts of Mr. Sen and Eliot's mother fail to motivate Mrs. Sen to learn driving in the U.S., a fresh fish becomes an irresistible temptation which ends up her driving venture in an accident. The mysterious, incurable disease of Bibi Haldar which could not be cured by all sorts of physicians was unwittingly yet successfully treated by an anonymous lover who made her pregnant. Mrs. Croft's lone struggle to survive till the age of one hundred three becomes a tale both educational and inspiring.

Most of the stories analyze the experiences, shocks and surprises which are encountered by the diasporas, and are marked by an undercurrent of pathos. For no expatriate, even if at the height of his professional success in the U.S., has been shown to be perfectly happy. It is the relative happiness and satisfaction, which keeps them tied to a foreign land by escaping from the difficulties of survival in one's native country with its monumental problems. A fragile attachment with the native people, native food, native culture, and even native dress and language makes them feel 'at home' in a place, which is thousands of miles away from home. Hence Jhumpa Lahiri writes some of her stories now and then in comic vein though it is not consistent and regular as one finds in R.K. Narayan, Khushwant Singh and Arundhati Roy. There are occasional flashes of comic touches in characterization, in descriptions, in images—particularly similes—in witty remarks, in strange perceptions of children, as also through depiction of cultural dissimilarities.

Jhumpa Lahiri introduces comic elements in character sketches by way of describing some of their oddities and eccentricities—a few of which each one of us has—but when such temperamental peculiarities outweigh the normal traits, they do give occasionally the impression of being caricatures. Mr. Pirzada, in *When Mr. Pirzada Comes to Dine,* is portrayed as a well-dressed Pakistani who comes to the United States on a Government scholarship to study the New England trees, misses his Dacca-based wife and children, and in order to get over the feeling of homesickness, frequently visits an Indian family in the U.S. For Jhumpa Lahiri, Mr. Pirzada, as seen through the eyes of a girl Lilia, was a compact man whose "feet were perpetually splayed, and his belly slightly wide, he nevertheless maintained an efficient posture, as if balancing in either hand two suitcases of equal weight. His ears were insulated by tufts of graying hair that seemed to block out the unpleasant traffic of life. He had thickly lashed eyes shaded with a trace of camphor, a generous mustache that turned up playfully at the ends, and a mole shaped like a flattened raisin in the very center of his left cheek" (28-29). Mr. Pirzada kept his pocket watch set to the local time in Dacca—eleven hours ahead of the U.S. time and usually placed it on a paper napkin of the dining table. He had seven daughters whose names began with letter A—Ayesha, Amira, Amina, Aziza—which always confused him. Even when he had gone back to Dacca after staying in the U.S., he wrote back that the names of his daughters were still confusing, as he could not remember them according to their age. At first, Mr. Pirzada's sketch appears to be exaggerated in which some of his physical features as well as his traits appear odd, distorted, and humorous. Comic phrases and images have liberally been employed to describe Mr. Pirzada's feet, belly, ears, eyes, mustache, and a mole on the check, a pocket watch, and seven daughters. Each described part by being humorous brings his character sketch to caricature, but what saves it from being unrealistic is the fact that the details have been observed and recorded by the child Lilia.

In addition, the way of describing things is quite pleasant. In *A Real Durwan*, Boori Ma was sixty-four "with hair in a knot no larger than a walnut, and she looked almost as narrow from the front as she did from the side" and "the only thing that appeared three-dimensional about Boori Ma was her voice: brittle with sorrows, as tart as curds, and shrill enough to grate meat from a coconut" (70). "A superb entertainer," Boori Ma was always narrating highly magnified version of her ancestral property, her daughter's marriage and her way of living. Any incident, any topic, any object of necessity or luxury could launch her into her imaginary past. Knowing well that her tales might not be believed as true, she would always punctuate her narrative with "Believe me, don't believe me." Her bathwater, she would say, "was scented with petals and attars. Believe me, don't believe me, it was a luxury you cannot dream" (73). Even though the story of Boori Ma is pathetic, for she has been a refugee two times—first as a Bengali refugee sent to Calcutta after India's partition, and now being a non-American doing menial jobs, Lahiri has made it fairly interesting by adding some humorous touches to it. Belonging to a lower caste and having no regular source of income for survival in the U.S., Boori Ma earns her livelihood by cleaning the stairwell and guarding the apartments where the Bengali people live. In return, she is given a place to keep her belongings and to sleep under the letter box. Not being allowed to sit on furniture when she went to the houses of others, "she crouched, instead, in doorways and half ways, and observed gestures and manners in the same way a person tends to watch traffic in a foreign city" (76). Miranda in "Sexy" had "silver eyes and skin as pale as paper, and the contrast with her hair, as dark and glossy as an espresso bean, caused people to describe her as striking, if not pretty. She had a narrow, egg-shaped head that rose to a prominent point. Her features, too, were narrow, with nostrils so slim that they appeared to have been pinched with a clothespin" (87). None of these characters could be taken completely as caricature, though certain features in their sketches have been disproportionately exaggerated. In a caricature, as in a cartoon, some traits of a character are highly exaggerated or prominently highlighted so that they cannot escape the notice of the reader. But whereas a cartoon is likely to be turned into satire, a caricature is purely for comic effects. Jhumpa Lahiri has taken up some traits or habits of these characters, such as, their shapes, their hair, their eyes, their skin and the way they talk and conduct themselves with others so that by making their personalities interesting, she makes her stories eminently readable.

Jhumpa Lahiri's descriptions too are occasionally marked by comic touches, which could be either in the form of a pictorial phrase or through short or extended images. Thus monkeys sat along the branches of trees in Orissa while their long gray tails "dangled like a series of ropes among the leaves" (47). Mrs. Das arranged her sunglasses "on top of her head like a tiara" (50). The plastic brush with which she stroked her hair "resembled an oval bed of nails" (54). Mrs. Dalai whose husband had purchased a washbasin which other residents did not have was rumored to be doing "nothing but wash her hands in her basin all day" (79). Miranda had a pair of black high heels "with buckles smaller than a baby's teeth" (92). Dev curved his hand around Miranda "like a big bracelet around her body" (94). There was around Goddess Kali a necklace which was "composed of bleeding heads, strung together like a popcorn chain" (96). These images are extremely uncommon, verging on the comic side, but with startling freshness. Lahiri could have selected for comparison numerous other objects, more appropriate, from her memory but the given examples carry an unmistakable comic strain to make the characters and descriptions lively and pleasant.

At many places, Lahiri makes a generous use of highly magnified details, comparing two objects quite disproportionate and unusual. Mrs. Sen, driving her car, "manipulated the automatic gear shift as if it were an enormous, leaky pen, and backed inch by inch out of the parking space" (120). If she passed a person, she waved, and if she happened to see a bird twenty feet ahead of her, "she beeped the horn with her index finger and waited for it to fly away" (120). On other occasions, her descriptions are so meticulous, her observations so sharp that the familiar and realistic by being tempered with her comic touches appears altogether new and marvelous. A letter received by Mrs. Sen from India was "a blue aerogramme, grainy to the touch, crammed with stamps showing a bald man at a spinning wheel, and blackened by postmarks" (121). Occasionally, a few comic strokes of her pen make the fictional characters or their features quite interesting. Bibi Haldar was "hotter than coals" (168). Mrs. Croft was "a tiny, extremely old woman. A mass of snowy hair was arranged like a small sack on top of her head" (177). Mrs. Croft stared at the letter, then handed it back to the narrator, carefully "gripping it with her fingers as if it were a dinner plate heaped with food instead of a sheet of paper" (178). The brief images in their casual forms present short yet sharp vignettes which remain so inextricably woven in the reader's memory that one chuckles in lonely hours as they invade the consciousness.

The innocence and simplicity of children can cause several humorous situations and hence their mischievous activities, their funny games, their casual conversation and queries, their understandings and misunderstandings, and even their seemingly wise and grave reflections have often been used by most writers for comic purposes. With their anxiety to know of things all around, children have a tendency to understand and to judge things in the light of their limited knowledge which creates sometimes distorted pictures, misunderstandings and eventually comic situations. Lilia puts in her mouth a chocolate, a box of which was given to her by Mr. Pirzada when he was in the

U.S. When she prayed for the safety and health of his family in Dacca, she only pretended to brush her teeth, for she genuinely feared that if she were really to brush her teeth and rinse her mouth containing the chocolate given by Mr. Pirzada, she "would somehow rinse the prayer out as well" (32). When Lilia had kept back a book on Dacca in the library, her teacher Mrs. Kenyon had checked "and lifted the book by the tip of its spine as if it were a hair clinging to my sweater" (33). For Eliot, Mrs. Sen's red sari leaped "like flames under her coat" (130). Rohin, a seven-year-old boy, told Miranda, "you're sexy." When she asked him the meaning of the word "sexy"—he said, "It means loving someone you don't know" and went on to explain, "That's what my father did. He sat next to someone he didn't know, someone sexy, and now he loves her instead of my mother" (107-108). In Mrs. Sen's, an eleven-year-old boy Eliot does not understand the significance of vermilion which married women use in India and the way he is made to understand appears interesting, even witty:

> Mrs. Sen applied a stroke of scarlet powder. When Eliot questioned its significance, Mrs. Sen replied, "I must wear the powder everyday," and that it was "for the rest of the days that I am married."
>
> "Like a wedding ring, you mean?"
>
> "Exactly, Eliot, exactly like a wedding ring. Only with no fear of losing it in the dishwater" (117).

An object, an incident or a situation can once in a while activate a child's imagination in such a way as to make him grave and reflective, and his reflections, his guesswork, his observations and conclusions appear funny to the adult imagination. The gravity of the children in such cases no longer remains the iron gravity of an adult mind but on being tempered with the children's ingrained simplicity and goodness, it turns into something pleasantly wonderful, tinged with a mild sense of humour. When there was a change in Mrs. Sen's behaviour towards Eliot's mother, the latter asked her son, whether he had noticed any change in Mrs. Sen's behaviour, and this is what Eliot reflects: "He didn't tell her [his mother] that Mrs. Sen paced the apartment, staring at the plastic-covered lampshades as if noticing them for the first time. He didn't tell her she switched on the television but never watched it or that she made herself tea but let it grow cold on the coffee table" (128). In *When Mr. Pirzada Came to Dine* the situation at one time was tense in Dacca in 1971. Lilia's father rang up some contacts in Calcutta to find out the latest development in the subcontinent, while at the same time arrangement was also being made for Mr. Pirzada to sleep in their house. Lilia, a child, found a serious concern about Mr. Pirzada's family in all of them—her father, her mother and Mr. Pirzada; she remembered "three of them operating during that time as if they were a single person, sharing a single meal, a single body, a single silence, and a single fear" (41). In the above cases, while the observations of the children are sharp, they have not made use of adjectives, adverbs or high-sounding epithets to describe the tension in Mrs. Sen or a heightened sense of anxiety about Mr. Pirzada's family among all the three people; instead, they have just taken a mental note of and described the outward behaviour of the concerned characters without any embellishment or comments but which in its simplicity tells eloquently of how much tension weighs in the house. The words used by the children are simple, carefully chosen and witty, and which evoke a smile and even a mild sense of humour with the face that in their simplicity, the children in both the stories have adopted such an intelligent mode of narration.

Children have also been known to indulge in mischievous activities and play the games of distorting words through change of spellings or by mispronunciations. Estha and Rahel indulge in such activities in Arundhati Roy's *The God of Small Things* by writing words backwards, by splitting a word in two or three parts, such as, "Lay. Ter" (1997: 146) or "Never. The Less" (1997: 55). One finds an occasional example of children's play with words in Jhumpa Lahiri's short stories. In "Sexy" the American children make fun of the Dixits. While waiting for the bus on the other side, they would say half audibly "The Dixits dig shit" (95), and then would burst out into laughter.

Cultural diversities have always been a good source of confusion and humour. The manners, the eating habits, the way of speaking including their different pronunciations have often been a good source of humour. Khushwant Singh has exploited this factor well in most of his short stories, particularly in *A Bride for the Sahib* and *Mr. Singh and the Colour Bar.* The Superintendent of the office in *A Bride for the Sahib* felicitates Mr. Sen on the latter's marriage in his provincial accents: "Saar, whee came to wheesh your good shelph long liphe and happinesh" (1967: 8) which not only disturbed Mr. Sen but provokes laughter. R.K. Narayan gives a few accounts of such humorous situations in *My Dateless Diary* when he had traveled within the United States Miranda had written "Motterry Dixit" (99) for "Madhuri Dixit" and had thought she was related to another character in the story having the same last name. Mrs. Sen pronounced the first part of "Beethoven" as "bee" like the insect, and not "bay" (120). The narrator in the story *The Third and Final Continent* notices many changes in the U.S.—that Americans drove on the right side of the road, not the left, called a lift an elevator, and an engaged phone busy. A flask was referred to as thermos because a flask was supposed to store whisky. Problems in communication have always been a source of humour because of the ignorance of terminology or pronunciation. The narrator of the above story calls an old landlady in the U.S. to have a room on rent:

> "Yes, good afternoon, madame, I am calling about the room for rent."
> "Harvard or Tech?"
> "I beg your pardon?"
> "Are you from Harvard or Tech?"
> Gathering that Tech referred to Massachusetts Institute of Technology, I replied, "I work at Dewey Library," adding tentatively, "at Tech."
> "I only rent rooms to boys from Harvard or Tech!"
> "Yes, madame"(177).

The same narrator was confused in London when the man had cried "piper" only to find out later that what he had pronounced was "paper." Similarly, the conversation between the narrator and his wife Mala on her arrival in the U.S. for the first time is interesting:

> I told her I had prepared some egg curry at home. "What did they give you to eat on the plane?"
> "I didn't eat."
> "All the way from Calcutta?"
> "The menu said oxtail soup."
> "But surely there were other items."
> "The thought of eating an ox's tail made me lose my appetite" (191).

Whereas the unpredictable reactions of the people because of the cultural gaps become a source of inconvenience, embarrassment, humour and fun, but no less tragedies, it is creditable on the part of Lahiri that she has also injected comic elements in what could have been mere tragic tales of the diasporas.

It is often by the use of comic images that the intention of the creative writers becomes clear whether they want their works to be totally serious or would like periodic flashes of humour in them. The comic images are often based on comparison of two objects which could be highly disproportionate, dissimilar, or full of exaggerated traits. A writer with the intention of provoking laughter makes small things gigantic or vice versa. The comparisons, thus, become incongruous, funny, peculiar and odd. Several examples of this type can be found in Jhumpa Lahiri's short stories. In *Mrs. Sen's*, the apartment was too warm and "the radiators continuously hissed like a pressure cooker" (114), Mrs. Sen used "a blade that curved like the prow of a Viking ship, sailing to battles in distant seas" (114). Mr. Pirzada grazed Lilia's "throat with his short, restless fingers, the way a person feels for solidity behind a wall before driving in a nail" (28).

While a comic image is an indirect display of the wit of a writer, wit by itself plays a significant part in injecting elements of comedy in literature. *Webster's New Dictionary of Synonyms* defines wit as "reasoning power or mental capacity [which] more typically implies intellectual brilliance and quickness in perception combined with the talent for expressing one's ideas in a sparkling effective manner," and goes on to explain that "sometimes the implication of a power to evoke laughter or smiles becomes prominent and the term without any loss of its earlier suggestions of mental acuteness and swift perception, especially of the incongruous, adds notions of verbal felicity, especially as shown in the expressions unexpectedness of turn and aptness of application" (1968: 876). Many examples of witty expressions can be found in Lahiri's short stories—in conversation, in repartees, in intelligent display of the power of giving an appropriate reply. When Mrs. Sen goes to purchase a fresh fish, she asks the salesman, "You are sure what you sell me is very fresh?" and he replies, "Any fresher and they'd answer that question themselves." When Mrs. Sen further asks the salesman to leave the heads of the mackerel on, he asks, "You got cats at home?" and she answers, "No cats. Only a husband" (127). In *This Blessed House*, Sanjeev's wife Tanima is nicknamed "Twinkle." To Nova, the name sounded unusual but Twinkle herself justified the name by saying that Bollywood too has such names in Dimple Kapadia and her sister Simple. Since "Twinkle" is the first word of a nursery rhyme, after some time, Sunil casually asked, "Is her last name Little Star?" (153). The father of Bibi Haldar wanted the latter to get married but for which her photograph was needed. Bibi Haldar urges her father to have her photographed, because "apart from my x-rays, I have never been photographed. Potential in-laws need to know what I look like" (164). Mrs. Croft wanted Mala's husband to say "splendid" when the American astronaut had landed on the moon; and he had grudgingly repeated the word after her. But when one hundred three year old Mrs. Croft had fallen down and had herself called the police for help, the narrator, as a token of sincere appreciation, could not help calling her act as "splendid."

It is particularly fascinating and delightful that Jhumpa Lahiri weaves in her short story little floating straws of details in such a subtle way and so meticulously that it becomes as ingenious, as artistic as a nest made by a weaverbird. This is what probably Arun Aguiar means when he writes: "Lahiri's stories bear the stamp of the same painstaking craftsmanship as Buddhist sages apply to the making of a mandala" *(Pif Magazine:* 1999). C.J.S. Wallia commends all her stories as "a showcase of elegant craft" *(IndiaStar Review of Hooks:* 1999). In each of Lahiri's stories, a number of details keep striking the face of the reader, making him wonder what significance do they have, till he comes to the end of the story and at that time the details become quite relevant, meaningful and significant by becoming an indispensable part of a well-crafted texture. Shukumar in *A Temporary Matter* becomes astonished by Shoba's capacity to think ahead when it comes to hoarding grocery and other items of use, but his astonishment turns to a sense of shock when during a five-day disruption of electric supply to their apartment, she rents a separate room, checks and rechecks its physical facilities, and informs him only at the end that she was terminating their married life. Mr. Pirzada, who was perplexed by being thanked at the bank, at the shop, at the library, and by the telephone operator, had professed not to know what the meaning of the word "thanks" was, while on finally reaching Dacca and finding his family safe and sound, he wrote back that he did not know whether giving "thanks" was sufficient enough to acknowledge his gratitude for the good Lilia's parents had done for him. The fact that Boori Ma had her life's savings tied to the free end of her sari keeps popping out repeatedly in the story and it is only at the end that she finds everything missing from it, and so also has the much talked about wash basin been stolen, bringing to an end her job and place of stay in the apartments of Bengalis. The above details in no way can be considered comic even if their end-result is the same in the sense of giving pleasure to the reader. For as various pieces of a jigsaw puzzle fall into their appropriate slots and the entire picture becomes clear, there is the same sense of fulfillment, of pride and of pleasure which one finds alter reading Jhumpa Lahiri's short stories. To me, Lahiri's *Interpreter of Maladies* becomes an interplay of mellifluous melodies.

WORKS CITED

Aguiar, Arun. "Review of Jhumpa Lahiri's *Interpreter of Maladies.*" *Pif Magazine,* July 28, 1999.

Lahiri, Jhumpa. *Interpreter of Maladies: Stories of Bengal, Boston and Beyond.* New Delhi: Harper Collins Publishers, 1999.

Roy, Arundhati. *The God of Small Things.* New Delhi: IndiaInk Publishing Co., 1997.

Singh, Khushwant. *A Bride for the Sahib and Other Stories.* Delhi: Orient Paperbacks, 1967.

Wallia, C.J.S. "Review of Jhumpa Lahiri's *Interpreter of Maladies.*" *India Star Review of Books,* 1999.

Webster's New Dictionary of Synonyms. Springfield, Mass: G. and C. Merriam Company, 1968.

4 Generational Differences in Diasporic Writings: Jhumpa Lahiri's *The Namesake*

Sunita Agarwal

Jhumpa Lahiri's Pulitzer Prize winning collection of short stories *Interpreter of Maladies: Stories of Bengal and Boston and Beyond* focuses on the lives of Indians in exile. She very subtly brings out the conflict of these immigrants between the traditions they have inherited and the day-to-day life they encounter. In her second work *The Namesake*, a fiction, she again deals with the theme of identity crisis and the problem of assimilation and adaptation in another country. The novel is a story of two generations—Ashoke and Ashima on the one hand and their children Gogol and Sonia on the other, and their life period of thirty years. The novel begins in the year 1968, the birth year of Gogol and stretches to the year 2000, depicting the different attitudes, outlooks and directionality of two generations in dealing with the problems in a foreign country. They face different problems as the meaning of culture differs for both the generation—the first being directly related to his/her homeland and second generation forming an image of culture based on the information transmitted by the first generation. The present paper proposes to deal with these generational differences in diasporic culture with reference to the novel *The Namesake*.

The novel opens in a nostalgic mood, Ashima, the wife of Ashoke, the protagonist, in her advance stage of pregnancy, is eating puffed rice with lots of spices and lemon, an Indian concoction sold in Calcutta's sidewalk for pennies, the taste being not the same brings her the memories of her homeland. Ashoke, an MIT engineer, has migrated to Boston to obliterate the memories of a train accident he met with, thus it is a self-imposed migration. Edward Said has defined it as an ascetic mode of 'Willed Homelessness'. Inspite of his well-settled life there, his return to India to marry a Bengali girl asserts his desire to retain his separate identity and solidarity to homeland. Ashima, for all her efforts to settle in a new way of life, felt homesick in that alien country. She felt uprooted and lived in a world of nostalgia. She spent hours in the apartment napping and sulking, rereading her parents' letters and the same five Bengali novels time and again. For Ashima "Being a foreigner is a sort of lifelong pregnancy—a perpetual wait, a constant burden, a continuous feeling out of sort. Like pregnancy, being a foreign, Ashima believed is something that elicits the same curiosity from strangers, the same combination of pity and respect" (50). The dichotomy between public and private sphere is almost tormenting to these woman immigrants who have to suffer double dependence. It becomes difficult for them to cope with multiple stresses of the two different cultures. They have to reconstruct their gender identity and locate themselves in the host culture.

Ashima gave birth to a child in a country where she is related to no one, where she knows little, where life seems so tentative and spare. The boy was named Gogol, after the name of the Russian writer Nikolai Gogol who is associated with the memories of the train accident. In fact Ashoke owed his second birth to him. At the time of the train accident, he was reading the story 'The Overcoat ' by Gogol and it was with the fluttering of its page that the attention of the rescuing party was drawn to Ashoke and he was saved. The choice of name Gogol is quite significant and appropriate. Through out the novel Gogol failed to establish his identity either as American or Indian. As Gogol grew, Ashoke and Ashima's circle of Bengali acquaintances also increased. The very fact that all belong to one country is reason enough for them to relate and form their own ethnic group and community. Thus distinct diaspora communities are constructed out of 'the confluence of narratives of the old country to the new, which create the sense of shared history' states Robert Cohen. "They all come from Calcutta, and for this reason alone they are all friends. Most of them live within walking distance of one another in Cambridge" (38). This diasporic community preserves their separate identity by observing their tradition. As Safran (1991) has observed, it is a general characteristic of diasporic that 'they continue to relate, personally or vicariously to the homeland in one way or other and their ethnocommunal consciousness and solidarity are importantly defined by the existence of such relationship' (84). These immigrants have to construct a sense of community, culture and nation (ality) in a country where they see themselves as different. They have to define both their historical legacies and their present geographic and social realities.

Ashoke and Ashima celebrated all the Bengali festivals and observed all religious rituals and rites with the ethnic community. When Gogol was sixth months old, they invited all of them for *Annaprasan* ceremony, the rice ceremony. Ashoke wore a transparent white Punjabi top over bellebottom trousers and Ashima wore a silvery saree. The first generation diaspora's adjustments and changes are expedient. They accommodate and adjust to create space and identity in a foreign country. The sense of uprootedness is disturbing to them, more so in the case of new immigrants. Said in his work *Culture and Imperialism* has elaborated on the journey of the exile from his 'homeland' to globe. The exile first becomes 'tender,' then strong and finally perfect: "The person who finds his homeland sweet is still tender beginner, he to whom every soil is as his native one is already strong, but he is perfect to whom the entire world is foreign place" (Said 1994 : 407). These new immigrants seek advice and suggestion from the ethnic group. "The wives, homesick and bewildered, turned to Ashima for recipe and advice, and she tells them about the carp that is sold in Chinatown, that it's possible to make halwa from cream of wheat. The families drop by one another's home on Sunday afternoons. They argue riotously over the films of Ritwik Ghatak versus those of Satyajit Ray. The CPI(M) versus the Congress party, North Calcutta versus South Calcutta. For hours they argue about the politics of America, a country in which none of them have right to vote" (38).

But for the second generation Diaspora, Gogol and Sonia, identity and problem are rather different, for they have a sense of pride and affinity to India, but it is America that is perceived as 'home'. In America they are born and educated. In America they want to be accepted on their own terms. It is here that they face a sense of alienation in the sense of 'insider' 'outsider.' On one of the fieldtrips in school, Gogol and his classmates are assigned a project—to rub the surfaces of the gravestones and find out the name of the dead person—the feeling of alienation and aloofness was doubly intensified because Gogol was old enough to know that there is no Ganguly there. 'He was old enough to know that he himself would be burned, not buried, that his body will occupy no plot of earth, that no stone in this country will bear his name beyond life' (69).

The first generation Diaspora wants to retain their homeland culture and transfer it to the second generation, it is through the eyes of the older generation that the younger generation perceives and learns about homeland culture. Ashoke and Ashima sent Gogol to Bengali classes and culture classes every other Saturday, held in the home of one of their Bengali friends. Though they do face some conflict with their children in this endeavor but the older generation makes certain compromises to maintain inter-generational relation. Ashoke and Ashima learnt to celebrate some of the main festivities of the dominant culture. "For the sake of Gogol and Sonia they celebrated with progressively increasing fanfare, the birth of Christ, an event the children look forward to more than the worship of Durga and Saraswati" (64). Ashoke and Ashima adjusted with food habits of Gogol and Sonia. It is Bengali food, that Ashima and Ashoke relished and preferred but for Gogol and Sonia she conceded and made an American dinner once a week as a treat "Shake'n Bake chicken or hamburger helper prepared with ground lamb" (65). Ashoke and Ashima gave in many ways but it was only to peripheral values, i.e. food, dress which were negotiable but not the core values such as their cultural and religious traditions. In fact, the first generation maintains a tangible link with the homeland by continuing tradition—an outward manifestation of its cultural tradition.

Ashoke and Ashima's reaction towards Gogol's friendship with a young girl Ruth, is typical of all first generation Diaspora. They disapprove and reject all such relationship. It is one accomplishment in Gogol's life about which Ashoke and Ashima are 'not in the least bit proud or pleased.' They tell him 'you are too young to get involved this way' (117).

Cultural displacement involves the loss of language, family ties and support, and is generally viewed by diasporic groups negatively. Salman Rushdie, in his novel, *Imaginary Homeland* talks about the turbulence and turmoil, a migrant goes through when he says, "A full migrant suffers, traditionally, a triple disruption. He loses his place, he enters into alien language, and he finds himself surrounded by beings whose social behaviour and codes are unlike and sometimes even offensive to his own. And this is what makes a migrant such a pathetic figure, because roots, language and social norms have been three of the most important parts of the definition of what it is to be human being." In the first generation Diaspora memory and nostalgia play an important role. They cherish and retain all the memories of their homeland and wait very anxiously for the moment of their visit to the country. Their ease and comfort with their own culture can be perceived in their behaviour. In one of the visits to India, Ashoke and Ashima's changed attitude is keenly observed by Gogol and Sonia, "Within minutes before their eyes Ashoke and Ashima slip into bolder, less complicated versions of themselves, their voices louder, their smiles wider, revealing a confidence Gogol and Sonia never see on Pamberton Road" (81). In contrast there are the second generation youngsters, the memories of Calcutta trip are wiped out from their minds "like clothes worn for a special occasion, or for a season that has passed, suddenly cumbersome, irrelevant to their lives" (88). In spite of their attachment to America and American ways they could not be one of them. They are Americans, but different.

Identity for the youngsters is much more complicated, for at the two levels, of private and public, there is dichotomy—Indian values and culture define identity at home, while outside, they are Americans but different. The generation gap is doubly problematic for them, for not only do they face the problems common to many teenagers in relationship to their parents but they also have the problem of the perceived 'Indian-ness'. The parents expect them to behave in an ideal manner and as most of them have migrated because of betterment in economic or academic field, they expect their children also to perform well academically and professionally. Ashoke and Ashima wanted Gogol to pursue engineering and Moushumi's parents wanted her to be a chemist. In this regard, Prashad comments "In the US, desi sunders the world into two, the outside world, the world of the workplace, is a world of capital that must be exploited as much as possible, and the inside world, the world of home, is a world of culture that must be protected and cherished...whereas morality is protected by the desi migrant within the world of home and culture, immorality is virtually sanctioned in the world of capital" (104). Contrary to this, the second-generation youngsters wanted to choose and adopt a career and a profession of their own liking. Gogol becomes an architect; Moushumi pursued a double major in French. Immersing herself in a third language, a third culture, Sonia becomes a para lawyer. They feel attracted and have an appreciation for the host culture. Gogol's shifting to live with Maxine's family, adopting and accepting her lifestyle, assimilating their cultural values point towards the second generation's desire of adaptation to the host culture. The first generation parents restrict and refrain such kind of involvement. They want to follow their own cultural values in these matters. As the younger generation could not understand this double standard, they, many a times, grow rebellious in nature. They hide their social relation to avoid confrontation. Gogol did not disclose his relationship with Maxine as long as possible and so did Sonia and Moushumi. It is ironical that Moushumi marries Gogol against her determination not to marry an Indian. Gogol's decision to change his name to Nikhil is also a way to reject his past, though he regrets it when the truth is out. Herberg (1989) argues that in general the second generation immigrants experience conflict even though there is variation in intensity of the conflict, the form it takes as well as the type of accommodation arrived at. Different ethnic groups may opt for different types of accommodation and there could be variation within ethnic groups.

Jhumpa Lahiri has, thus, very successfully delineated the poetics of exile. The exile has to deal with the two centers, external colonial or modernist and the internal or national filtering into a personal identity. The chief feature of the poetics of exile is the trial during which it deals with these centers, sometimes rejecting and sometimes accepting them. She has, deftly, narrated the struggle of these immigrants to assimilate and adapt the host culture and in the process of alteration they give up the rigid hold of their past and alternate his/her behaviour with the need of situation. During their stay in the new country and in interaction with the representative culture the subjectivities and modes of thinking of the Diaspora also change and they intervene in the cultural discourse of the dominant culture. Thus 'hybrid identities' are negotiated. Ashoke and Ashima's acceptance of Maxine in his son's life, Ashima's consent for Sonia's marriage to Ben, a half Jewish and half Chinese boy, all indicate their changed perspective. The death of Ashoke brings a change in the life of Sonia and Gogol also, the second generation. Now they can experience the trauma and pain their parents have undergone during the death of their parents. Now they can share the agony and pain their parents felt for being far away from their home. At the end of novel, Ashima's decision to live six months in Calcutta, in India and six months in America with Gogol and Sonia make her realize that she belongs nowhere and at the same time everywhere "True to the meaning of her name, she is without border, without a home of her own, a resident everywhere and nowhere (276), and so with 'Gogol' who is an alien both in India and America.

WORKS CITED

Cohen, Robert. *Global Diaspora: An Introduction.* UCI Press, 1997.

Herberg, E.N.T. *Ethnic Group in Canada.* Scarbourough Ontario: Nelson, 1989.

Lahiri, Jhumpa. *The Namesake.* India: Harper Collins Publishers, 2004.

Prashad, V. (2000), *The Karama of Brown Folks.* Minneapolis: University of Minnestoa Press, 2000.

Rushdie, Salman (1991). *Imaginary Homelands.* New Delhi: Penguin, 1991.

Said, Edward. *Culture and Imperialism.* London: Vintage, 1994.

Safran, William (1998). *Nationalism & Ethnoregional Identities in Chilka* (Nationalism & Ethnicity). Frah Cass, 1998.

5 Immigrant Experience in Jhumpa Lahiri's *The Namesake*

Anju Bhatt

Jhumpa Lahiri, the Pulitzer Prize winner and author of *Interpreter of Maladies* (a collection of short stories), is the daughter of Indian immigrants who settled in America for the sake of "greater opportunities, perhaps a better standard of living" (HMC). She had received huge critical acclaim for her warm and complex portrayal of family life and Indian immigrants trying to straddle the two cultures—their Indian heritage and the American dream, in her first collection of short stories. Being born in a family of immigrants, Lahiri from the childhood had experienced the conflicts, experienced by an immigrant who is continuously struggling with his surroundings and himself in order to find his real identity in the world, where he is given dual identities—identity based on the roots (the country to which his parents belong) and the place of his birth.

In *Interpreter of Maladies* Lahiri's painful depiction of people struggling to understand each other as well as themselves is universal in scope. The death of family members, disappointments in love and the inability to adjust to new ways of living and thinking are poignantly drawn. What sets her apart is overwhelmingly simple yet richly detailed writing that makes the heart ache as she meticulously unfolds the lives of her character. The crafted beauty of short stories stays in

Lahiri's first novel *The Namesake* where she continuously develops further the themes of cultural alienation and loss of identity that the immigrant faces in making a new home in foreign country. *The Namesake* revolves around the life of an Indian immigrant couple Ashima & Ashoke Ganguli who have come to create a new life for opportunities for themselves in the University of Suburbs in Boston. The novel opens with Ashima Ganguli trying to make a spicy Indian snack from American ingredients—Rice krispies & Planters peanuts—but "as usual, there's something missing" (1). Ashima, who is pregnant when taken to the hospital for delivery does not find anything normal in America—a country, where she is destined to spend her rest of life and even in labors she is terrified to raise a child in country where "Life seems so tentative and spare" (6).

The novel begins with pathetic portrayal of anxiety, uneasiness and various psycho-sociological problems such as nostalgia, rootlessness, alienation, schizophrenia experienced by Ashima who at a young age has migrated to a country where "she is related to no one" (6). Motherhood for Ashima does not bring only happiness but also the threat of raising the child all alone in a country of strangers. The child's birth was a lonely celebration and the realization that his entry in the world was "so alone and deprived" (35) laid the foundation of that dilemma that small child had to experience throughout his life. Ashima's struggle to adjust in a foreign country, to adapt herself to the newly found environment, is the struggle of every immigrant, for the universal issue of identity.

Being an Indian woman, Ashima had learnt from the childhood to sacrifice her own desires and cravings in order to please her husband and family. So for her, the pain, the yearning for going back to her own country, own land was to be kept hidden away in some remote corner of her heart, to herself. She keeps the "disappointment to herself" (30), not wanting to offend Ashoke or worry her parents, Ashima gradually adjusts herself to the new surroundings and devises a routine for herself where she completely merges herself in looking after Gogol, her son, who demands her utmost devotion and "last ounce of strength" (35).

She starts accepting the American ways of living but Indianness in her is kept intact by adhering to the Indian culture and rituals. By the time Gogol is six months old, they know enough people to entertain on a proper scale on the occasion of Gogol's *Annaprasan*. The connection, the contact with Indian culture is kept intact by strictly following the rituals that are part of Indian culture. Ashoke and Ashima create a "mini-India" for themselves, by getting them acquainted with all the Bengali families living around. She maintains address books in which the name and address of every Indian whom she comes across is recorded and she prides herself on each entry and feels privileged to "had the fortune to share rice with them in a foreign land" (160). Her discomfort with the life around her represents the bewildering world of American immigrants who are born in one country but spend their life either gracefully immersed or hopelessly drowning in the culture of another people. The anxiety, the fear of losing one's identity in an entirely foreign land, is passed on to the next generation also. Ashoke and Ashima's son Gogol who emerges as the central figure in the novel is the classic example of this phenomenon. The fears, the uneasiness, the restlessness, which his mother had experienced, when he was in the womb; passes genetically to him. He inherits not only his parent's culture or looks, but also inherits the pain of being lost in an alien culture. Gogol is unhappy with his name and hates it for lacking dignity or gravity. A name is an introductory ID tag to the world but Gogol, when he in his teens, despises his name so much so that "he came to hate question pertaining to his name, hates having constantly to explain. He hates having to tell people that it doesn't mean anything 'in Indian...'. He hates that his name is both absurd and obscure, that it has nothing to do with who he is, that he is neither Indian nor American but of all things Russian" (76).

In fact the title *The Namesake* reflects the struggle Gogol Ganguli goes through to identify with his unusual name. His struggle for establishing his identity is dual. The name that ultimately defines a person's individuality becomes a burden for him. It does not give him an identity but puts him in a dilemma about his original identity. Secondly as a child of immigrants in America, he constantly has to fight with conflicts arising due to his Indian roots.

The novel is autobiographical in portraying the repercussions of what the children of immigrants have to experience when they are destined to born in a country which does not belong to their parents. Jhumpa Lahiri who herself is a child of an immigrant couple had admitted in an interview, "I wanted to please my parents and meet their expectations, I also wanted to meet the expectations I placed on myself to fit into American society. It's a classic case of divided identity, but depending on the degree to which the immigrants in question are willing to assimilate, the conflict is more or less pronounced. As a young child, I felt that the Indian part of me was unacknowledged and therefore somehow negated, by my American environment and vice-versa, I felt that I led two separate lives" (HMC).

Gogol who hates his name, for the first time in his life, takes an independent decision and decides to get it changed to Nikhil. It is as Nikhil, Gogol faces the crisis of establishing his real identity. He finds it difficult to acknowledge that Gogol and Nikhil are both a part of his ownself and torn between this struggle he feels as "If he's cast himself in a play acting the part of twins, indistinguishable to the naked eye yet fundamentally different" (105). He is having twin sets of personality now—Gogol is the son of Indian parents who want him to live, behave and act according to Indian culture and values; Nikhil is the free liberated person, who has left his past behind and has nothing to do with Gogol. It is as Nikhil that Gogol forgets all the cultural restrictions imposed on him by his parents, who even after spending twenty years in America cannot bring themselves to "refer to Pemberton Road as home" (108).

His parents can never reject their old cultural values and one can sense the presence of deep-rooted nostalgia in their behavior, Gogol and Sonia view their multi-cultural life differently. After their annual enforced visit to Calcutta, they yearn to go back to their western ways. Gogol as compared to Sonia is the one who feels a life long disconnectedness to his family and culture. Gogol spends his immigrant life feeling as if he is on a river with a foot in two different boats. Each boat wants to pull him in separate direction and he is always torn between the two. His parents expect him to adopt a life based on Indian culture and the moment he boards a train to Boston, his home, "Nikhil evaporates and Gogol claims him again" (106).

He manages to have a dual existence—an existence having both Indian and American cultural values. Gogol represents the Indian part in him whereas Nikhil is the embodiment of all the cultural values that America has given to Gogol. It is while living these two lives, that Gogol realizes the need of an identity, which is not based on his roots. The predicament that Gogol experiences is the symbol of that wretchedness which every immigrant experiences when he has to answer any question based on his identity. Though he is born and brought up in America yet to Americans he is still an Indian. And when he comes back to the country of his roots he is referred to as an NRI. The feeling of belongingness, the urge to be claimed by one's root is universal and perhaps it is the only reason that a person eventually returns to the country of his birth. The pain, the anguish, the inability to adjust to foreign surrounding, compels the immigrants to long for their own country where their own people surround them. But in the *The Namesake* Lahiri had poignantly portrayed the pain of the next generation, who has no land, to be called as their own. They are living in a land, which they 'own' by birth, but to which they can never 'belong' because of their roots.

Gogol's experiences, his quandary cannot only be limited to Indian Diaspora, living in America. Even in India people who are migrating from their native state to other states in order to earn their living face the same problem. We can take the example of the people migrating from hills to different parts of India in the search of lucrative jobs. Immigration takes place yet it is at a smaller scale, but the pain, the suffering that the people experience can be well compared to the agony experienced by Ashoke and Ashima. This feeling of loss of identity is not only prevalent in the Indian Diaspora but can also be felt in the hearts of those Indians who even though living in India, find themselves disconnected from the land of their birth.

The immigrants' experience portrayed by Lahiri in the novel forms the core theme of the novel. Throughout the novel through various characters, we get an exhilarating and liberating view of the Diasporic situations often experienced by the immigrants. Gogol wants to be liberated from his Indian backgrounds but after his father's death, the Indian values which he had inherited from him make him move closer to his mother and his sister resulting in a strain with his relationship with his girlfriend Maxine. The sudden death of his father makes him turn his back towards his family and unknowingly he donned the responsibility of an elder son, as he would have done if he had lived in India. Gogol's quest for identity is a never-ending search; he cannot reject the Indian culture and cannot even fully accept the American values. This turns out to be on going, draining and difficult process for him. He cannot reject the demands of tradition and cannot afford to accommodate to the temptations offered by a new culture. He belongs to postmodern world which is defined as "the age of refuge" and modern man as "the new nomad" not being able to put down roots anywhere.

In her interview with Houghton Miffen Company Jhumpa Lahiri has remarked that "the question of identity is always a difficult one, but specially for those who are culturally displaced as immigrants are who grow up into two worlds simultaneously" (HMC). *The Namesake* vividly portrays what Lahiri had expressed herself and she never allows her characters to sink under their tribulations thus making *The Namesake* a subtle medium to remind us that "the pain of assimilation lasts not just a generation—the children feel it as much as the parents do" (BCL).

WORKS CITED

BCL: www.bookreporter.com.

HMC: www.houghtonmiffin.com.

Lahiri, Jhumpa. *The Namesake*. London: Harper Collins, 2003.

Steiner, George. *Extra-Territorial Papers on Language and Literature*. London: Faber and Faber, 1968, 10-11.

Toffler, Alvin. *Future Shock*. New York: Bantum, 1970, 74-94.

6

Manju Kapur's Nowhere Women

Sudarshan Sharma

Indo-English writing, as said by Manohar Malgonkar has, "a mystical structure. It is a strategy to blend the factual and the fabulous sustaining at the same time reality consistently." It is so structured that its variant identity has added to its richness. There is only a thin line of demarcation between the various sections projected by different writers like Naipaul talking about expatriate Indianness, Ruth Jhabvala talking about heat and dust, Anita Desai talking about aesthetic attachment, Mulk Raj Anand talking about social evils and Kamala Markandaya talking about poverty and compatibility of eastern spirituality. Quite a few authors like Raja Rao, Nayantara Sahgal, Bhabani Bhattacharya, talk about the evil effects of a colonial Raj and the struggle for freedom under the impact of Gandhian ideology. Recently, there has been an addition of Dalit Literature, Subaltern Literature and Literature of Feminism. These new voices are representations of marginalized sections of community and attract attention because of their profundity and veracity. They are forceful, compelling, vibrant, and distinct and have won global recognition. Winning various awards has brought them to the forefront.

Manju Kapur is one of the prominent new voices making its presence felt. She won the 'Commonwealth Award' for her first novel *Difficult Daughters* in 1999 and it was a runner up for the 'Crosswords Award.' Women writers form a major chunk of Indo-English writing. Gender discrimination and male chauvinism can no longer push them to the background. Whatever the drawbacks of British rule in India, they definitely created an atmosphere of awareness by enlightening people about their rights. Exposure to English literature written not only by the English but also by the other English speaking countries made people realize the need to assert themselves.

Women by nature are very sensitive, sacrificing and great home makers. Their suffering has mellowed them down and given them an edge over their male counterparts when it comes to depicting confusion created by clashing values and thoughts. The so-called Feminist literature is a cry from their heart. They want to assert themselves and at the same time they don't want to upset the applecart. That explains why a major preoccupation in recent Indian women's writing is a peep into the innermost recesses of the mind and a delineation of interpersonal relationships. Though the Constitution has given women equal rights, double standards of morality are the order of the day. Their expression of individuality and protest is either feeble or suppressed. The central focus still remains marital bliss. As a result, we find an emergence of an essential Indian sensibility along with an expression of cultural displacement. Manju Kapur is one of the women writers from India whose protagonists are women trying to maintain a balance all the time. Their suffering has made them strong and they are struggling to set themselves free from the shackles of tradition and various prejudices.

Manju Kapur lives in Delhi and teaches in a college in Delhi University. Her first novel *Difficult Daughters* is set against the historical background of India's partition. The novel covers the colonial period chronologically yet the crux is anti-colonialism. It highlights the problems of marginalisation suffered by Indian women whose major concern is maintaining their individuality and dignity. It portrays that a woman's search for identity is crucial to her perception and it does not necessarily presuppose defiance of time-tested traditions and cultural norms. The most readable of the novels published in

1998, it is the result of five years of research at Nehru Museum and Library at Teen Murti and was rewritten eight times. It was received really well for its simplicity of style. It manifests autobiographical data and explores pertinent and persuasive subjects like self-affirmation, man-woman relationships, family feuds and above all the mother-daughter conflict and contradictions. It is a first-rate realistic novel about a daughter's reconstruction of her troubled past hinging on her mother's story describing how she was as a daughter. It covers three generations of women against the backdrop of India's partition. It is the story of Virmati seen through the eyes of her daughter Ida, from whom her mother's past has always been kept a secret. Virmati, the daughter of a staunch Arya Samaji family of Amritsar, falls in love with a married professor and marries him against the wishes of her family. Motivated by a search for true love, independence and self-actualization, she realizes that values change and nothing is ever the same. Her own daughter is very clear that "the one thing I had wanted was not to be like my mother." Virmati herself was difficult to manage. Manju Kapur elaborates, "Conflict between daughter and mother is inevitable and I supposed I was a difficult daughter." The conflict carries on from one generation to the other perhaps because mothers want their daughters to be safe.

Realizing the value of higher education Virmati goes to Lahore to study further. She is convinced that one has to look outside to education and freedom. Even the professor's wife realizes that, "It is good the girls of today know so much." Double standards of morality are highlighted when nothing is said to the professor whereas Virmati is locked in a godown. She protests, "they still lock me in the godown. Each time I hear the door shut, I burn with anger and humiliation. I am just like the sacks of wheat and dal." She has to get her pregnancy terminated because the professor is away for the 'mundan' ceremony of his legal son. She wonders, "How many new beginnings had her relationship with the professor led her to?"

Virmati decides to forge her identity in a life of service and dedication and is fully determined to carve her own niche.

Unfortunately, fate has some other plans. By a queer quirk of fate, the professor is in a jam and can no longer postpone getting married to her. Disowned by her own family and resented by his wife and mother she writes to the professor, "I am my own mistress. I will relate to you with dignity or not at all." These are only futile proclamations, as she has to adjust, compromise and adapt. Finding herself going nowhere, she is driven to a stage when she does not care whether she has a home and children or not. Despite her efforts to find an identity, she is a victim of conditioned conventionality. After her first sexual encounter with the professor, she tries to justify by saying that there was no point in foolishly denying what was his on the basis of an outdated morality. At the same time, she is pleased with her marriage to him because it gives her a recognizable pattern in her life.

Though the novel can be considered a Feminist literary work, it tackles the problems faced by an educated Indian woman with authenticity and insight. It symbolizes a fight against taboos, social restrictions and manmade code of conduct in a traditional society. The woman of the forties depicted as a dependent woman symbolizes the modern woman as well. She is still struggling to establish her identity and gain self-expression and self-assertion. Though Virmati frees herself from old shackles, she becomes a prisoner of new ones. She realizes that, "men do take advantage of women." This is what Swarnlata had also told her. She represents the modern woman torn between desire for self-assertion and her helplessness. The novel explores the possibility of change in attitude through exposure to literature. According to Dennis H. Wrong, Virmati is looking for her roots having lost her spiritual and social moorings like the modern man. The novel deals with concern over the problems of women in a male dominated society. Born out of typically Indian situation, Virmati is caught between tradition and modernity, self-aggrandizement and self-realization, and self-assertion and confrontation. It only results in self-alienation and she becomes a symbol of female imagination responding to pressures and oppressions of patriarchal culture where marriage is seen only as a compromise. It does not become very clear whether a girl should make her own choice or not. The male chauvinists subscribe to the biblical view that the woman has to play a subservient role. At the other extreme are the feminists who condemn the idea of a woman taking the husband's name after marriage as they insist that she must retain her own identity. *Difficult Daughters* is the story of struggle for freedom at various levels. When India was fighting for freedom from the British Raj, Virmati was struggling to live life on her own terms. It ceases to be important somewhere towards the end as she is torn in two halves, one of which is on the side she is fighting against. As India attained freedom at the cost of partition, at the cost of losing half its soul, Virmati is able to exercise her choices at the cost of family ties, dignity and self-respect. Even today, women are victims of gender discrimination and sexual exploitation. Though the subject is stale, the novelist has dealt with the problem very naturally, authentically and convincingly.

Kapur's preoccupation with the female revolt against deep-rooted family values and the institution of marriage is followed through in her second novel *A Married Woman*. It is the story of love set against the background of the aftermath of the demolition of Babri Masjid. The theme of challenging the constraints of middle class existence has been handled very sympathetically and intelligently. Astha, the protagonist, is a typical middle class woman brought up in Delhi. She agrees to an arranged marriage and initially exults in passionate sexuality within the bounds of marriage. Though she seems to be quite happy being a teacher and a mother of two kids, there is always an undercurrent of resentment against being treated as one of the inferior sex. Hemant, her husband, shares the burden of looking after his first-born and is quite liberal in his views. Gradually the outer sheen wears off, and he fits into the mould of a typical Indian husband. After the death of Astha's father even her own mother trusts Hemant and not her as far as handling the finances is concerned. Hemant is quite autocratic in dealing with money matters at home and even her mother-in-law considers it to be only a male prerogative. Astha objects and pleads, "Surely, equals could relate better than master and slave." She had a good life only as long as she asked no questions. After retirement her mother goes to Rishikesh and sells most of the stuff at home. Astha wants to keep the books but they are donated to a library because Hemant does not want them. She is not taken into confidence even when their plot of land is sold. Though the air tickets for Goa are bought with the money earned from the sale of her paintings, she is not allowed to buy an antique silver box worth Rs. 5000 because Hemant considers it to be a waste of money.

Astha is introduced to Aijaz Akhtar Khan because of the street theatre. She is entrusted with the task of writing the script for a street play based on the demolition of Babri Masjid. She does a lot of research at India International Centre and becomes really knowledgeable about the historical background of Babri Masjid. She fantacizes making love to Aijaz and drifts towards lesbianism where the center of attraction is Reshana; though the attraction is short-lived. Her main crush turns out to be Pipeelika, the young widow of Aijaz. Unfortunately, the fanatics burned him alive when he had gone to Ayodhya to create awareness about the right approach.

A Married Woman can be considered a sequel to her first novel. Whereas in *Difficult Daughters* the focus is on the relationship between the mothers and the daughters with marriage as the ultimate goal, her second novel focuses attention on the relationship between the husband and the wife and the physical attraction between members of the same sex. The bond between Astha and Pipeelika gradually becomes so strong that the latter resents when the former has sex with her own husband. Hemant is very upset as he senses his wife drifting away. Perhaps in every marriage, the voice of protest and rebellion ultimately results in lengthening of silences and the two gradually drift apart. The author seems to be advocating the cause of the gays and the lesbians though in a very subtle and suggestive way. She does not seem to be very sure about it being the only solution, hence, the status of 'nowhere woman' for Manju Kapur's protagonists.

The silently suffering woman ultimately becomes strong enough to go with Pipeelika on a tour of the country to create an awakening and awareness. The two do come back but Pipeelika does not want to let her go. Astha cannot make up her mind. She is unable to tear herself apart from her husband and children and at the same time she does not want Pipeelika to go to America. Torn between the two choices she becomes a true symbol of a nowhere woman. Against the aftermath of Hindu-Muslim conflict over the issue of Babri Masjid in Ayodhya, Manju Kapur projects the unrest in Astha's mind. Sense of commitment to her marriage comes in the way of open protest and rebellion. The grieving widow of the Muslim professor and Astha find comfort in each other's arms. The description of their expression of love for each other goes beyond literary inhibitions, which are quite unnerving and passionate. It leads the reader nowhere as both the women go their own ways, since they cannot have a future together.

Thus we find that Manju Kapur has displayed a mature understanding of the female psyche and the inner subtlety of a woman's mind. She has been highly disturbed by the suffering but stoic woman trying to set herself free from meaningless chains. However, occasionally her rendition of a lesbian relationship distracts the reader from the tensions of the situation and the core sensibilities of the characters. Her preoccupation with the female revolt against deep-rooted family values and the institution of marriage is the focal point of interest in both the novels.

WORKS CITED

Kapur, Manju. *A Married Woman*. New Delhi: India Ink, 2002.

—— *Difficult Daughters*. India: Penguin Books in association with Faber and Faber, 2002.

7

Manju Kapur's Astha: A New Woman

Anuradha Verma

Manju Kapur, a new Indian voice, won laurels for her first novel *Difficult Daughters*. She received huge international acclaim and was awarded the Commonwealth Writers Prize for the best first book (in Eurasia region) in year 2000 and was a number one bestsellers in India. At present Manju Kapur is teaching at Miranda House College, University of Delhi. She is married to Gun Nidhi Dalmia.

Manju Kapur's Virmati and Astha are the two protagonists who are the reflections of a new woman.

Till yesterday we discussed and talked of feminism and feminist writers. Now a new concept has emerged which is a by-product of feminism, i.e. "a new woman." According to Sharad Srivastava as discussed in his book *The New Woman in Indian English Fiction,* "A new woman is 'new' if her basic concerns are deeper than merely seeking equality with men, asserting her own personality and insisting upon her own rights as a woman and as an equal being" (97).

This second novel *A Married Woman* of Manju Kapur takes a deep and satisfying look at the sense of displacement often felt by women in the traditional institution of marriage and family. It is the story of Astha, a young woman brought up in Delhi in a typical middle-class household. Astha succumbs to her parents finding her husband in a traditional arranged manner. Within the bounds of marriage, she discovers a latent sexuality, which is driven by love and passion of her husband. She leads a seemingly blissful life, finding her feet in the teaching profession, painting as well as bearing two children. Yet somehow, underneath all this, lies a life of repression and anguish.

Astha is Kapur's new woman "conscious, introspective, educated, wants to carve a life for herself, to some extent she even conveys a personal vision of womanhood by violating current social codes" (Malik 171). Right from her childhood she protested against the niche of traditional trappings of social customs and values. She never imbibed in her the values of her mother. Her mother often declared:

> "When you are married, our responsibilities will be over. Do you know the Shastras say if parents die without getting their daughter married, they will be condemned to perpetual rebirth" (1).

At this Astha reacts strongly:

> "I don't believe in all that stuff and I think as an educated person neither should you" (1).

After the death of Astha's father, Astha becomes very concerned for her mother. She wants her mother to stay with her family. When she constantly requests her mother for it, her mother says:

> "It doesn't look nice."

Astha replied with a grieving heart to her mother:

> "I wish you wouldn't be so stick-in-the-mud, Ma. Why didn't you have a son to look after you when you were old, if you cannot take anything from a daughter? Why did you stop with me?" (85).

Astha envied Hemant, his straightforward relationship with his parents.

The life of Astha as depicted by Manju Kapur reveals her torrential quest for equality, for considering her an equal being and a worthy member of society. Astha becomes very emotional for the books of her father that express her devastated and outburst anger. When she learnt that the books had been donated to a library, she quarreled with Hemant and shouted at her mother:

> "Why did you do that, they were mine as well, I loved them" (87).

She feels shattered as she was not consulted before taking any major or minor decisions.

One more instance is when Astha's mother sells her plot and gives the balance to Hemant to manage. We again find that this type of behaviour considering women weak and inferior aggravates her. It is not that Astha wants to take the position of a man. She accepts her duties at home as well wants to be partner in sharing all the undertakings and managements. This aspiration makes her a new woman. Her statement testifies it when she says:

> "Really Ma, don't you think women can be responsible for their own investments?" (97).

This urge to be treated as an equal being is fully imbibed in each of her remarks. It appears as if Manju Kapur through the medium of Astha demands the niche which is equal to man in a society. Ashta sadly finds fault in her father who thought his wife, i.e. her mother, inferior in managing money matters. She finds fault in her mother-in-law who brought up her son "for bringing up Hemant to never regard women as beings so to be consulted in their own lives" (98).

Hemant, an America return, was very caring, loving husband. When Astha was pregnant he himself said to his mother who hopes the child to be a son:

> "But Ma, I want a daughter. In America there is no difference between boys and girls, how can this country get anywhere if we go on treating our women this way?" (57).

This same man who no doubt promoted Astha for teaching loved her but treated her as an Indian wife, who is the second being after a husband. He himself later on discriminates between a boy and a girl. When Astha is pregnant second time, he also desires for a son and finds nothing wrong when his mother engages a priest to perform rituals to ensure that she gives birth to a son. "Like every married woman, no doubt she has a liking for motherhood but she does not like a sex-subjugation of her in-laws. She is surprised at the reaction of the family and society when they remain cypheric of Anuradha's birth but gets an overwhelming approval of motherhood after the birth of Himanshu" (Nayak 130). Not only this but his Indian male-ego is outpoured when Astha considers her job important. He talks of teaching in derogatory terms:

> "Hardly a serious job, you just go, talk to some children about poems and stories, organise a few clubs and come back" (68).

Thus Astha is hurt again and again by the male dominated treatment.

For Astha marriage meant union not only physically but spiritually and socially in all the spheres of their life. For Astha it meant a union of two partners. For her physical relationship with her husband is a sort of fulfilment both at the emotional and spiritual level. In the mid-last part of the novel she meets Pipeelika, the striking widow of a political street theatre actor. A rapport is quickly established between them. The relationship with Pipeelika grows and the two women become intense lovers. The intimacy and comfort she revives from this affair, contrasts strongly with the distance she feels in her rigidly defined role as a wife and mother. But this new kind of relationship disturbs her and she is at times in turmoil. She finds herself in the dilemma to make a decision to choose either the radical, liberating option of following her lesbian lover or to stay within the safe bonds of her family. I would like to point out here that a new woman is not a rebel. At the end, her duties called her and made her feel that this relationship cannot have a future altogether. She didn't want to ignore her family. This is a 'new woman,' who accepts her household duties and also wants to be treated not as an inferior being but as an equal creature though with a different body structure.

While assessing the emerging new woman's character in Astha, I am reminded of Great Rani Jhansi who was yet a new woman because she was the one who showed the world that for being a female she could not be confined to the four walls, she could rule and this she proved as she fought and made the Britishers feel bitter.

Indira Gandhi, the former Prime Minister of India, was also a 'new woman' for she not only held her role as a woman but also proved to be a good administrator, an administrator who is still remembered to deal with those crucial issues like "Kashmir-issue" which is yet not resolved. Jijabai, Shivaji's mother, is also a new woman as she proved by discharging her duties completely.

Studying Astha we find in her a true reflection of contemporary Indian woman, who is satisfied not only with the right to franchise but also wants to be treated as being equal to man in society.

Although Manju Kapur is against an extra-marital affair or more precisely against lesbianism yet she uses this relationship in order to convey the intense quest of Astha as a 'new woman.'

Manju Kapur has delineated Astha's character as a woman who seeks a space in her life, a woman who asks a bit more of life than tradition will automatically give her. Astha is, thus, a new woman who instead of security, comfort and respectability wants her emotions and spiritual needs to be recognized. Through Astha, Kapur offers "a frontal challenge to patriarchal thought, social organisation and control mechanism" (Nayak 137). Like Shashi Deshpande, Dina Mehta, Anita Desai and Bharati Mukherjee, Kapur expresses her concern for women "with a missionary zeal and seems to suggest that a married woman's job is not to complete wifing, child-bearing and housekeeping but to do something more. Her Astha appears to be an Ibsenite who raises her voice against the ages old customs and trends" (Singh 65). Astha is like Nora, the protagonist of Ibesen's play *A Doll's House* who tells her husband Helmer,

"Let us sit down and discuss."

For Astha a marital life meant participating in all activities, discussing all issues with her husband but for Hemant this relationship meant physical relationship and just fulfilling the needs of his wife.

Thus, this new insight of being treated with equanimity makes Astha a 'new woman.'

WORKS CITED

Kapur, Manju. *A Married Woman*. New Delhi: India Ink, 2002.

Malik, Seema. "Crossing Patriarchal Threshold: Glimpses of the Incipient, New Woman in Manju Kapur's *Difficult Daughters*." *Indian Writing in English*, ed. Rajul Bhargava. Jaipur: Rawat, 2002.

Nayak, Bhagabat. "Feminine Assertions in Manju Kapur's: A Socio-Ethical Perspective." *The Indian Journal of English Studies*. Vol. XLI, 2003-2004.

Singh, Sushila. "Recent Trends in Feminist Thought." *Indian Woman Novelist*, ed. R.K. Dhavan. New Delhi: Prestige, 1991.

Srivastava, Sharad. *The New Woman in Indian English Fiction*. New Delhi: Creative Books, 2001.

8 *Roots and Shadows*: Shashi Deshpande's Moral Prescription for a Reformed World of Relationships as the Basis of the Indian Traditional Dream of *Vasudaiva Kutumbakam*

Krushna Chandra Mishra

Shashi Deshpande's very first novel *Roots and Shadows* in its own right is a work of great merit—it won the author the Thirumati Rangammal Prize in 1984. Later Deshpande has been the recipient of the Sahitya Akademi Award for 1990 for her *That Long Silence* and of the Nanjangud Tirumalamba Award for 1990 for *The Dark Holds No Terrors*. These recognitions have proved that she wields her pen with a mastery that she stands out as an unrivalled artist in her own creative spheres. She is concerned about the world as she finds it. She sympathises with it and sorrows for its present woeful state of degradation. She shudders at the violence that in the world of human relationships sets her questioning the very purpose of existence and searching hard for devising a means whereby the humanity could find in some definite gainful way of honest soul-searching the very crucial role for it, out of which the meaning of life, so long diabolically withheld from it, could flow out in an endless spontaneity in its natural sweetness and joyous sustaining candour and splendour. She mixes facts of life with a salient aesthetic purpose to invest reality with a power to redeem the world of its present state of suffering. To her more useful is the ideal of association and service than that of detachment and passive withdrawal, a coward and dull and, hence utterly dead act. In *Roots and Shadows* (henceforward throughout this paper referred to as only *Roots and Shadows*), she looks critically at the way the Hindu marriage institution has missed its focus on the ideals of association and selfless action and thereby moved away from making any direct and effective contribution to the cause of continuity of life and the world. To be detached, to her, as in Indu's further understanding of the life in general, is to be dead. To touch and be touched, to be contacted, to be loved and loving are to her the only right ways to make life a true and laudable success. To fail in this is to fail in life, to die while failing others and imposing both failure and death on them. To assume a detached and exclusive approach to protect the self under the lure or motivation to achieve success is illusory. It is a virtual act of self-deception and a path paved the clearest to doom, death, destruction. Marriage must not mean clash of ego, confusion of the mission of life, erasure of identities, lost in absurd infighting, but it must make room for independence at the level of individuals, between man and woman as husband and wife, between castes as social equals, between generations—older and younger, and thus make love possible to help co-existence and contribute through innocence and non-violence towards achievement of the perpetually eluding goals of humanity to deserve peace, progress, prosperity, happiness and fullness. Through strategic indirection, but a neat and detailed presentation of facts, events, people and purposes and motives, Deshpande very convincingly drives home the point that in the face of the grim horrors of reality—and to Deshpande reality refers to us in our human world amidst our limiting conditions, we must appropriately and intelligently work to prevent every apprehended act of disintegration that may signify an irresistible colossal cataclysmic collapse for our kind of a collective that is capable of society, friendship and love, and thereby of remedying its own lot that otherwise, in absence of hard investigative reflection, is obscure and incomprehensible. Towards this capability-rebuilding in the humanity and towards making it see sense in responsible action in a bid to save from a dangerous identity-assertion exercise in its negative egoistic way, Deshpande's creative oeuvre in *Roots and Shadows* in its magnificent promise is a real splendid first success.

Deshpande's View of Literature as a Social Moral Project

Literature for Deshpande is an awareness-effecting tool in the hands of a writer. It propagates the writer's "Idea of Morality." It endeavours in a certain way to convey to the readers "The human consciousness of something that exists beyond this mundane existence, beyond mere survival." It attempts to establish "an understanding that there is the possibility of a better existence, that there are better selves concealed within us, that there is a voice that speaks to us of these things and of right and wrong" (Deshpande, 2001: 31-32). Literature has got a moral purpose in so far as the social cause thereby could be better served—a better order of existence could be given shape to. Writing itself being "an act of protest...against the state of world as the writer sees it," "against reality" in such a way that a purposeful kind of "constantly engaging with the world" (*Ibid*) is possible. Deshpande says, "I write because I want to change the world. I would like to change it, certainly in some areas especially where I see grievous wrong. And my writing does come out of dissatisfaction with the world. But I know...that no writing can change the world. I can at the most raise questions and doubts about things" (*Ibid.*, 31-32). She is one with Camus in search of a world of "innocence" and of a "life untainted by the guilt that comes from the transgression of a moral law". She is convinced that the *Mahabharata* or *Gora* or *David Copperfield* or *Anna Karenina*, each one as a work of great literature deals essentially at its very core with a moral world. But soon she finds her view of art is also that of Arthur Miller, the American dramatist who feels that art is "linked to morality." She feels the writer does not outrightly "preach a moral life" but works "to present the struggle of a human to get closer to the moral world," trying to communicate "meanings" in the line suggested by John Gardner, "discovered by the process of the fiction's creation" (*Ibid.*, 33-35).

About her own method of writing, Deshpande says, "When I begin a novel, I never start with a plot. There are only people. I knew them, or at least their predicament at a certain given moment. I don't know what will happen next. The events unfold in accordance with people's nature, in accordance with their own beliefs" (*Ibid.*, 33-35). She is never worried if a good character dies. She is convinced—"Morality is never the purpose of literature; it is the guide, the maker, the lights that show where the run-way is. The death of a good character is not a defeat of morality...literature is riddled with the death of the innocent and the good. But this does not mean that goodness is defeated, it does not spell out of the triumph of evil" (*Ibid.*, 33-35).

About presentation of reality in literature Deshpande avers: "Literature presents reality, but it is not just a mirror image of reality, it goes beyond that to present the hidden truths, the complexities of human existence that are under the surface of life" (*Ibid.*, 36). Concerned about the presentation of "the moral voice" which "within remains steady and consistent through all the confusion" (*Ibid.*, 36) when our motives remain "often incomprehensible even to ourselves," thus, literature discusses to a degree our hidden and incomprehensible motives so that when its call "to live a moral life" could float up distinct and abiding, "it never justifies a moral wrong." This is due to her optimism about the regenerative character of human life. With Evelyn Waugh she agrees: "...there is a moral purpose, a chance of salvation in every human life" (*Ibid.*, 36-37).

Deshpande rejects the view of "art for art's sake" since she sees a distinct social purpose for her art, but while linking "social justice" to "morality" and "literature," she feels a work should be so "shaped" that it emerges as being "aesthetically convincing" otherwise "it will fail to communicate what it wants to" (*Ibid.*, 37-38). Seeking to secure that balance "between the values of creations and the values of humanity" as after Camus, she feels in order to be edifying as well as of worth across ages, the aesthetic considerations involving form, setting, presentation need be given highest attention (*Ibid.*, 38-39). In this she assigns primacy to "content" subordinating "style" to it—"the style comes out of the content" and too much of a preoccupation with style leads to a loss of real focus of art—its communicative intensity gets diluted and as a result communication suffers and ultimately art fails. Thus aesthetic preoccupation in itself is a powerful precondition inadequate consideration of which could inevitably lead to thorough artistic failure. Insisting on Jane Austen like example of "a perfect writer," Deshpande sees the role of "integrity" to the moral vision and to the self (of the writer), of "having faith in what one is saying," and of being "true to one's art" in the success of any communication courtesy art or literature (*Ibid.*, 39).

What disturbs Deshpande is how "we seem to have grown inured to cruelty and horror," how "between good and evil" the line of difference "is getting blurred as we continue to find fresh excuses for evil" (*Ibid.*, 39-40). She agrees with Prof. U.R. Ananathamurty that "a great creative writer would never simplify this phenomenon (of the fight against evil forces). There is always a tension between the values of order and the forces of violence and anarchy" (*Ibid.*, 41-42). She finds for the writer the need to go beyond the level of "facts" that makes the search for truth different from the TV talk shows and journalists. For the writer there is the need to bring to the issues "the complexity and density" which, as Hemingway considered, "could make things true than anything true and alive" (*Ibid.*, 42).

Linking morality and freedom, Deshpande quotes an Egyptian saying—"Behold there is no calling that is without a director except that of the scribe and he is the director," and observes: "It is the writer who is in a sense the truly free person, the freedom that is much more than the legal freedom that society gives a writer. For while writing, the writer stands aside from the spectacle of humanity, sees it from the outside and from this perspective tells us about ourselves, our reality, our possibilities, our dreams and our nightmares. No one else can do this. It is with this freedom and the urge to create the writer begins to write. And if, as Hemingway says the writer is able to create something true and alive, it will survive" (*Ibid.*, 43). Deshpande considers that it is the writer's philosophy from which her writing issues taking her integrity, her faith in what she writes, and, most important, her freedom together and granting her art an authenticity and a power making it both "true and alive."

Reading *Roots and Shadows*

The Ch. 6 of *Roots and Shadows* is a central piece considered from the point of view of the main discussion taken up in the novel. The issue in question is marriage—its relevance, its significance, its use and its promised contribution to life in terms of granting it coherence, continuity, consistency and meaning. Old Uncle and Indu in their exchanges show that the theme drags in reflection on the theme of universal interdependence as after Huxley's formulation and again it enthusiastically ponders over the un-contradictable appropriateness of the assertion by the patient in the Cancer Ward that "not all of me shall end" and Pushkin's prime contention that human entity in its entirety is not for the fierce and irrevocable dissolution—human essence is a matter of existence across eternity, and again it relates to Camus and the idea of the inexorable human destiny, the idea of human predicament.

Thus weaving in many apparently dissimilar threads of intensely perturbing as also disconcerting thought, *Roots and Shadows* tries to emphatically place the author's point of view—life in freedom must seek for its fulfillment of the human essence, the human dignity, the human worth. Towards this crucial criterion of freedom in its potential to give rise to happiness as in the context of a married life the issue gets gradually more subtly drawn. Thus, the meaningful aspect in any marriage as a vital issue further embraces the questions of happiness and success. Happiness further is discussed in relation to the issue of identity, in relation to one's needs—material and mundane, and emotional and spiritual.

Questions on caste and marriage, property rights and marriage etc. are very deftly put in fit sequence. Now happiness—in its material *vis-à-vis* its psycho-social/spiritual dimensions—is deliberated upon through examples of Aka's marriage and her expectation and experience as well as horrible encounters of a tragic proportion, through Indu's marriage to Jayant by her own choice that attracted the virulent criticisms involving the caste-question in its traditional unquestioned adherence and honourability as also in its questionable status in the age of modern secular and democratic set-up, through Naren's marriage with (Pad) Mini that remained only at the proposal level and could not materialize especially due to a brazen obduracy on the part of both Kaka and Kaki, Mini's parents, who in their place wanted to find Mini a working and well-to-do groom as against a "loafer" that Naren in their consideration was, through Mini's marriage and dowry deals as an unsavoury devilish social practice, and again through the interrelationship and therefore influencing role of marriage in socio-legal considerations involving property rights of the women in a Hindu Undivided Family around the inheritance question.

A simple everyday life's very common facts as that of marriage approached with care and deep caution goes to unearth the multi-layered complexities that constitute the very customary and conventionalised aura around it. Deshpande's competence at confidently critically investigating the problems inalienably associated with the institution of marriage in the Hindu Society of India, especially amongst the Brahmins, has emerged as uniquely superb, vying only with a reformer and activist's majestic arrogance and meek, but unwavering determination. The concern very mightily expressed in *Roots and Shadows* on the plight, especially traditionally, generally held in store for women in marriage or for girls being proposed/betrothed for marriage—in case of married women the question of happiness is a worthy matter to grapple with whereas it is no less important to consider with sympathy the case of suffering which marriageable age girls unwittingly have to undergo with hardly any one coming to bother about them or to help them out in their woes and distress.

Roots and Shadows in a very subtle way comes to lay bare the shame that is euphemistically glossed over the institution of marriage as it today obtains in the Hindu fold. In Indu's opinion—and this is very important since Indu happens to be the central figure in the novel, marriage and happiness are two very different and quite unrelated ideas. The traditional view that marriages automatically lead to happiness, in the modern context of a materialistic Hindu society, does not stand scrutiny. Indu says: "But marriage.... It makes one so dependent" (106). Again, she says: "Faith, love, devotion...do they always have to be unbalanced, obsessive, unreasonable" (106). To Old Uncle's simple acceptance of life: To me, life seems simple. You work, you earn a living, you have a family, you look after them, you are cared for.... And what more can one want? (107) She (Indu) does not take time to throw back: To care for anyone too much.... It's all pain. A punishment." But the old man in his usual calm comforting way argues out: "That's not right, Indu. That's the coward's way. Attachment...we can't escape it. It's the law of life. You can never protect yourself against love" (107-108). Again, he also says: "It's (marriage) the only thing that matters. It means continuity. It means I'll never die" (108), and further: "That's the hope that keeps us going" (108).

Against the secure serenity-inspired soothing view of life turning happy through a renewal of hope, Indu has got her own exclusive reaction; she is worried about 'my dream, my ideal of detachment.' She says: "I don't know why, but my mind keeps harping on this theme of detachment and loneliness. Will I never reach that stage.... No passions, no emotions, an unruffled placidity?" (108). The attachment-detachment dichotomy as brought out in an impeccable and astounding neatness with reference to marriage provides for us a greatly satisfactory image of Deshpande as a writer in line of true greatness after her ideal—Jane Austen, the perfect writer, true to morality, true to herself, true to her beliefs and truly interested in unravelling for her reader the deep mystery of life conveyed through a whole impenetrable complex array of motives and intentions of the people among whom our predicament-ridden lot is most woefully cast. The world, she feels, looks dreadful, horrible in its intimidating strangeness, entirely due to a gross and complete absence of "innocence". Hemingway's "more true than the true and alive" kind of penetrating analysis and aesthetically convincing presentation makes her a truly great writer. In her ideal moral hero's model she brings up her protagonist (in *Roots and Shadows*) Indu as intelligent, smart, unhesitating, uncompromising and outrightly assertive. In this she is very true, in that she follows the norms she lays down in talking of morality's role in life in the modern world and its place in literature. Further, *Roots and Shadows*, in its presentation of Indu in the midst of an aggressively arrayed hostile hoard of selfish people who claim to be belonging to one and undivided family, vehemently pooh-poohs at the idea of family as it has come to stand today. The suggestion is that the self-seeking people under the cover of the family-idea virtually remain firmly hoisted so that the simple, uncritical, pliable and cow-down-able could be hoodwinked and bamboozled to the extent of losing their right of self existence as sovereign and dignified beings. Indu is, thus, not allowed to be a dumb cow that anybody could drive out at mercy or a whimper. The hugely damaging, debilitating, destabilising, devastating, devouring and almost obliterating will and fancy of everyone claiming identity with her in common thereby flashing out a deeply entrenched right to the property traditionally accumulating to the family's reserve thus hardly leave her sighing or shying. In a very potent way however she guards her own self—her authority, power and status—that not only she emerges unscathed and unruffled, but she gains an acquaintance of each one to an extent where acquaintance leads to a situationally saving kind of understanding of relationships almost by a way of a sudden revelation in absence of which perhaps one might have to wash off with empty hands. A family tragedy—the death of

Akka—provides the occasion for all the members of the family spanning three generations to gather together ostensibly to mourn, but obviously and also more importantly, to have each one's potential fully exercised so that the family could become several independent, isolated and apparently unrelated individual families. Indu's "dream," "a recurring dream" with which Ch. 1 of *Roots and Shadows* begins has got a significance which deserves to be noted for its relevance in the overall context of this novel—the dream of Indu is the fact of her parting from her family members: "I am not the only one. There is a large crowd with me. I get in. The bus starts and suddenly I remember I have left someone behind. I panic. 'Stop, stop,' I yell and scream. But the bus moves relentlessly on and suddenly in the midst of my despair, I know who these faceless people are. They are my people" (10). The episode of the family quarrel in Ch. 10 is revealing in most ways especially as it makes "sva-janam...My people. Our people" (167) their unpalatable estranged variants as "such people" (Indu-169), "them" (Govind, Indu's father-169) etc. It makes the accusation by Hemant against Indu involving her having "Aka's money" offer a crucial turning point 'to show how even one is seen to have lost her right to say in matters involving a Hindu Undivided Family after one's marriage.' A marriage—by choice of the people of the family or in defiance of it by one's own choice (as in Indu's case)—ultimately connotes the increasing practical value of others as compared against one's real old parental family with the realisation that "Their faces are blur, as if I am flashing past them at great speed" (10). Indu says: "I had rejected the family, tried to draw a magic circle around Jayant and myself" (10), but not very late she discovered to her utter dismay—"I had pulled in my boundaries and found myself the poorer for it. Alienation, I know, is not the answer. On the contrary, too much of it and we can die of a terrible loneliness of the spirit. I am alone ...they seem to me to be the most poignant words in any language" (10). Purportedly, *Roots and Shadows* in an equally poignant manner endeavours hard to come out with an antidote to 'I am alone' kind of oppressive and shattering feeling by proposing in all sincerity a method of not progressive alienation that puts one irretrievably on the brink of disaster and doom leaving one in inconsolable grief at the irreparable loss one's apparently irremediable situation has brought one. This is the method of possession and accumulation and the gradual "thingification" (Ami Caesaire) of the human being which implies increasing loss of contact, correspondence and responsive belongingness with as well as towards others. Such a process prevents the world of human relationship from becoming cordial and vibrant.

The *Roots and Shadows* is a kind of a treatise on marriage as a typically Hindu Social Institution though its assessment and criticism has been presented following the liberal model brought in by modern education—Indu as an educated woman, a talented and enterprising journalist quite well aware of the world of facts is sharp in her grasp of the issue in hand. She also has much to contribute by way of her personal experience as a woman married as after her own choice out of an enthusiastic pursuit of love in a rigid bid of being a "success" (105) and not cowed and "castrated" (105), not made to part with her own cherished ideals of freedom and individual dignity. And, thus, *Roots and Shadows* emerges as a powerful critique on the institution of marriage—its traditional sacrosanct and lofty objectives on one hand and its present deplorable degradation on the other are weighed against the real order of things and their desirable modification in the light of an artistic vision that at one and the same time is a mocking outsider like Naren whose intrinsic worth is realised once the great end arrives, and a powerful and gracious awe-inspiring presence like Indu herself whose mission as an insider at all costs is to integrate and chasten and save. With a definite, determined, persuasive yet firm presentation, Deshpande very ably exposes the vulnerability of the married woman while side by side not failing in the least to critically dwell on tremendous possibility for the woman exercising her own powers to an advantage and achievement which traditional scheme of things usually might not allow. The moral victory of innocence scored against the oppressive and adamant forces of male arrogance conniving in all mean ways possible to perpetuate the tale of woman's subjugation and her subsequent inevitable miserable languishing is something very special to Deshpande's conception whereby she finds justification for exposing the "tension in creative writing of a high level between the values of order and forces of violence and anarchy" (Deshpande, 2001, 41-42). It is also in being true to her belief and philosophy that she draws up her figures of innocence as strong, resolute and inherently dynamic people who could not only withstand the challenges of an awing and subduing nature but turn the adversities to a rarely hypothesised advantage. Towards this end, in *Roots and Shadows* she has endowed her characters with acumen, insight, agility and firmness. The intricate web of manipulation, aggression, moral transgression and exploitation is so immaculately designed in the Hindu society almost exclusively to the male advantage in terms of sexual malpractice that in Deshpande's view it has to be blasted from inside if "conscience" be rendered awake and "freedom" (Deshpande, 2001) in its right implication be given to play its real role to help effect a world in which not confrontation of an unsavoury nature would occasion estrangement of a totally devastating potential involving man-woman relationship, but cooperation of an exalted order achieved through a true understanding of each other could lead to the individual progress material, moral and spiritual—at all levels of temporal consideration. As it stands out in *Roots and Shadows*, the novelist has not followed an anti-Hindu approach and argument so far as the ideal is concerned, but her frankness is about the crooked and immoral practices that the Hindu world has in course of time fallen into thereby unwittingly driving the wedge into its very social entrails and leaving scope for the section suffering in the Hindu fold to lash out at the very society that justifies the practices as patently Hindu. To this end her estimate of the writer as "a rebel and a social reformer" (2001: 31-32) also very aptly applies to her in her recognition that "writing itself is an act of protest—a protest against the state of the world as the writer sees it" (*Ibid*). About her own writing she says: "and my writing does come out of a dissatisfaction with the world. But I know...I can at the most raise questions and doubts about things...I can offer my meaning of life. My truth, which embraces not just social laws and social wrongs, but also the eternal laws that govern human behaviour, ideas of right and wrong. The truth which also involves an understanding of the relationship between human beings, the relationship of a human to the inner self, of humans with society, with the physical universe and the other unseen universe we know we are also part of" (*Ibid*). Her writing is based on as well as geared to arouse "an understanding that there are better selves concealed within us" (*Ibid*). She is aware, as after Camus, that "the world of novel is a rectification of the world we live in pursuance of a man's deepest wishes," as she finds "connected to a moral world" (*Ibid.*, 33-35). One with Arthur Miller, she holds that art is "not founded" on morality, "but linked to morality." She finds herself "not set out to preach a moral life," but "to present the struggle of a human to get closer to the moral world" (*Ibid*). She thus is convinced to have at the heart of her work "conflict between the belief in a moral world and a denial of it" while she does not "resent the death of a good character" as for her it does not mean "a defeat for morality," it does not mean that "goodness is defeated," "it does not spell out of the triumph of evil" (*Ibid*).

What then does Deshpande truly find in her mission to offer to her readers in *Roots and Shadows*? Speaking of so many marriages, so many collapses, so many possibilities *vis-à-vis* so many ifs and buts emerging around them, Deshpande in *Roots and Shadows* very skillfully brings "alive" the phenomenon of evil that in the sense of Hemingway undoubtedly underlines her rich "invention" (*Ibid.*, 36): ...Hemingway, when asked "what is the function of your art?" said: 'from things that have happened and from things as they exist and from all things that you know and those you cannot know you make something through your invention that is not a representation but a whole new thing truer than anything true and alive and you make it live and if you make it well enough, you give it immortality' (*Ibid.*, emphasis presently added). What is evil in the Hindu marriage? How has the institution become kind of a means to deny "social justice" which can be linked to morality?" (*Ibid.*, 37-38). How could in such a situation that practical spheres of life in Hindu India be adequately remedied? How could art especially be an adequate medium to suggest with force the very nature of such a remedy and point out the unwishawayable kind of urgency that this remedy warrants today? Deshpande is however superbly conscious about her own responsibility as an author to display the exact order of "commitment to social reform" as unequivocally "the driving force" of her writing (*Ibid*) and in this she is careful about making her presentation: "aesthetically convincing" (*Ibid*) knowing it deeply well that otherwise she would fail to impart her work the communicative thrust it wants in its zealous bid to strike the conscience of people whose callousness and whose folly have made the Hindu social practices sink to such abominable depths due to introduction of materialistic considerations—dowry system and the like practices unthinkingly glorified as the tradition or custom. Attacking the social morals and customs as found firmly embedded in the Hindu order, Deshpande, almost in a rage prompted by despair, very strongly, as it may be, urges the Hindu fold to take stock of the reality in the face of all its present debasement and to wake up and act such that the very ideals behind the Aryan conception of family, society, caste, marriage, equality and prosperity could be further more presented back in their original pristine splendour and grandeur. Thus *Roots and Shadows* offers a powerfully persuasive plea for an imminent critical self-examination of the Hindu reality as it obtains today against its rich heritage of a civilizational past the fabric of which was woven out of a selfless seeking for knowledge by the seers to throw up a system of Power that inherently should be endowed with the dynamism to ensure accural of ever accumulating social good. The concept of *Kalyan* (well-being) of *vyakti* (individual) and *vishwa* (world) capable of making of *vasudha* (the whole world) one single *kutumbakam* (united family) as inherent in the *Vivaha-bandhan-sutra* (marital ties), it appears, is what stirs the imagination of the novelist in *Roots and Shadows*, and thus, by showing how ugly an originally planned beautiful social system of integration, association and attachment has unfortunately become, Deshpande leaves the readers' minds re-engaged in the mysteries and methods of universal well-being such that a firm commitment to overhaul and cleanse the system may emerge across the constituent units of the Hindu society, and re-dedication to ring in the good by ringing out the unwanted and wicked elements corrupting the system may ensure that marriage be re-installed in its hollowed pedestal of peace, pleasure and plenitude.

Concluding Notes

Shashi Deshpande at the core of her mission has the issue of innocence. Her concern is for the plighted humanity that stands exposed to the tough inclement weather of inadequate understanding of individuals who in their various forms of relationship or of being related to one another in the socially traditionally approved ways convolute and corrupt innocence and thereby weaken the moral basis of the society. She is clear that the world stands to benefit if it makes of innocence a culture and a way of life without any petty and clumsy consideration of denominational affiliations. Innocence is to be firmed up and the truly innocent have to be presented as not dominated and exploited and suffering or dying. Morality then is sure to triumph in its own right as innocence emerges as a might in itself, as a permanent and inexhaustible source of this might ready in its indefatigable way to fight on against corruption in every minute form that undermines human strength and ridicules its firm and determined will to bring in the rule of good and of practical wisdom. The writer in Deshpande is keenly aware that corruption is a brazen assault on the morality mission of innocence, and because it is the mind of man which legitimizes corruption under any shade of logic and is a relating agent contributing effectively to its perpetuation across generations and under the banner of tradition, the barbaric potentiality to inflict cruelty and violence inherent in the acts of corruption needs to be in full calm resolutely opposed at the level of mind itself. This unboomeranging action has to be exercised by way of thought, which should spring from an astute optimism about the self-correcting and self-regenerating potential of the humanity. Innocence thus germinating would lay the foundation of a world where peace abides and love fostering freedom and self-development at the universal level is certain to assert itself. The kind of revolution this onerous task implies could then be accomplished if the mind-set of the people is appropriately changed. And this kind of change is possible, among a host of other possible ways, through literature. Deshpande's acute understanding of the role and power of literature in this transformative project is of crucial importance in this regard. Not condemning and chiding, but guiding and goading, persuading and pleasing, appealing and pleading, she wooes her readers explaining the necessity of their conscious undertaking of the job to allow innocence a free and fair play as against the faking and foul play of corruption, manipulation and exploitation. If colonisation of women as under Hindu Marriage System is to be prevented, colonial mind-set present in countering the institution of tradition is also to be effectively changed. Women then must not be anti-colonialist in their approach adopting the coloniser's basest of debasing, devaluing, dehumanizing and deforming ways. Rather, the proper way of fighting, opposing and frustrating male colonial ways would be in exposing inhuman colonialist strategies and arranging for the education of the colonised colonising mind of the Indian people in general and of the Hindu male mind in particular that is long conditioned to colonial ways in remaining servile as a colonised people so that true freedom's enlightened thousand ways promising cooperation, peace, prosperity and happiness would be desirably rendered open to work out equality, justice and dignity at all significant levels of human relationships, of man-woman relationships. *Roots and Shadows* is a definite achievement in this direction of leading the crises in man-woman relationships along the reconciliatory and emancipatory lines promised by an aching aesthetic vision informed in full by the practical experiences of the crude world of facts and of dull and uninspiring realities. Deshpande in her bid to usher in the prospects of a happier moral world has scored a definite laudable success in her *Roots and Shadows*, her first eloquent manifestation of her profound compassionate artistic vision. *Roots and Shadows* is a dedicated in-depth exposition of the fact that what reconciliation achieves is squandered away by dull-headed headstrong confrontation—the spirit of reconciliation is a proof of human capacities for accommodation, for being open-minded and judicious about the pressing demands of changed circumstances, for seeing reason for changes when they are the most needed, for remaining ever prepared to be forward-looking and hopeful about the positive gains that are always there for those who are able to reconstruct for immediate as well as eternal purposes the pro-life meaning of human relationships. To this end literature as relationship-studies (Mishra, 1997) is indubitably magnificently illustrated in Deshpande's *Roots and Shadows*. *Roots and Shadows* in Barthesian sense is a fit example of writing as "invention" (Sontang, 1993)—words as depicting reality while imposing a certain fixity on the facts interestingly as words in new situations and under new considerations for need-dictated uses lift up their limited referential value in their relation to the spatio-temporally frozen facts and thereby grant to the words immense as well as inexhaustible possibilities to marshal into service meanings as could be appropriate for almost all anticipated occasions of subjecting the narrative in *Roots and Shadows* to analysis. And happily *Roots and Shadows*, thus, like the Eiffel Tower in Barthes provides interesting reading-interpretation possibilities. *Roots and Shadows* is a powerful cultural text, a strong post-colonial text, a text dealing with social problems and pleading for impending social reforms, an oblique and effective critique of the Hindu Marriage tradition, a feminist text, and the like. Thus rich of use and meaning possibilities, *Roots and Shadows* is a unique creation of Deshpande in its vivid and vociferous clamouring involving the claim of the reform-minded artist for making room for "innocence" and for her "moral world" if the world is to be spared of undue and unwarranted duress, drudgery, dejection, disintegration and disaster and doom. Providing pleasant reading on issues and facts of a decidedly unpleasant nature, *Roots and Shadows* in a way sensitises the readers about the distinct role that they must unfailingly play if they are genuinely convinced that their knowledge of the problem and also of its solution in itself is hardly of any avail in case they are not jumping into the action that is the most proper in the present set of circumstances. In this also one could easily find Deshpande as being in true conformity with the Indian ideals of *karma* falling short of which by any whit might smack of the whole store of unproductive knowledge as sheer vanity and vice. A Deshpande novel like *Roots and Shadows* is, thus, a siren call to the reading public to get united in sort of an unswerving bid in the manner of the civil society to work out the rescue of all concerned now found caught up in an almost sure fatal mess.

WORKS CITED

Ahujha, Ram. *Social Problems in India.* Jaipur: Rawat Publications, 2002.

Atery, M. and V.K. Kripal. *Shashi Deshpande: A Feminist Approach*, 1998.

Deshpande, Shashi. *Roots and Shadows.* New Delhi: Orient Longman, 1983, Disha Books, 1992. Subsequent references to the text are from the 1992 edition and are indicated in parentheses.

Deshpande, Shashi. "Literature and Morality." *The Literary Criterion.* Mysore: Dhvanyalok, Vol. 36, No. 4, 2001, pp. 28-44.

Dhawan, R.K. (Ed.), *Indian Women Novelists*, Set-I, Vol. 5. New Delhi: Prestige, 1991.

Gandhi, M.K. *Constructive Programme: Its Meaning and Place.* Ahmedabad: Navjivan, 1945, Reprint 2001.

Mishra, K.C. *Literature Studies for Introduction as Relationship Studies.* In the Arunachal Front, Naharlagun, A.P. Issue dtd. 1 May 1997 and continued subsequently.

Mongia, Padmini (Ed.), *Contemporary Postcolonial Theory: A Reader.* New Delhi.

Sontang, Susan. *A Ronald Barthes Reader.* London. Vintage, 1993. For the idea of writings as "Invention" please see the chapters—The Eiffel Tower; Introduction to the Structural Analysis of the Narratives; Writers, Intellectuals, Teacher; and The Third Meaning.

9

Mother-Daughter Relationship in the Short Stories of Shashi Deshpande

Abha Shukla Kaushik

The family in India, during the last few decades, has been under a process of social change, thus substantially affecting the various relationships in a family unit. There is a conspicuous change in the spheres of roles and values. Due to growing enlightenment and movement for women's emancipation, socio-economic conditions have changed and so have the patriarchal attitudes to gender. Literature plays an important role in raising the readers' consciousness by providing a glimpse into female psyche with the full range of female experience. Indian writers, in their works, present an image of woman, which is totally different from the image of the past, according to which woman was viewed as an evil counterfeit and a weak vassal. Karen Horney writes, "Men, have certain fixed ideologies concerning the nature of woman, that woman is innately weak, emotional, enjoys dependence, is limited in capacities for work,—even that woman is masochistic by nature" (231).

Woman's struggle in the context of contemporary Indian society is to find and preserve her identity as wife, mother and most important of all, as human being. She has got to go beyond the socially determined role of 'wife' and 'mother' and find out her real identity. The present-day Indian woman seeks to be emancipated; her aim is to be a whole human being, regardless of the difference in sex. In this task, writers, who have been writing about it, help her. The impact of the west and the emergence of feminist literature have considerably shaped Indian life and literature. Woman's quest for identity is a recurrent theme prevalent in women's fiction, which involves writing of materials and literatures that deal, in a direct or implied fashion, with women's improvement and their general enlightenment. This has given a great impetus to the growth of creative writing in English.

Shashi Deshpande is one of the major voices in the Indian English fiction. She has to her credit ten novels and many collections of short stories. She has ushered in a new era of psychological realism into Indian writing through her writing. She makes gender central to her writing. She writes about ordinary women in ordinary urban situations depicting women from a perspective that stems from a firm belief that our lives are to a great extent influenced by myth. "To be as pure as Sita, as loyal as Draupadi, as beautiful as Laxmi, as dogged in devotion as Savitri, as strong as Durga—these are ultimately the role models we cannot entirely dismiss" (Afterword, *The Stone Women,* 87).

Deshpande's stories give a perspective on women in their complex and real relationship. They are about mothers and daughters, grandmothers and wives, women working outside the home, negotiating a balance between tradition and modernity, analyzing and expressing their insecurities, fears and desires.

While communicating that the mother-daughter relationship is rarely dealt with in traditional stories and legends, she feels that her portrayal of the uncompromising relationship, at times, makes some readers uneasy. She is of the opinion that this is so because "we have this stereotypical image of what a loving mother is like that we find any variation to be lacking in motherly feelings. It seems to me we need to get rid of these images to be able to release ourselves from guilt. We had to wait for women to write to bring out the truth of this relationship" (Telling Our Own Stories, *Writing from the Margin and Other Essays,* 97).

Some of her stories depict poignantly the mother-daughter relationship from the perspective of a mother trying to reach across a barrier to her daughters. These stories are first person narratives of a woman's real concern at her inability to be an ideal mother—the epitome of succor and comfort, and her difficulty in communication. Deshpande examines the problems of the mother-daughter relationship in several of her stories.

"Why A Robin" is one such story in which a mother and daughter reestablish their links. When the story starts, there is nothing common between the two. The mother is justified in thinking that her twelve-year-old daughter has an attitude of rejection towards her. The feeling of subjugation by her husband is so strong in her that she feels that she has nothing that she can offer her young daughter. Even physically there is little common between them. The mother asks herself "How did I, so plain, so common, get a daughter like her?" (*Collected Stories,* Vol. 1, 45). The story starts with a confrontation between the mother and daughter. The daughter comes home from school and wants the mother to give her ideas and points for a two-page essay on robin. The mother, unsure of herself as ever, stammers, "I don't know...I know nothing about it. Except that it's a pretty bird. With a red breast...and it comes in winter..." (45). She understands as much about robins as she understands her own child. The bird, robin, stands for the child, for an unfamiliar, untreadable ground and the daughter makes it clear that the mother has again failed her.

On being offered help and information, irrelevantly as it appears, on sparrows, mynas and finally on peacocks, the daughter stamps out of the room, saying, "I will ask Papa. He's sure to know, he'll help me" (46). To escape from this rejection, the mother is lost in the memories of her own childhood and of the peacocks in a temple, which she, as a child used to visit with her grandmother. She recalls how she would quiver with anticipation, wonder breathlessly whether the peacocks would come out and dance for her. Peacock becomes a symbol for something familiar, comfortable, and for a world that the mother hankers after, a world that is no longer there. But it is the robin that is strange, exotic and desirable in this world, not the peacock. Shashi Deshpande has summarized the mother's utter helplessness by making her cry out in exasperation in the following words—"It is as if I am, in my own house, confronted with two closed rooms I am condemned to sit outside and gaze helplessly at the closed doors" (47).

Later that night, after her husband has shown the daughter different books from which she could get information on robin, and has withdrawn himself to listen to music alone as he does every night, the mother goes to bed. It is during the night that the mother, who is feeling very vulnerable, confused and depressed, hears sobs from the daughter's room. Though her first impulse is to check herself from going to her daughter, thinking it would be the father that the girl wants, as always, she finally gathers courage to go and see what ails the kid, leaving her husband in deep sleep. This gathering of courage, this taking a bold step towards the daughter is the determining factor in breaking the barrier between the two. It was on this night that the daughter, no longer a mere child has crossed the threshold to womanhood. In those painful and bewildering moments, the mother and daughter find each other, re-forging the links, which had snapped long before. It is then that the mother, trying to comfort the daughter, tells her about the peacocks, tells her about her childhood and about herself. For once the daughter is ready to listen to the mother, to acknowledge that she is after all a person worthy of notice. The bridge over the gaping gap is finally complete when finally the daughter sleepily says, "I'll ask the teacher—why not a peacock?" and the mother responds, "Why not a *robin?*" (52). In the end both the mother and the daughter are ready to take the necessary steps to understand each other's needs, to enter each other's worlds.

"It Was Dark" is another such story, which deals with the feelings of a mother whose fourteen years old daughter has been brought back home after three days of anonymity after abduction. The story explores the mind of the mother whose daughter has probably been raped and the fears and apprehensions, the guilt, memories, anger, frustration and feelings of hopelessness and helplessness have been so poignantly described that it immediately touches the heart. The story begins with the protagonist coming out of an ugly dream to come face to face with an even uglier reality. Her kid daughter is too traumatized to react to anything. The mother's frantic efforts to make her say something are only able to elicit a single expression "It was Dark" from the daughter who keeps staring at a point on the ceiling. The changes that the child shows after those three days of being away are not only beyond the comprehension of the mother but also horrific. She tries to reach out to her daughter, trying to find the child of old times in her but fails miserably.

Her agony is increased by the suggestion of a possible pregnancy and the course of action—an MTP—that would have to be taken in the eventuality, by her husband who has been told about it by the police and the doctor who had examined the daughter. The thought is sickening to her. She says "...he couldn't have found words more innocuous sounding, but relating them to my fourteen year old daughter, I found them obscene" (*Collected Stories*, Vol. 2, 126).

She is unable to accept the reality of the situation, which to her is almost fiction like. When the neighbours come visiting the enormity of the reality strikes her—"A few lines in the newspaper—I had read the thing so many times myself. But this time it was my daughter" (127). She wants to escape the ordeal of facing them although her husband tries to reason by saying, "Get it over with. You can't hide yourself forever" (127). She hates those visitors comparing them to the 'condolence visits' paid by people after her father's death. The agonized mother sees enemies all around the visitors, the fear, the loneliness, the dark. In her furtive attempts to bring her daughter out of the stupor and back to normalcy, the exasperated mother pulls back the curtains. Sunlight pours into the room filling it with brightness. And now that the room is no longer dark, the daughter's eyes move from the fixed spot to look at her mother. The story ends with a very suggestively eloquent short sentence "She saw me" (132). Thus at last she is able to reach out; to her daughter as a woman and as a human being.

Another story, "My Beloved Charioteer" depicts the story of a woman who is able to come to terms with her own loneliness and widowhood but is unable to make her daughter see reason in a similar situation. She had been living alone for seven years before her widowed daughter and her daughter come to live with her. She says, "I had got used to this silence...it was a friendly silence, filled with ghosts of so many voices in my life. They came back to keep me company when I was alone—my younger brother, my aunt who loved me when I was a child, my two infant sons who never grew up, and even the child Aarti who seems to have no connection with this thin bitter woman who now shares the silence with me" (*Collected Stories*, Vol. 1, 182).

The mother tries to bring back her incessantly smoking daughter [whose "face has the arid look of a desert no smile, no happiness ever blooms there" (184)] to normalcy by engaging her in small talk but all her efforts are rebuffed curtly. She hopes that her daughter will talk and laugh again one day. Her failure to understand her own daughter amazes her. She feels that her daughter is hiding even her sorrow from her, guarding it jealously and would not let her approach. She realizes her daughter has closed all the doors on her. Her utter helplessness is conveyed with full force when she says—"Nine months I carried this daughter of mine in my body. I had felt every beat of her heart, every movement of her limbs within me. But and my doctor had told me this then—my pains and shocks could never penetrate to her, she was insulated against them. Even now, I have no protection against her pains. I suffer with her, but, like all my other emotions, it is a futile suffering for I cannot help her. I can only fumble and blunder and make things worse" (183). She tries to build bridges to reach out to her daughter, to tell her "You cannot hold on. You will have to let go" (188). But the lack of communication is so immense that she only keeps struggling. Opportunity comes when the daughter knocks down a photograph of her late father accidentally and the glass on it cracks. She seizes this opportunity to tell her daughter, who feels as if she has committed a crime towards her mother, that she let go her husband the day he had died. She recounts some oddities in the character of her husband. At the end of it the daughter springs up and glares at her mother. Thus the mother at last succeeds in making the daughter to 'look at' her. It does not bother her if the change in the attitude of the daughter will be for the better or for worse. What satisfies her is that the channel of communication has been opened. The monotony in the life of her daughter has been broken and she will now be able to respond to things around her in a normal way as she has to her mother.

Corresponding to these mothers' narrative is the portrayal of her mother by a daughter and her effort to understand her mother in the story entitled *Memorabilia.* In this story a daughter, the youngest of siblings who is on an ostensibly usual, normal stay at her mother's house, finds it difficult to convey to her mother that her daughters wanted her to give up her home of forty years, around which most of her life centered, and live with them in turn.

The daughter starts with apprehension, fearing resistance in the form of anger and tears. The mother's ready acquiescence surprises her and they start clearing up instantly. She is unnerved by the silent, passive apathy of her mother willing to let the daughter tell her what to do next. After sorting things out when the mother-daughter duo is about to retire for the day, the daughter catches sight of her mother's wooden 'kumkum' box and when her mother sees it, she wishes to keep it with herself. The box opens up a door of memories to her and she is lost in her past. Later that night the mother wakes up after having a bad dream about her own mother. Unable to go back to sleep, she tells the daughter about her own mother who had died in childbirth. She tells her that her mother went to her parents' house in a remote village, without any medical aid, every year for delivery because as her aunt had told her, she wanted to be away from her husband. She is supposed to have said, "If I get away, I'll get some more time between babies. Six months away means that the next baby will come six months later" (*Collected Stories,* Vol. 2, 111).

She still remembers and fully agrees with her aunt's comment on her sister, "My sister was a strong woman but what choice did she have?" (111).

This sentence serves as an eye-opener for the daughter. She realizes that her mother may be ageing, isolated, friendless and incapable of living alone but she is reluctant to give up her home and by forcefully making her do so her own daughters are leaving her no choice. The story ends with the daughter giving up her idea of winding things up at her mother's place, hoping that her sisters too would understand. There is a new understanding in the relationship between the mother and daughter. This bridging of gap, the re-establishing of links, the new found appreciation of each other's feeling by a mother and a daughter are an interesting aspect of Shashi Deshpande's stories which is rare in the writings of other writers.

Corresponding to mother's narratives are the daughter's portrayals of their mothers in some of Deshpande's stories. Though the mothers in most of Deshpande's stories try to build bridges, trying to understand their daughters, in these stories the daughters see their mothers in a negative light. The antagonistic attitude of the daughters is sometimes due to the almost villainous attitude of the mothers when they were younger. At other times it is the unreasonableness of either party. These daughters are portrayed as being closer to their respective fathers. Shashi Deshpande breaks the immensely powerful mother myth in these stories. She negates the concepts and ideas that have made it impossible for us to get past the image of the ever forgiving, the always sacrificing mother. She says at a place, "When I became a mother, I found such a discrepancy between what I was told about how mothers felt, and what I really felt, that I was deeply disturbed. It was only as a writer that I could get across this disturbing split and approach reality. And I realized that motherhood does not turn you overnight into a different person, it does not make you a nobler, stronger, more loving and lovable individual. You are the same person, except for the enormous bond that suddenly appears between you and the newborn. In fact we know that mothers can be selfish, jealous, possessive, that they can even at times be cruel" (Telling Our Own Stories, *Writing from the Margin and Other Essays,* 97).

The story entitled "A Liberated Woman" portrays one such mother, who is unable to forgive her daughter for marrying against her parents' wishes. In place of feeling happy for her daughter on her marriage, she curses her. In fact the daughter attributes her own unhappiness to these curses of mother. The mother disowns her daughter and does not meet her or talk to her for the rest of her life. She dies of cancer but is unwilling to let her daughter be informed about it although she is a medical practitioner. The story being short does not divulge the details of the relationship but Shashi Deshpande later expanded the story into a full-fledged novel *The Dark Holds No Terrors* wherein we find the causes and effects of this strained relationship etched out in detail. Mother in this story is contrary to what is usually the stereotypical picture of one.

Similarly in the story "The Awakening" the mother figure is an aggressive, frustrated, and cribbing woman, who is partial in her attitude towards her son. Her own daughter thinks of her in the following words, "God made mothers because He could not be everywhere himself. What nonsense! There are mothers and mothers and mothers. Mine is a woman with a heavy, sullen face (but when she looks at Shirish) and a tongue like a serrated knifė (but when she talks to Shirish)" (*Collected Stories*, Vol. 1, 115).

The story is about a family of a postal clerk who has a bright child in Alka. She wants to have a proper education and become something in life so that she would not have to continue with the drudgery of this life of clerks. Unlike her, her elder sister thinks that clerks are also people. After Alka's SSC exams are over she is offered the job of a typist by an acquaintance. Her mother wants her to leave her studies and take up the job while she wants to continue with her studies. This becomes the cause of a constant quarrel between the two. Unfortunately her father dies suddenly and, in the words of

Alka, her way of escape is 'closed up'. She has to shoulder her father's burden, howsoever unwilling she might be. The story ends with Alka finding a letter in her late father's briefcase in which he had expressed his faith in the abilities of his daughter and hoped that unlike him, she would be able to achieve something in her life. The letter restores her faith and gives her courage to continue working not only to share her father's burdens and responsibilities but also to realize her own dreams.

"Madhu" is another story, which depicts a mother who is not exactly cruel or negative but is on the point of exasperation at being unable to understand her own daughter Madhu. Madhu is a young woman who is impertinent, casual, careless, impatient and intolerant of her parents. She is doing her B.A., which in her own view is pointless, only to please her parents. Her real interests lie elsewhere and she spends most of her time out of the house either freaking out with friends or working on the magazine she and her friends are bringing out. Her father says, "She treats this house like a hotel, a place to eat and sleep. We can't even ask her where she's going or when she'll return home. She flares up. And no help at home at all." (*Collected Stories*, Vol. 2, 95).

The mother's opinion is no better, "It's funny when your daughter treats you like a stranger. Almost an enemy...the only thing we do together is fight" (94). Madhu on her part has her own complaints. She thinks that her mother is always ready to misunderstand her. But the same Madhu changes drastically when her father has a heart attack and is admitted in a hospital. She behaves in a very mature way and seems to have suddenly grown up.

She even pledges to sacrifice something dear for her father's good health and then gets her beautiful long hair cut when her father gets well. However, once the father is back home and everything falls into routine, she is back to her old ways. The story portrays the differences between two generations very touchingly.

"And Then" is another story where the mother is not precisely a sacrificing, forgiving, understanding or loving one.

Once again the mother figure portrayed here is that of bitter and disillusioned woman who knows very well that she is not the priority of her children. She feels like an outsider in her son's house where she has come to live as a result of her daughter's departure to the US for further studies and career advancement. She does try to stop her daughter from leaving but the daughter is determined to go. The mother realizes "I could rage, throw a tantrum, burst into tears—nothing would stop her. And yet knowing I could change nothing, I went on arguing until irritation began to creep into her words, desperation into mine" (*Collected Stories*, Vol. 2, 174).

She uses her last weapon on her daughter, saying that her late father would not have liked his daughter going abroad without getting married first, but is deterred by her daughter telling her about having talked to her father about it when he was alive. She realizes to her horror that both of them are actually using a dead man to put forward their view and withdraws. But this does not stop her from seeing her own children's selfishness. Even small gestures of her children are enough to indicate to her their real thoughts. Thus Deshpande takes a more realistic view of motherhood exposing not only the excitement and wonder of being a mother but also the frustrations and disappointments.

The women portrayed in her stories, whether as a mother or as a daughter are authentic, credible and realistic. These women react to every situation and are sensitive to every event. They try to reason out each and every action of theirs, struggling hard to understand life in reality. These characters are not just mothers or daughters, or even just women; first and foremost they are humans in different circumstances, living in different conditions and with different personalities. They have their own desires, frustrations and ambitions. They express them in their own way and each looks for her way of realizing her ambitions and each comes to terms with her problems in her own way.

WORKS CITED

Deshpande, Shashi. Afterword, *The Stone Women*. Calcutta: Writers' Workshop, 2000.

——. *Writing from the Margin and Other Essays*. New Delhi: Penguin, 2003.

——. *Collected Stories*, Vol. 1. New Delhi: Penguin, 2003.

Horney, Karen. *Feminine Psychology*. New York: Norton, 1967.

10 Promotion of the Patriarchal Cruelty Through Female Agency: A Study of Shashi Deshpande's *The Dark Holds No Terrors*

Monika Bhatnagar

Name of Shashi Deshpande needs no introduction. Gifted with a rare literary bent of mind, she has made a niche of herself among Indian English novelists. Beginning her career at the time when Indian women (especially the middle-class educated woman who is financially independent) were struggling for liberation, Shashi Deshpande has become well aware of her plight. In fact, the awareness is well revealed in the projection of the inner picture of women in her novels. She is rightly placed above to her contemporary Indian women novelists because of the meticulous introspection and psychological probing of the subconscious and unconscious of her characters.

Most of the Indian novels that deal with woman's issues offer a peripheral treatment of the cruelties inflicted upon a woman by another woman; rather those sum up in establishing the stereotypical tortures hit upon the woman by Indian male. *The Dark Holds No Terrors* by Shashi Deshpande is a new phenomenon in the sense that it vibrated the typical patriarchal image of Indian male by substituting it with a woman who does her best to add the agony of the female protagonist. In this paper, my aim has been to treat the concept of 'female-female' polarity as a natural and inherent factor in a social and psychological framework. Central motif is the family relationship which establishes the construction of the female gender by the females.

The novel proposes the pitch for the Post-Modern dilemma of an educated woman who refuses to internalize the generally accepted norms attacking female individuality and identity. The origin of antipathy is another woman in the novel, Saru, the female protagonist's mother, who is the main representative of the values and canons fixed by a patriarchal society. The irony lies in the crucial factuality that a female can be made an agency for the elevation of a male point of view. The mother-daughter relationship is based on the ever increasing estrangement.

The novel *The Dark Holds No Terrors* begins in a captivating manner with the female protagonist's (better known as Saru) coming back to her parental house apparently to stay with her widower father, but the fact correlates with Saru's attempt of escapism from the nightmarish brutality of her sadist husband, Manu. During stay in her father's place, Saru is provided with the opportunity to ponder over the happenings of her life, comparing and contrasting those with her present-day life. In this way, the layers of the past are unfolded to the readers with the simultaneous knowledge of the present. The stream of consciousness made her recall the childhood experiences, her estranged relationship with her mother, Kamalatai, her marriage with the handsome versatile looking young poet, Manohar, the suffering which follows, and her daughter Renu and son Abhi.

The problem commences with the belittlement of Saru's rank in the family in comparison to her brother, Dhruva. When alive, he is being mother's darling and Saru is perfunctory. Later she is held responsible for Dhruva's death. She has been continuously accused of her brother's death by her mother: "Why didn't you die? Why are you alive when he is dead?" (29-30). This leaves an indelible impression on her soul. Various events are inscribed on her mind to indicate how she had been treated second to Dhruva. She recalls one of her dialogue with her mother:

"Don't go out in the sun. You will get even darker. Who cares?"
"We have to care if you don't. We have to get you married."
"I don't want to get married."
"Will you live with us all your life?"
"Why not?"
"You can't."
"And Dhruva?"
"He is different. He is a boy."

The values of the male-dominated society are being projected by the mother.

Saru is offended again and again even for her body:

> "You're growing up; she would say. And there was something unpleasant in the way she looked at me...."
>
> "And it became something shameful, this growing up so that you had to be ashamed at yourself..." (55).

The predicament is not associated with generation gap; it is a power struggle in which a woman is robbed of her right of individuality and identity by another woman. The institution of home has become a snatching factor in the case of a female child, while at the same time, fostering the growth of a male child. In fact, our society structures females in such a way that they work against even those of their own gender. The male-female relationship is not so much responsible as the female-female relationship is for the enthralment and enslavement of the female sex. Saru remembers how the mother had strongly opposed her admission in Medical College. Contrary to her expectations, it was the father who has come-up to support her. Though unsuccessful, her mother attempted her best to dissuade him from sending Saru to study medicine:

> "You don't belong to that class: and don't forget, medicine or no medicine, doctor or no doctor, you still have to get her married, spend money on her wedding.... Let her go for a B.Sc. You can get her married in two years and our responsibility will be over" (130-131).

This proves that girls are considered a weight; a responsibility which has to be disposed of as early as possible. They have to be socialized in a way as to be perfect in the roles of wives. For this a girl has to adjust herself twice; first in her parent's house, and then in her in-law's house. Goffman terms these as the "primary adjustment" and the "secondary adjustment." These adjustments, especially the later, bring a number of bondages, under whose restrains a girl has to pass her life.

Even before marriage, Saru has reached the state of non-existence in the eyes of her mother. Later on, her mother has revengefully removed her from her life with the exception of a photograph only because her brother was also in it. Saru's mother abhorrently condemns her: "Daughter? I don't have any daughter. I had a son and he died. Now I am childless. I will pray to God for her unhappiness. Let her know more sorrow than she has given me" (178). Being impressionable and haunted by the terrifying memories of her childhood, Saru often feels that she is suffering due to the curse of her mother. Due to obsessive remembrance of her mother, a mark of guilt is imprinted on Saru's psyche. Ironically, the door of reconciliation is rushed with the entry of death. Dead or alive, her mother has been an empowering force, denying to Saru any happiness.

The early life experiences are so horrifying that Saru starts hating her own womanhood. She feels abhorrent and fears to be another Kamalatai: "A kind of shame that engulfed me, making me want to rage, to scream against the fact that put me in the same class as my mother" (55).

There exists an authority—a conflict between the mother and the daughter, where the daughter is the representative of modernity and the mother, as said above, is the mouthpiece of the male-orientation. Breaking the umbilical cord—leaving home—Saru announces her first war-cry to challenge the patriarchal hard power-system. Her relationship with her mother prepares the foundation for the structure under which she stands after being mature. Viewed as rival in the power game by Saru, her mother has been a threat to her individuality.

Saru's self-will was always at the point of demolishing. The archetypical terrible mother considers her daughter only as a person aimed to fulfill certain family responsibilities, having no choice of her own in her life, and supposed to follow the track which has been already prepared for her by her mother.

The deep-rooted repugnance is exhibited by the comment Saru makes: "If you're a woman, I don't want to be one" (55). Her mother's presence always perturbs Saru as she apprehends to be observed and investigated for final disapprovation and possibly for ultimate exclusion. Consequently an ardent desire develops in Saru to prove herself to the society as well as to that family which had been responsible for her pretty low self-esteem. But this childhood pressure lingers with her when she enters adulthood. Her act of marrying Manu, a promising young poet and the secretary of the Literary Association of the college, is another step to display her defiance and prove her strength. Being orthodox, Saru's mother is not in the favour of pratiloma marriage (Kane, 52). She condemns the idea rudely:

"What caste is he?"
"I don't know."
"A Brahmin?"
"Of course not" (87).

The mother's Parthian shot—"I know all these love-marriages. It's love for few days, then quarrels all the time. Don't come crying to us then" (62)—is a prognosis of the malfunctioning of Saru's married life.

Saru was ecstatic during the early years of her marriage as Manu was her husband—hero, whom she has chosen. Lower economic or social status does not matter at that time—but slit in the married life becomes visible with the passage of time when the initial 'role-playing' of Mrs. Manohar has been metamorphosed into a popular doctor. Manu's job of a teacher has been considered as trivial. The tenants of the chawl start giving more importance to Saru, the doctor. This marginalization from centre to periphery is replenished further when an interviewer reminded Manu of his perfunctory status:

"How does it feel when your wife earns not only the butter but most of the bread as well?" (182).

Saru's financial unswing and social rise give way to Manu's emasculation. The only alternative he can go for the assertion of his potence is through sexual aggression upon Saru, which is resulting in the 'dual personality' of Manu: a rapist at night and a loving, cheerful husband during the day. This transformed sexual relationship of the husband and wife encourages detachment and aloofness. The transition brings in its train the shifting of Saru from husband's home to father's house. But this shifting of Saru can be placed as a belated one on the part of a girl who has been a rebellion throughout her previous life. There is a reference in the novel to a woman who, ill-treated by her in-laws, drowns herself in a well. There is a reference to yet another woman victim who is tied to a peg by her in-laws and fed in the cattle shed. Saru detests the cold-blooded verdict announced by her mother: "she perhaps deserved it." Not only this, Saru dislikes the very idea of changing the name by one of her friends after marriage. On the other hand, she has lot of appreciation for her friend, Neelu, who is living a life of independence. All these reactions establish Saru as a vehement pleader for the cause of woman. Now, a woman with such a bent of mind is shown silently bearing the nightmarish brutality of her husband. The paradox lies not in Saru's personality, rather her repeatedly hurt ego by the mother does not allow her to admit miscalculation and defeat in conjugal life. It is only when the onslaughts became unbearable and she gets the news of her mother's death, Saru takes shelter in her father's house. For woman who has passed one phase of her life as a loveless, insecure existence, it is really difficult to accept the romantic ideal hero of her choice turned to be a sadist.

Conventionally, the mother-in-law is seen as a domineering figure by the women writers but in the novel the figure of the mother becomes a disintegrating factor. The thrust is more on woman's cruelty to woman than man's cruelty to woman. The emphasis is on the internalization of the patriarchal cruelty by woman. Saru's impetuous speech in the women's college highlights her vigorous reaction against such traditional norms which are taught to a girl as primary lessons by her mother:

> "Listen girls...whatever you do, you won't be happy, not really, until you get married and have children. That is what they tell us. And we have to believe them because no one has proved it wrong till now. But if you want to be happily married, there's one thing you have to remember. Have you girls seen an old-fashioned couple walking together? Have you noticed that the wife always walks a few steps behind her husband? That's important, very important, because it's symbolic of the truth. A wife must always be a few feet behind her husband. If he's an M.A., you should be B.A. If he's 5'4" tall, you shouldn't be more than 5'3" tall. If he's earning Rs. 500 you should never earn more than Rs. 499. That's the only rule to follow if you want a happy marriage. Don't even try to reverse the doctor-nurse, executive-secretary, principal-teacher role. It can be traumatic, disastrous" (124).

In the traditional sense of the term, this may be acknowledged as the way of the world by the females like Saru's mother, but Saru would opt for the unfrequented route. The hurdles and scrape do not deter her from striving, seeking, finding and not yielding. Being an educated woman, Saru cannot accept anything without reason. The females like Kamalatai do not understand that time has changed now and there is no use of putting all the restrictions on that growingly enlightened class which belongs to their own sex. In many cases, as Maria Mies says:

> "The non-conforming conduct of the woman is not the consequence of an external necessity but of changed consciousness. They are not satisfied with the rhetoric of equality between man and woman but want to see that the right to an individual life and the right to development of their individual capabilities are realized in their own lives."

The Dark Holds No Terrors focuses on the notion of non-acceptance of sexist discrimination ironically popularized by females. The novel centralizes on the independent social image of the woman, interdependent conjugal relationship of husband and wife, and impartial filial affection of the parents. Shashi Deshpande does not glorify woman's suffering; rather she maintains commendable objectivity. What the novelist simply tries to establish is that a woman, first of all is a human being, she too, has a right of choices in her life. What is wrong if she wishes to be recognized more as a person than as a woman. Today's society does not run on the idea of 'internalization of phallocracy' to borrow Spivak's phrase, but on the slogan of 'Yatheechasi Tatha Kuru,' in which there is a possibility of interdependence.

Towards the end of the novel, Saru remembers Madhav's words: "I cannot spoil my life because of that boy (his brother Satish). It is my life after all" (189). It is enough to make her realize the inner strength which she has forgotten for the time being. The fear of proving her mother right vanishes and we encounter a new, more energetic Saru who goes to Manu not to seek help but to complement him. Now her nights would no longer terrify as the dark holds no terrors to her.

Saru's coming back to her real 'inner space', i.e. her husband's house, is not indicative of submission to patriarchal edifice constructed by her mother; rather she comes back to reconstruct her emotional role(s) without deconstructing her gender identity.

REFERENCES AND NOTES

Deshpande, Shashi. *The Dark Holds No Terrors*. New Delhi: Vikas Publishing House Pvt. Ltd., 1980. All textual quotations, given in parenthesis, are from this edition.

Goffman, Erving. *Asylums*. New Delhi: Penguin Books, 1968.

Kane, P.V. *History of Dharma Shastra*. Poona: Bhandarkar Research Institute, 1941, 52. The union of a female of a higher *Varna* with a male of a lower *Varna* was termed as *pratiloma* marriage, *i.e.* against the proper order.

Maria, Mies. *Indian Woman and Patriarchy*. New Delhi: Concept, 1980.

11 Vedic Vision in the Poetry of Krishna Srinivas

K.A. Agrawal

Krishna Srinivas is the most outstanding name among the contemporary poets. He has addressed his poetry to the people of the whole world. His poetry breaks the limits of the boundaries of race, colour, clime and country. It blends the consciousness of the modern age with the ancient sublimity of great *rishies*. His poetry is read and enjoyed not only in his land but in foreign countries also. His poetry contains the essence of humanity. He is a poet of spiritual unfoldment. It moves from darkness to light.

Krishna Srinivas is an Indo-English poet of distinction, undoubtedly he is a classic of our times. His poetical works like *Dance of Dust*, *Everest*, *Five Elements*, *Beyond*, *Maya*, *Water* and *Sonnets* etc. are poems of "excellences." They contain human culture. His other poetry-books are *Sankara*, *Ramaneya*, *Vallalar*, *Madhavs*, *Christ*, *Muhamad*, *Tamil Vedas*, *Buddha* and *Mahavir*, etc. They are inspiring poems devoted to human values and world-unity. They transcend all barriers of religions, castes, creeds, colours and nations. Prof. Syed Ameenuddin rightly observes: "His life is a journey from darkness to illumination; a quest to know the blaze of realities; a tireless exploration to discover newer horizons; a task to lead others to lofty thoughts; to reach the core of the cosmos."

Dr. K.V.S. Murthi, a great critic on Krishna Srinivas, has also praised his poetry in these words:

> "The poetry of Krishna Srinivas, an internationally reputed poet admired as fiery cosmic articulator, is replete with multidimensional sensibility and energetic expression, idealism and cosmic sweep."

In his poem *Water* he says that the present world is a highly mismanaged world. He writes:

I cry with the river,
I grow with the river,
I frolic with the river,
I age with the river,
I regenerate with the river.

Here Krishna Srinivas has presented a poetic vision, water has been symbolised. It is the source for life but its purity has been polluted by the ever-crowded civilization.

Dance of Dust was published in 1946. This poem is one of his early epical poems which established him as one of the living greatest poets of the contemporary literature. It is an extraordinary poem with the utterances of humanity. It moves from darkness to light. In fact the darkness is because of the ego. Of course our true nature is divine but ignorance and sense of pride cover our divinity. So unless we cross the river of ego we cannot reach the bank of light. This poem reminds us of the Vedic declaration, *Tamso Ma Jyotirigamaya*. It means O Lord lead us from darkness to light. It is a wonder that in spite of the neat floor and clean lamp with full oil there is no light. The human being is not able to get light. The poet tells his readers that through ignorance the common people keep themselves separate from God. Ignorance is a strong rock which does not allow to see the Divine Light. It hides our true nature and through ignorance the true self becomes the fantasy of an age. The poem moves from common and worldly life experiences to uncommon and divine experiences. In this way *Dance of Dust* is philosophical and symbolical poem. In other words, the theme of the poem is *destruction and construction of the world*. It reminds us of wars. The poet himself says:

"The war came—carving cemeteries of cities, planting fevers in the arteries of our world.... And this long poem 'Dance of Dust' is the pouring of my agonising soul.... Past is my born, I hunger for the reign or everlasting peace and Paradise Regained."

The poem has the development of religious sensibility. People are ignorant of their own actions. Their lives are loveless confusion of struggle and flight. The whole world is suffering from the disease of ignorance and scepticism helplessly. The modern people are suffering from religious uncertainty because they are on the darkling plain. The poet says:

Man kills man in sport,
And flags dripping with blood;
Flutter over peaks of flesh;
And ships loaded with gold and ivory,
Sweep the seven seas in revelry,
Babes torn from women's breast,
Are sold as slaves to silver might;
And raped to honey dew;
In silken chalice of juicy crevice,
In the name of art, religion and rule.

The lines are the cry of agonised soul of the poet. He revolts against the existing culture and social norms of the world:

Culture sleeps in many beds,
In vagrant shades and truant times,
Ravishing connoisseurs
Feeding genius with fires from many hearths,
Snug silent, antediluvian.

The poem exposes the drawbacks of modern society. We are coloured in western culture which has renaissance spirit and teaches us only to lead a materialistic way of life. But *Dance of Dust* inspires us to embrace Vedantic-Culture of purity. Auden declares, "We must love each other or die" while Arnold says, "Oh love! let us be true to each other." Krishna Srinivas has conveyed the message of "World Peace" and "spiritual unfoldment" through this poem. For the immortal preaching, it has been liked by the scholars. It has been accepted by a host of readers because it exposes violence against women, children and innocent people. It must be stopped otherwise all culture and social progress will come to an end. It is in every inch an Indian poem characterised by the qualities of Beauty, Truth, Goodness, Love and Power.

Here *Dust* has symbolical meaning. It stands for unrest, violence, exploitation and terrorism. The poet prays to God that the people should realize their mistakes and there should be a cultural-revolution. He dreams about the economic, cultural, social and intellectual emancipation of the people.

A storm of conquest,
Taming the wrath of seas to ply the oars,
Accumulating the filth of bloody wars,
Pricking the bubbles,
Pinning the babes,
Tearing the rainbows from heavens,
Fluttering banners of bureaucratic pride,
India gleams as lea of quietude.

There should be no discrimination between man and man because caste, creed and colour are based on falsehood. All are children of God and therefore the ruling class has no right to oppress and exploit the masses. All types of oppressions like physical, economic, social, religious or cultural must be stopped. This poem cultivates Indian values of life, art, literature and culture.

Christ crooned commandments;
Buddha dreaded dust
And counselled caution, Nirvana,
Exhilarating Transcendence.

Both Lord Buddha and Lord Christ had worked for the spiritual gains of humanity. Here gods and human beings play with each other. The poet has full faith in the Divine Nature. He writes:

Despair not:
You and dust anon must
Fix the lease of rigmarole

And hush the wrath of wormy wars
And crack its typhus in an iron tomb.

He advises to take the journey from dust to divinity. The different types of wars, conflicts, quarrels and disputes are in the world because we have forgotten our divine nature. We should realize our divinity and we should follow the goal of human upliftment. It is possible only through national and international integration. He gives the gospel of human unity in this poem because *Earth is the best space for love.*

In the *Five Elements* the poet deals with five elements—water, wind, fire, earth and void. These elements are present from time to eternity. Here the poet has energized his spiritual resources for the future generations. Here he criticises terrorism, violence, horror and nuclear wars because they are mounting upon the humanity. The poet writes:

In passion I am born
In passion I live
In passion I perish
So too, you, my Kaveri.
* * * *
At Kaveri ghats
Sages and saints chant their beads
And lisp a million Om
Grow million fires
Char million desires.

The poem emphasises upon the need of human unity to solve the tension between different human groups. In this poem the poet wants to convey the philosophy of ONENESS. His approach is bound to be synthetic. The poem bridges the gap among politics, religion, philosophy, science, mythology and theology. The poet is conscious of the fact that anger, greed, passion, arrogance, hatred, terrorism, violence, exploitation of man by man, national and international prejudices, tension, hypertension, cultural ignorance, other ignorances, communalism, pollution, ecological imbalance and other evils are challenging the very existence of mankind. So the poem preaches the solution for all these evils. It can be possible only through human unity. This poem is a precious document of humanity. Rapid technological growth has brought moral degeneration. The chilling moral stagnation has eaten the bones of our civilization. The global catastrophe is increasing day by day. The mankind is suffering from a transformational crisis. It takes the reader to the long cultural and poetic journeys which will enlighten us with self-knowledge, spiritual wisdom and universal message of oneness and it is read and enjoyed as a precious document of humanity. It transforms, the hearts and minds of human beings from darkness to light. The references of vedic literature and ancient sages in the poem are the sources as nectar to the morally degenerated world of today. The poem raises its voice loudly against vulgarity and profanity of world culture.

In this poem Krishna Srinivas shows his intelligence, a sound sense of culture, history, philosophy and rare genius of aestheticism. It touches classical heights.

Maya is a socio-philosophic poem. It reveals the mystery of all existence. Krishna Srinivas has taken *maya* into a new vision. He says that those who denounce *maya* are ignorant because *maya* can never be seen as distinct from *Brahman*. Often people call *maya* as *avidya* but we should keep this fact in mind that both *maya* and *vidya* are properties of *Brahman*. Whenever there is failure to see the world as creation of *Brahman*, there arises *moha*, *shoka* and *dukh*. Poet Srinivas believes that the self and the entire world are nothing but the absolute *Brahman*.

The poem *Maya* is an interesting narrative poem which deals with the relationship between man and woman. The poet begins this poem in a socio-philosophic way:

From the Unreal lead me to Real
From languor lead me to light.
From death lead to eternity.

The poet has considered *maya* in the human shape and narrates her story. A mythical character Maya is the 19 years old daughter of Geetha who works in an office. She showers her love, affection and kindness on Maya. The teenaged girl also regards the soft sentiments of her mother. But their temple like house is collapsed when one day the girl is informed by her maid-servant about the questionable life of her mother. Her mother has illicit relations with her office-boss. Here we are reminded of the typist lady in T.S. Eliot's poem *The Waste Land*.

Like T.S. Eliot, Krishna Srinivas also discovers the modern myth of corruption. It is a general belief that when the woman becomes corrupt, she produces corrupt children and then the whole civilization becomes corrupt. The purity of human race surely depends upon the purity of the mother. But here Krishna Srinivas does not believe the old rotten belief. He does not agree that corrupt mothers produce corrupt children. There have been many corrupt mothers but their daughters have adopted the path of purity and virtue. The poem *Maya* deals with the theme of the man-woman and mother-daughter relationships. The poem reminds us Goldsmith's famous lines on Woman-character. He writes:

When lovely woman stoops to folly
And finds too late that men betray
What charm can soothe her melancholy
What art can wash her guilt a way.

The answer is only to repent for her wrong deeds. The poem is a beautiful narration about the character of 19 years old girl Maya who in spite of her mother's corrupt life comes out as a woman of purity and virtue. The poet has emerged here as an experimentalist. He has dealt here with man and woman relationship as creative endeavour and co-operative action. It is in their creativity, co-operative attitude, confidence, and purity that the future of the world community depends. The whole poem has been written in a philosophical mood, vein, tone and language. It is an innovative poem. Dr. R.K. Singh observes:

> "Through *Maya*, Krishna gives the message of liberty, restraint and truthfulness."

Dr. Syed Ammeruddin's words about *Maya* are most worthy to be quoted here:

"The institution of marriage has been created not only to streamline the way of flesh and the hunger of ravishment but also to blow off the last particles of broken dust paving way to serene calm and thrushing man and woman into a dual heaven...everlasting Eden...perennial paradise."

Krishna Srinivas advocates for conjugal love. Man and woman should lead the life of purity as husband and wife. This poem emphasizes the importance of the divine characters which are possible as an ideal couple—husband and wife. Only then they can see and realize the purity and divinity in their inward parts. Thus they can find the spirit of truth and realize the kingdom of heaven upon this earth. Such a couple can find peace and harmony on this earth. In fact, man's true nature is divine and the knowledge of the self can make the man and woman illumined. The poet's discovery of Maya in our modern world is praiseworthy. His Maya stands for purity and a symbol of woman-virtues.

His next poem *The Everest* has the theme of the fusion of various elements. The poet develops a theory of human history in the poem. He fuses the human history with that of geographical birth of the Everest. He fuses the image of the past and the present into a unified whole. It is a systematic study of both the histories for more than fifty millenniums. The poet closely watches and interprets the links of the Everest and the mankind. It is the witness of many human civilizations of the past. The poem shows underground connections and seeds of comparative religion, philosophy, culture and anthropology.

And that day will dawn
When gods churn again
An Everest morn

The poet uses in this poem the images of vast abyss, darkness, magic zodiacs, fossilized earth and image of the past and present into a unified whole. For him the Everest is a natural beauty.

I searching Me
And Me searching Thee
And I and Me

Mirrored in He
I and Me no different He.

He sings of 'Eternity' with philosophical ideas. He emphasises to keep alive India's prime principle of equality, liberty, fraternity, universal brotherhood and love for humanity. The poem achieves the aesthetics of impersonality. It emphasises the need for multi-culturalism. The various religious thinkers, prophetic genius and literary giants bestow the best elements of tradition of multi-cultures:

Mohameds and Christs
Dantes and Shakespeares
Blakes and Eliots
Bubbled at the brim
** ** ** ** **
Vyasas and Badaryanas
And sagely tribes
Seeded in Manna icicles
Drip Vedic Chants
And Upanishads
In words heard and memorised

He thinks that Everest is a cup of *som rasa* of wisdom. It is a symbol of the harmonies of heart, mind and soul. It represents Indians' sublime culture and civilization. It creates an enchanting world of eloquence, harmony and genius, the poem is a store-house of Indian-philosophy. The poet has used befitting references of the Ganges, the Kaveri, the Yamuna, the Upanishads, the Bhagavad Gita and the incarnates of Indian life like Lord Krishna and Lord Buddha. He has also referred to the great contributions of great contemporary personalities like Mahatma Gandhi and Pt. Jawahar Lal Nehru. The poem pleads for human justice and it is possible only by accepting the principles of equality, liberty, fraternity, love and universal brotherhood.

Present echoing the past
And becoming ravished beyond
Fifty millenniums ago
From rage of atoms rose

Cephalized metazoa
Rolled up and enveloped
And god burnt to bone
Rose over fossiled earth

The musical expressions and the philosophical ideas of the poem move our hearts as nothing has moved them earlier. It watches the cycles of civilization. It also represents the multi-culturalism which is the need of the time. It is a classical poem having sublime thoughts of world-unity, world-peace and world-order.

His poem *Tamil Vedas* shows his great mastery over Tamil literature and language. In Tamil the four thousand lyrics are very famous and the Tamils all over the world sing them as a part of their prayer, they are the soul of *Vaishnavism*. Krishna Srinivas has presented the gist of the *Tamil Vedas* in beautiful poetic form. Dr. Syed Ameeruddin has rightly observed:

> "Since all the four Vedas are sung in Sanskrit, these Aposetles, called Alwars, have transported into Tamil all the countries where Tamils live, these immortal lyrics of Alwars are sung with great devotion every morning. Especially in East, descendants of Tamil, who migrated into these countries millenniums ago, sing with gusto these soul stirring verses."

The poet has used very simple but harmonious style in composing verses in his poem *Tamil Vedas*. Like a *Sadhaka* he has devoted his true sublimity to this poem. He has followed the Vedic dictum *Charaiveti, Charaiveti*. Some of the lines in the poem may be read like *mantras*.

Krishna Srinivas is not only lover of India but he is also a staunch lover of the entire universe and mankind and so the scope of his poetry is not a prison-house of one ideology or nation or culture but it is as vast as the open sky. He believes in *Vasudev Kutumbhkam*.

His poetry achieves the power of the *mantra* to register and master experience. He often repeats words, phrases and sentences to emphasise his viewpoint and depicts his experiences. He has done a lot of translations from Sanskrit, Tamil, Arabic and other languages. But he is not a mere translator or borrower, he has the Shakespearean quality. Whatever he borrows from other sources, he totally absorbs it and makes it as his own. We can say in bold words that Krishna Srinivas is a great modern poet. In the end I quote the words of Dr. Syed Ameeruddin which is the true appreciation of this great Indo-Anglian poet:

> "Krishna's *Divine Blaze* illumines the most universal theme—KNOW THYSELF. It is to discover one's archetypal being through complexity of imagery and thought, uniting life and pursuit. His imagination transcends the permutation of aradoxes used to uncover the mysteries of existence."

WORKS CITED

Ammeerudin, Syed and Krishna Srinivas. *A Colossus in World Pannassus.* Madras: World Poetry Society, 1995.

Benegal, Som. "A Bold Peace Approach." *The Hindustan Times*, August 2, 1996.

Dwivedi, Suresh Chand. *Krishna Srinivas: A Poet of Total Experience.* Madras: World Poetry Society International, 1997.

Filler, Buckminster. *Modern Poetry*. Delhi: OUP, 1985.

Gokak, V.K. "The Concept of Indianness with Reference to Indian Writing." *Indian Writing in English*. ed. Ramesh Mohan, 1994.

Iyenger, K.R.S. *Indian Writing in English*. Bombay: Asia Publishing House, 1973.

Mahadevan, T.M.P. Western Vedant in *Vedant for Man*. Ed. Swami Yatishwamand. London: George Allen and Unwin Limited, 1952.

Murthi, K.V.S. *Krishna Srinivas: A Poet*. Madras: World Poetry Society International, 1980.

Parthasarathy, R. (Ed.), *Ten Twentieth Century Indian Poets*. Delhi: OUP, 1984.

Shields, M.E. *Krishna Srinivas and His Poetical Works*. Delhi: OUP, 1987.

Singh, R.K., Krishna Srinivas and S.C. Dwivedi. *Krishna Srinivas: A Poet of Total Experience*. Madras: World Poetry Society International, 1997.

Srinivas, Krishna. *Poetical Works*. Madras: World Poetry Society International, 1979.

Yatiswamand, Swami. *Spiritual Unfoldment in Vedant for Modern Man*. London: George Allen and Unwin Limited, 1952.

12

Quest for Identity with Shashi Deshpande

Sangeeta Das

Shashi Deshpande is a present time author in Indian writing in English, her valuable contribution dates back to the 70s and 80s. Her main subject of discussion is adjustment problems and conflicts of educated middle-class women who have to reconcile to the traditions and customs in spite of their desire to prove their individual identity in the society.

Shashi Deshpande's women vehemently reject whatever comes from past. They do not wish to look back but move on and make a place of their own in the male-society.

Shashi Deshpande has given a clarion call to the women through her novels to awaken them to their worth in the society. Educated middle-class women are focused in her novels which form the bulk of our society. She cannot be called a true feminist as per the definition put forth by her foreign counterpart because she stresses feminine freedom without open revolt and exclusion of male from their life. Abiding by the norms of our culture and society, Shashi Deshpande does not deny the necessity of the existence of man in a woman's life in our country but at the same time, she defies total subjugation of woman before man absolving herself of her responsibilities towards herself as a human being.

In *That Long Silence*, Shashi Deshpande discusses the mute supplication of Jaya not only to her husband Mohan but her continuous obeisance to her father then to her elder brother and finally the most to her husband. Jaya's life is a living example of a middle-class educated woman of today's society who compromises at all the stages of her life in order to secure her position in the family.

Jaya was a good writer who had won a prize which was snubbed by her husband who looked hurt instead of elated at her achievement. In order to quell her husband's irritation, she goes as far as giving up her writing. She was driven by an internal fear of jeopardizing her marriage.

Reluctantly she reconciled to a stereotyped life of a housewife who would arrange the sheets, wash the utensils, prepare food and send children to school. Her weakness to defy such a bonded existence makes the reader feel disgusted at the helplessness of her position.

Shashi Deshpande has held a mirror before us. Most of us are prototypes of her characters. Adjustments to such an extent of plummeting the very flowering of a woman's life and career has to be fought against. But fighting so, we do not wish to downgrade the men-folk nor are we doing so just out of prejudice but for our existence and upliftment. Awareness and awakening are two milestones, which have to be memorized by each woman of today. We alone can uphold our identity and march on shouldering the hardships and hurdles which come in its wake. This campaign is not easy for us but writers like Shashi Deshpande have provided us with enough insinuations through their novels in which each protagonist is one amongst us and has found a way out at the end. In *Roots and Shadows*—Indu and in *The Dark Holds No Terrors*—Saru present themselves as the women who want to go in self-quest and in the process, free themselves from the inhibitions of the society, culture, nature and also from their own conflicting emotions.

Traditional barriers and cultural shackles have no place in the life of Shashi Deshpande's heroines. Even Jaya who had kept silent since childhood till the day her husband forsakes her to clean himself from the charges against him, decides to resume her writing and establish her own existence because though her son Rahul comes back to her in the end and her husband's return is confirmed, she realizes the fact that life goes on and instead of pining for what had not been achieved, one has to make it worth living as one cannot escape from it.

Too much of importance of a man's existence in our life makes us vulnerable to their whims and our compliance to them is misconstrued by them as total dependence on them. Without looking upon them as our enemy, we should make them realize the truth that they are not our masters but companions in life who cannot exist without each other and are equally dependent on each other for a complete and accomplished life. In *That Long Silence* Mohan though did not wish Jaya to have an individual identity of her own could not bear the thought that she should remain indifferent to his problems and troubles. Misconstruing her reticence as indifference, he throws up tantrums and allegations that Jaya has not been a supportive wife to him when he had gone out of his way to give comforts to her and their children.

Mohan's unjust anger and enraged remarks and consequent desertion of Jaya though temporary, proves to be a turning point in Jaya's life. She realised the futility of subservience and relinquishing her docile attitude she tries to stand on her own legs and socks to break the age-old silence by deciding to refuse to dance further to the tune of her husband.

The protagonist Jaya of *That Long Silence* is a perfect representative of the modern woman of today. Her ambivalence and consequent mental turmoil make her a perfect picture of present women. Though Jaya can be intercepted in many different ways, I would like to figure her as a present-time woman of indecision who wavers between family and self-assertion. An Indian woman, I agree, cannot survive peacefully by denouncing her family but she cannot also flourish by quelling her desire to spread her wings and scale the sky of achievement. To strike a balance between the two crucial choices of a woman, she has to wriggle out of the pressure of the family and asserting herself, should perform both the duties—satisfying herself and enabling herself to prove her worth.

Shashi Deshpande has discussed two different images in the novel, which put a big question-mark on the relationship of a husband and wife. She has compared the husband and wife to a pair of bullocks yoked together which means the two have to go together in the same direction, violation of which would result into pain. Secondly, the two bullocks in spite of sharing the burden do not know whether one loves the other or not. The pair of bullocks goes together under compulsion whereas, the marital relationship should be based on love and affection. It involves two lives of opposite sexes who unite in love to form a family and no happy family can be formed under compulsion. Thus, such a comparison puts forth a bizarre picture of a husband-wife relationship. The two are expected to be considerate and compassionate towards each other and do the utmost to keep each other happy. But such a temperament is not shown in *That Long Silence*. Here the husband, Mohan, expects everything from the wife and never peeps into his heart to see if he was showing any feeling and compassion towards his wife. Many such pairs co-exist in the society today, who are emotionally aloof from each other. The wife being the worst sufferer because though she is educated yet is not allowed to establish her identity and thus the resulting clash becomes disgusted and indifferent.

Through Jaya's character, Shashi Deshpande has tried to portray the picture of a contemporary educated independent minded Indian woman who undergoes a mental ordeal as she cannot reconcile to her husband's ignorance of her ambition and also cannot forsake him simply because a husband in our society is like a sheltering tree without which life of an Indian woman becomes tedious.

Jaya, like a practical woman, wards off any comparison with mythical woman. She believes that these women have nothing in common with the demands of an educated, independent, progressive and ambitious woman of today. She regretfully accepts the fact that she herself had accepted everything about Mohan by blinding herself to the consequences like Gandhari and was also ashamed of her ignorance and inaction.

In our country of traditional background, a marriage between two persons does not necessarily have its foundation on love, which is important for a stable and permanent relationship. A loveless married life causes the wife and the husband to drift away from each other, resulting into a total failure. An understanding between the two is only possible with love for each other. A marriage without love is like a picture-drained of its colour. Mohan's acceptance of Jaya in his life as a matter of fact has been disastrous. He did the blunder of crushing both the woman and writer in Jaya, which proved that he had never loved Jaya. Her relationship with Mohan was casually accepted with their marriage but the patriarchal hierarchy in our society has always posed a hurdle in an even relationship between a man and a woman. Male ego has forever prevented a woman from exerting herself and prove her mettle. The *Sheltering Tree,* i.e. the husband has taken a wife to be a mute supporter and companion in his life disregarding her feelings and desires. They have never considered her to be a human-being of flesh and blood with emotions like themselves. Though the modern-educated woman of today has advanced far ahead of her predecessors, still she cannot deny the fact that even today man decides her destiny to certain extent. The man always believes that woman is vulnerable and can never survive in the society without their aid.

Many competently educated women of today have to compromise their career for their family in order to save their marriage and avoid the risk of annoying their husbands.

Shashi Deshpande shows through Jaya that the role assigned to a wife in our society, which is to stay at home, look after the children, cook the meals timely and keep out from the affairs of the world is resented by the woman of today. She being educated and armed well to face the cynic society does not agree to such conditions and wishes to fight her place out.

Shashi Deshpande and other women writers have dealt with the predicament of the modern-educated women in the traditional society which though has been said to have progressed yet has not slackened its stringency towards the women. As a consequence, the self-willed and individualistic women have to face disgrace and suffering caused by broken relationships. Nevertheless, there is no dearth of progressive women who are striving to achieve fulfillment against the defiance of male chauvinism.

With the up thrust of women writers, various problems and injustices against women have been spotlighted and has also proved to awaken women to their capabilities and rights.

In *That Long Silence*, Jaya rejects the mythical women who are the symbols of women supplication and edification. Though women have been edified in the past, they have also been tortured on equal grounds. For example, Sita has been edified though she led a miserable life and had to give an evidence of her sanctity. Consequently, Shashi Deshpande's protagonists stridently fight to come out from being framed as such and live a full life on the earth and on equal footing with men.

Deshpande upholds marriage as the social infrastructure of a healthy society, what is painful is the persona of the wife and not the institution of marriage. When the protagonist compromises with the family she does not do so as a mere person to be taken for granted but as an individual with personal aspirations and desires. Jaya accepts her role as Mohan's wife not on the terms of docility but with the determination to establish her individuality and shun vulnerability.

She had hidden desires for fulfillment, which had been spurred by her father who wanted her to go as far as Oxford for higher education. This dream was nipped in the bud by the untimely death of her father, to her utter disappointment. Her dynamic personality was stunted and truncated by Mohan's selfishness and reprehensive behaviour towards her. Her participation in anti-price campaigns, adopting a child, writing forthrightly about man-woman relationships and finally aborting an unwanted third child came to stern rebuff from Mohan except the last, which she did secretly.

Saru in *The Dark Holds No Terrors* shows another phase of male-degradation. Her husband tortures her mentally and physically like a sadist beast just to satiate his male ego. Saru's success as a doctor was greatly resented by Manu and he unable to refute openly, fearing to become a laughing stock, spills his hatred over her at night making her life miserable.

Man in spite of being educated can never come to terms with a woman's success. Manu, himself being a junior professor and thus no doubt an educated man, could not free himself from the shackles of inferiority complex. At one time, Saru had offered to give up her work, which was also not acceptable to Manu for he was not ready to forego the heavy pay-packet brought in by Saru. The predicament of a woman is apparent at this juncture. Saru got a break to escape such a situation with her mother's death. Change of place and circumstances gave Saru time enough to review her relationship with Manu and coming to a formidable decision. Her existentialism helps her to accept the truth that every individual is alone but has to put up with social and inter-personal relations. After such a realisation, Saru could go back to her marriage with the merging of persona and self.

Shashi Deshpande has very adroitly dealt with the double-personality aspect of every modern educated middle-class married woman. In *That Long Silence*, Jaya undergoes a psychological tousle when the compliant Suhasini, her new name after marriage, is confronted with defiant Jaya whose animus had been sharpened by her father when young. Her period of married life comprises of confrontations between the two phases of her personality where the latter had to be trumpled in order to appease her husband's ego and save her marriage. But as comes off an inevitable outcome, Jaya is forced to choose between the two and put an end to a continuous struggle between the two phases of her personality which has totally left her thwarted and uprooted. In the end, she comes out to be a decided and determined woman who now knows how to strike a balance between her family and her identity in the family.

Through Shashi Deshpande's novels, the fact that we women are also partially responsible for our pitiable condition dawns on us. If we let the men fond for their own needs without making a doormat out of ourselves, they would know that they are not our sole masters and we, their bonded labourers. Vulnerability on our parts is also responsible for doubts of our capabilities. We educated women are at a more advantageous position than illiterate predecessors then why should we not come forward to take up the cudgels for uplifting our identity. Actually though we are educated and financially stable, we fear to lose the comfort of a well-supplied and well-supported home. But nothing has been achieved without sacrifice. Even our freedom fighters had to sacrifice much and forego enough to attain freedom for the country. Likewise, to attain the freedom of women and establishment of their identity, they have to relinquish the comforts and forsake compromise at the cost of their self-identity. Man has to be made aware of the capacities of a woman and accept her as a human being and his counterpart and not as a foil or a slave. Old Uncle's words to Indu in *Roots and Shadows* neatly sum up Deshpande's vision: "The whole world is made up of interdependent parts. Why not you?" Deshpande's heroine Jaya on reverting to her role as angry young writer with new revelations breaks that long silence which has shackled the women and had made martyrs out of them.

> "If I were a man and cared to know the world I lived in, I almost think it would make me a shade uneasy—the weight of that long silence of one-half of the world."
>
> —*Elizabeth Robins*

The women should, therefore, not belie their importance by compromising on the grounds of a social recognition because both a traditional and an unconventional woman suffer. The unconventional suffers for flouting the social norms and their aggressiveness while the traditional suffers for undue importance to male-ego and a consequent high-handedness of patriarchal male-oriented culture. However, there have been such males too, who have not underestimated a female-power of whom Swami Vivekanand was one who once said, "Educate your women first and leave them to themselves for we want that education by which character is formed, strength of mind is increased, the intellect is expanded and by which one can stand on one's own foot. With such education women will solve their own problems."

In the end, it is suffice to state that courage and not escapism is what woman of today requires. She should have the courage to uphold what is right for her and adhere to it with firm determination and tenacity. A headlong plunge into the social milieu with pertinacity can alone bring harmony and fulfillment in her life.

13 Gender Bias in Shashi Deshpande's *The Dark Holds No Terrors*

M.L. Garg

In this era of women empowerment, it is sacrilegious, if not dangerous, to speak of gender bias against women. Gender bias, however, has been a fact of life since time immemorial and we cannot wash it away. According to the Bible, God created man in His own image. And then the Lord God created Eve out of Adam's rib. Woman is taken out of man (though it is the mother who gives birth to a baby). God is male (created man in His own image). Man is created first. From the Bible to this day everywhere one can see a deep-rooted gender—bias; the bias has become part of the historical/textual tradition. Whether it is the popular saying that ten measures of a speech descended on the earth and man took only one while woman took nine or the common belief that a baby girl starts speaking earlier than a boy, or the notion that boys are good at mathematics and girls at language, there are all kinds of conceptions and misconceptions about the sexes expressed through language/literature. In all traditions women have always been considered inferior and incapable of any serious thinking; irrespective of religion, country, race, the period in which they live, more or less the same perception and sex—stereotyping is seen in language and literature.

"I want to reach a stage where I can write about human beings and not about women or men," claims Shashi

Deshpande, a leading Indian novelist writing in English today. In spite of the avowed aim of her creative writings, Deshpande's novels project a realistic picture of the middle-class educated women who are financially independent, who represent a larger part of the contemporary Indian society. Her novel *The Dark Holds No Terrors* is a harrowing tale of gender-bias prevalent in Indian society since centuries. It is the story of Sarita (Saru) who is a victim of her mother's biased behaviour towards her. Her mother's bitter words—"Why are you still alive.... Why didn't you die?"...uttered when as a little girl she was unable to save her younger brother Dhruva from drowning, leave an indelible scar on her soul.

Since her childhood Saru has always felt that to her mother, when compared to Dhruva, she herself was nothing. Throughout her life the childish grief of being unwanted swamps her unreasonably again and again. Saru is haunted by the words she had once written in a notebook: "Nobody likes me. Nobody cares for me. Nobody wants me...." (*The Dark Holds No Terrors*, 83). There was always a *puja* on Dhruva's birthday, while on Saru's birthday there was no *puja*. After Dhruva's death there were no more celebrations. Saru's mother held her responsible for Dhruva's death and refused to be reconciled to her till her dying day: "What daughter? I have no daughter" (108-09). Saru feels that she has been disowned. Her father never took any interest in her school or college. After Dhruva's death she just didn't exist for her mother. "I died long before I left home" (32).

Saru's father keeps fast on Dhruva's birthday. Saru revolts against her parents for cherishing Dhruva's memory; "Just because it is Dhruva's birthday, and because he happened to die, must I punish myself all my life like you do?"(180).

A son is regarded as something indispensable in an Indian family. The absence or death of the son makes the parents' world empty. Saru's mother holds her responsible for Dhruva's death. Till her death she is unable to reconcile to the fact that he has died. Her only consolation at the time of her death is that Madhav—a paying guest—is there to look after her husband. If there is no son, there is a son substitute. Madhav—

the paying guest—easily assumes Dhruva's place/role in the family. Kaka is more solicitous about him than about his own daughter. Saru questions—"All this concern for a boy who is nothing to you" (209).

Girls can't live with their parents after a certain age. Parents regard them as *Paraya Dhan*, something to be handed over, given to the rightful owner. They are not allowed even to move out in the sun lest their colour should get darker. Saru cannot avoid the pang of envy that shoots through her as she watches the sunlight fall full on Madhav's face, making his fair skin almost transparent, and she recalls her own experience with pain:

> "Don't go out in the sun. You'll get even darker.
> Who cares?
> We have to care if you don't.
> We have to get you married.
> I don't want to get married.
> Will you live with us all your life?
> Why not?
> You can't.
> And Dhruva?
> He is different.
> He's a boy" (45).

A woman has no right to a room of her own. She has right to choose nothing, not even her career. Saru's decision to take up medicine as a career stuns her mother who opposes it tooth and nail. She objects to Saru's becoming a doctor because she is a girl. Saru, however, knows the truth: "Yes, I am a girl. But it is more than that. I am not Dhruva" (144). A girl is just a responsibility to be performed, "But she is a girl...you can get her married in two years and our responsibility will be over" (144). Saru rightly protests: "Is that all I am a responsibility?" (144).

Shashi Deshpande portrays many women who have no identity of their own. There is Vidya, the incipient women's libber who finds gender bias even in Shakespeare's treatment of women. Shakespeare has a typical man's view of life—the man at the centre, the woman always on the periphery. "But it's not just their roles. It's the way he made the woman's personality merge into the stronger colours of man's personality" (156). Later Vidya turns a housewife as her husband does not like the idea of her going on the stage. "Everything in a girl's life, it seemed, was shaped to that single purpose of pleasing a male. But what did you do when you failed to please?," Deshpande indignantly asks (163).

After marriage a girl is never allowed to do things she wants to do. She has to do what her husband wants her to do. Saru's friend, Nalu, complains: "There is always time to do all the things 'he' wants to do, but never any time for doing the things you want to do. You just tag on to him and drift, a small boat towed by a larger ship..." (117). A husband even changes the name of his wife. A girl surrenders herself so completely to her husband that she does not mind sacrificing her identity to please him. Smita's husband changes her name to Gitanjali and she does not mind. The novelist protests: "This drastic change of identity, changing both the names that identified you for so many years...how then do you know yourself, and who you are?" (118).

Saru had once said in an inane interview to a woman's magazine: "It's all a question of adjustment, really. If you want to make it work, you can always do it" (118). But now she does not want to think of that, neither the interview, nor the girl who had done it, nor what followed after. Perhaps she does not want to admit that it is always the wife who has to do all the adjustment. A wife does not have the financial freedom to spend a small sum to purchase a small gift for her relative. She has to save a bit from what the husband gives for the household expenses. Smita considers Saru lucky as she does not have to ask anyone for money. She, however, does not realize the problems a working woman like Saru has to face.

It is thought that education and economic independence will go a long way in ensuring woman's emancipation. But women's emancipation is merely a mirage and Saru realises this bitter truth only after her marriage. After a torrid romance, Saru marries Manohar, a handsome romantic poet for love.

For sometime, all goes well. Manohar shows off his wife—a lady doctor—as a prized possession. But soon as Manohar's career moves nowhere, he suffers from inferiority complex and turns a sadist. He begins to attack Saru in the darkness of night inflicting untold physical and mental suffering on her. Once upon a time, Saru felt angry with those women who are a willing party to their humiliation..."all the indignities of a woman's life, borne silently and as long as possible because 'how do you tell anyone about these things?' Everything, kept secret, their very womanhood a source of deep shame to them" (107). But now she hates herself for letting her husband do it to her. "What he does to me he does it not because he hates me but because he hates himself. And I...I hate myself more for letting him do it to me than I hate him for doing it to me".

Saru's pride in her professional status evaporates soon after her business. There is only the work left. And that is now sheer necessity: the only thing that holds her together. But if it is her anodyne, it seems to be the cause of her disease as well. Saru ruminates: "It is because I am something more than his wife that he has become what he is. If I can go back to being nothing but his wife...and yet was I ever that?...he may no longer resent me" (78). Saru is prepared to sacrifice her profession to please Manu and save her marriage. However, the kitchen has to be run, the children have to be sent to a decent school so there can be no going back. They have to go on.

Saru realizes the futility of her surrender to her husband's tastes. Her abnegation to his tastes had seemed wholly natural at first. "Now, for the first time she found herself, wavering, hesitantly, making her way back to her real self. I, as I would like myself to be. But hunting for the real self had become rather like a dog scrabbling for a long buried bone. Piles of earth flew up, but where the hell was the bone? Or, had there been a bone at all?" (124).

There is no escape from a loveless marriage. Saru meets Padma in the hope of finding an escape but she has miscalculated. Padma wants what Saru cannot give. Suddenly Saru feels cold as if she was left alone in the middle of nowhere, one more hideout discovered, one more illusion shattered.

Saru is invited to give a lecture to the girls of a college in which Nalu teaches. She agrees:

> "Listen girls, she would say, whatever you do, you won't be happy, not really, until you get married and have children. That's what they tell us. And we have to believe them because no one has proved it wrong till now. But if you want to be happily married, there's one thing you have to remember. Have you girls seen an old fashioned couple walking together? Have you noticed that the wife always walks a few steps behind her husband? That's important, very important, because it's symbolic of the truth. A wife must always be a few feet behind her husband. If he's an M.A., you should be B.A. If he's 5'4" tall you shouldn't be more than 5'3" tall. If he is earning five hundred rupees, you should never earn more than four hundred and ninety nine rupees. That's the only rule to follow if you want a happy marriage. Don't ever try to reverse the doctor-nurse, executive-secretary, principal-teacher role. It can be traumatic, disastrous. And, I assure you, isn't worth it. He'll suffer, you'll suffer and so will the children. Women's magazines will tell you that a marriage should be an equal partnership. That's nonsense. Rubbish. No partnership can ever be equal. It will always be unequal, but take care that it's unequal in favour of your husband. If the scales tilt in your favour, god helps you, both of you.
>
> And so you pretend that you're not as smart as you really are, not as competent as you are, not as rational as you are, and not as strong either. You can nag, complain, henpeck, whine, moan, but you can never be strong. That's a wrong which will never be forgiven.
>
> Don't struggle, don't swim against the tide. Go along with it and if you drown nevertheless, well, that's an easier death after all. They will tell you about economic independence and an independent identity. Forget the

words. If Draupadi had been economically independent, if Sita had an independent identity, you think their stories would have been different? No, these are things that have been voluntarily surrendered, consciously abandoned that is the only way to survive. And what, in the long run, matters more than survival?

And it is your own teacher, that same Nalu, who told me once indignantly, an episode in Kalidasa's 'Shakuntala'. Of how Shakuntala, when rejected by the King, was advised by the escorting ascetics to stay on nevertheless in the King's harem, or as his slave, because he was, after all, her husband. And when the girl, weeping, shamed, humiliated, tried, in spite of this noble advice, to follow the ascetics back home, one of them turned round and thundered at her.... What, wanton girl, do you desire independence?" (137-8).

And then she had done. As she sat down there was a spurt of applause, and she realized with an honest astonishment that she had not made this speech after all.

WORK CITED

Deshpande, Shashi. *The Dark Holds No Terrors*. New Delhi: Penguin Books India Pvt. Ltd., 1990. All references are from this edition.

14 Writing from the Margins: A Study of Shashi Deshpande's *That Long Silence*

Ram Sharma

The bulk of post-colonial New English Literature has been generally preoccupied for the last few decades with the marginalised and the underdog. In India the focus naturally falls on women and backward classes.

Edward Said suggests that the canons of the center should be read contrapuntally with the work coming from the margin. Thus the binary exists even though Said's vision for the future is more utopian in nature. Shashi Deshpande's novels reveal the inability of the woman to speak and the positive movement is always the movement towards speech, towards the breaking of *That Long Silence*.

That Long Silence, which won Shashi Deshpande the Sahitya Akademi Award for 1990, tells the story of an Indian housewife who maintains silence throughout her life. The novel ends with her resolve to speak, to break her long silence. The novel depicts the life of Jaya at the level of the silent and the unconscious. It is a sensitive and realistic dramatisation of the married life of Jaya and her husband Mohan. It centers around the inner perception of a female protagonist who finds her normal routine so disrupted that for the first time she can look at her life and attempts to decide who she really is (King Debonair, 97) But could she decide?

The question "Who am I?" (24) haunts Jaya so obsessively that she fails to find herself. She is "an utter stranger, a person so alien that even the faintest understanding of the motives of her actions seemed impossible" (69), hence her agonised cries "I can't hope, I can't manage. I can't go on". In such a stifling and suffocating domestic ambience and patriarchal set-up, she finds her female identity effaced.

Gayatri Chakravorty Spivak writes in her article "Can the Subaltern Speak?":

> "Between patriarchy and imperialism subject-constitution and object formation the figure of the woman disappears, not into a pristine nothingness, but into a violent shuttling which is the displaced figuration of the 'Third-World Woman' caught between tradition and modernization."

Jaya is Suhasini and also "Seeta," the pseudonym she assumes to write columns about the plight of the middle-class housewife. Both "Suhasini' and "Seeta" are, as Jaya says, "the many selves waiting to be discovered, each self attached like a Siamese twin to a self of another person, neither able to exist without the other" (69). Hence if life is "to be made possible (193), she is to live neither as 'Suhasini' or 'Jaya' nor as 'Seeta' or 'Anti-Kusum.'" She is to live but not in fragments. Deshpande reveals the consciousness of Jaya through an exposition of her mind in the process of thinking, feeling and reacting to the stimuli of the moment and situation. In doing so, she goes on to assert the feminine psyche of the protagonist, that strives to break away from the stranglehold of a quagmired social fabric, rooted in patriarchy which repels as it attracts.

"And I was Jaya. But I had been Suhasini as well. I can see her now, the Suhasini who was distinct from Jaya, a soft smiling, placid motherly woman. A woman who lovingly nurtured her family. A woman who coped" (16).

Jaya is not totally a silent and mute sufferer. She is an active participant as well as an observer in the novel. She steps out of the narrative as a witness as it were a critic to perceive the tenor of the story filtered through a female consciousness.

"Sensual memories are the coldest. They stir up nothing in you.... These emotions and responses seemed to belong to two other people, not to the two of us lying here together...whatever my feeling has been then, I had never spoken of them to him. In fact, we had never spoken of sex at all" (95).

Jaya is a modern predicament and the flood of consciousness that ensures out of it a silent stream of thoughts and feelings. Jaya succumbs and surrenders to Mohan without revolting. Silently she wills to his will. She never says 'Yes' when her husband asks her whether he has hurt her. She endures everything, tolerates all kinds of masculine oppression silently, "in the emotion that governed my behaviour to him, there was still the habit of being a wife of sustaining and supporting him."

Simone De Beauvoir expresses his own views on man-woman nexus—"man represents both the positive and the neutral, as is indicated by the common use of man to designate human beings in general, whereas woman represents only the negative, defined by limiting criteria, without reciprocity" (534).

A woman is never regarded as an autonomous being since she has always been assigned a subordinate and relative position.

"Man can think of himself without woman. She cannot think of herself without man. And she is simply what man decrees...she appears essentially to the male as a sexual being. For him she is sex...absolute sex, no less. She is defined and differentiated with reference to man and not he with reference to man and not he with reference to her, she is the incidental, the inessential as opposed to the essential" (De Beauvoir, 534).

Shashi Deshpande uses a beautiful image to describe Jaya's married life. "A pair of bullocks yoked together...a clever phrase, but can it substitute for the reality? A man and a woman married for seventeen years. A couple with two children. A family somewhat like the one caught and preserved for posterity by the advertising visuals I so loved. But the reality was only this. We were two persons. A man and A woman" (8).

Jaya does not immediately react to the situation but the reader is insinuated through the flash back technique used by the author.

Jaya being renamed as Suhasini after her marriage is not a case of the loss of identity since Jaya and Suhasini are the two facets of the same coin and these two collateral names of the Deshpande protagonist are symbolical in their socio-familial import. Jaya, her premarital name, means 'Victory' and Suhasini, the post-marital name, given to her by her husband, means a soft smiling placid motherly woman. A woman who lovingly nurtured her family, A woman who coped (15).

"Jaya is a woman who adjusts and accommodates unlike the modern women who find themselves" forced into the background by the claims of culture and hence they adopt "an inimical attitude towards it."

She is not the structurally patterned woman of the traditional Indian society where woman was the follower and man the leader, where woman was the sufferer and man the ordainer. Jaya flounders to break out of the yoke.

"Stay at home, look after your babies, keep out the rest of the world, you are safe. That poor idiotic woman Suhasini believed in this. I know better, now I know that safety is always unattainable, you are never safe" (17).

Jaya's drift of thought and her evanescent mood are captured through the broken and fragmentary stream of consciousness. "A husband is like a sheltering tree." "Take on it, don't let it escape."

Jaya's self-questioning attitude comes as a split in the narrative. She broods over the metaphor of the 'Sheltering tree'.

"A sheltering tree, without the tree, you are dangerously unprotected...equally logically and vulnerable. This followed logically" (32).

Jaya desperately needs to protect herself from dissipating and sinking in the crumbling world around her. Deshpande thus presents the subterranean and subliminal impressions of human life, through digressions in the narrative.

In their stream of thoughts both Jaya and Mohan look at their marital relationship where there is nothing but suppressed silence. Jaya wants to flee from the cribbed confines of an incarcerated domestic life in order to find a new identity for herself, a new mooring for her fugitive self-communication at the domestic and personal level.

"Nothing between us...nothing between me and Mohan. We live together but there had been only emptiness between us" (185).

Jaya had never confessed her frenetic feelings to Mohan as it has seemed "like a disease, a disability" (97) which he had to hide from everyone. Jaya pines for social communication but the society is impervious to her spiritual need.

There is hardly any communication between Jaya and Mohan, neither verbal nor emotional. Mohan wanted a well-educated and cultured wife, not a reciprocating and loving one. There develops disheartening silence between the husband and the wife. Mohan's queries remain unanswered by Jaya for she is unable to find a word of response. She is unable to speak her trouble out for she is a woman who faces sufferings and opposition of the milieu in the true spirit of ideal Hindu womanhood where obedience and loyalty have degenerated to the state of dogged subservience. Could a modern woman, nestled in tradition like Jaya understand a traditionalist like Mohan who is rooted out and out in customs and whose repressive use of silence pressures Jaya into conformity with his expectations? Deshpande presents here not a woman who has a desire to revolt but the one who ultimately reconciles to her hapless lot. Having failed to discover the truth, she remains silent and reticent about revealing her most personal and private thoughts in her writings. Mohan wonders as to how could women be so rebellious and esoteric, so angry and recalcitrant. To him, it is unwomanly to be angry for it is against the ideals of feminism.

"A woman can never be angry she can only be neurotic, hysterical frustrated. There is no room for despair, either. There is only order a routine, today. I have to change the sheets tomorrow, scrub the bathrooms the day after, clean the fridge...." (147-148).

Marriage subjugates and enslaves women and it leads her to "aimless days indefinitely repeated, life that slips away gently towards death without questioning its purpose" (De Beauvoir, 1974: 500).

Women pay for their happiness at the cost of their freedom and De Beauvoir emphasised that such a sacrifice on the part of a woman is too high for anyone because the kind of self-contentment, serenity and security that marriage offers woman drains her soul of its capacity for greatness.

"She shuts behind her the doors of her new home. When she was a girl, the whole countryside was her homeland, the forests were hers. Now she is confined to a restricted space...." (De Beauvoir, 502).

It is against this encoded and pre-ordained role of a woman that Jaya revolts. For her "in this life itself there are so many cross-roads, so many choices" (192).

But a married woman has a few or practically no choice left to her save what her husband wills and desires. Unlike other married women, slavishly tagged to tradition, she has her own say. She unfurls and unburdens herself to activate the creative impulses smothered within her artistic self. Deshpande has laid bare the psyche of Jaya which is reluctantly responsive and passively secluded. The author's unrelieved stress on obliterating herself from the novel as a story-teller, giving full freedom to the protagonist to unveil herself, using her resilient mind to document her vision to life has imparted an unquestionable credibility of the realism of the stream of Jaya's consciousness.

The metaphor of silence under which the novel is organized helps to impose a quietude and discipline the inner dynamics of a self, cut off from human communication. *That Long Silence* is not an intrusion into the world of silence but a silent communion with the oppressed self-straining for articulation, for a voice. Jaya and Mohan hardly spoke to each other of love and sex. Love-making for them was silent and inarticulate affair.

"God, how terrible it was to know a man so well. I could time it almost to the second, from the first device wooing to the moment he turned away from me, offering me his hunched back" (85).

In the process of self-revelation through writing Jaya comes to recognise herself as a failed writer because when she had continued writing, her stories had been rejected for lack of genuine feelings which she had laid aside. In other words, she is self-alienated. Jaya's creative urge and artistic zeal frees her from her cramped and dubbed domestic and societal roles. At length she resolves to break that silence by putting down on paper all that she has suppressed in her seventeen years silence...that long silence which had reduced herself to fragments.

"I am not afraid...any more. The panic has gone. I am Mohan's wife. I had thought, and cut off the bits of me that had refused to be Mohan's wife. Now I know that kind of fragmentation is not possible" (191).

Through the image of a woman crawling into a hole, Deshpande describes the woeful plight of Jaya, unprotected and unshelled. Jaya says:

> "Distance from real life scared of writing, scared of failing oh God I had thought, I cannot take any more. Even a worm has hole it can crawl into. I had mine as Mohan's wife as Rahul's and Rati's mother" (148).

Towards the end of the novel Jaya consciously acknowledges her writing as a kind of fiction and quotes Defoe's description of fiction as a kind of 'lying' which may make 'a great hope in the heart'. Hence she decides to 'plug that hole' as said earlier by speaking and listening and erasing the silence between her and Mohan. It is this erasing of the silence that symbolises the assertion of her feminine voice, a voice with hope and promise, a voice that articulates her thoughts. The novel doesn't depict Jaya's life as a totally dismal and hopeless struggle. It suggests "hope" and "change" for the better.

"We don't change overnight. It's possible that we may not change even over long periods of time. But we can always hope without that life would be impossible" (193).

WORKS CITED

De Beauvoir, Simone. *The Second Sex*. Trans. and ed. H.M. Parshley. New York: Vintage Books, 1974.

Deshpande, Shashi. *That Long Silence, 1988*. New Delhi: Penguin Books, 1989. All textual citations in the article kept in parentheses are from this edition of the novel.

Spivak, Gayatri Chakravorty. 'Can the Subaltern Speak?' *Colonial Discourse and Post Colonial Theory*. Harvest Wheats Heaf, 1994.

15 Portrayal of Womanhood in the Post-Colonial Indian English Fiction: A Journey from Self-Effacement to Selfhood

Malti Agrawal

From time immemorial, a woman in India has been deified. She has been considered the embodiment of Shakti. The Vedic period observed no discrimination between boys and girls. She enjoyed an honoured place as she enjoyed equal opportunity of getting education. But gradually in the post-Vedic period, there had been decline in her status in the society. She was deprived of education and eventually all pleasures of life. She was treated as the second sex who was supposed to be obedient to her husband whether he be a leper, wife-beater or a sadist or indulged in polygamy. She was indoctrinated into firm believing that the real virtues of an ideal Indian wife are self-effacement, unusual tolerance and submissiveness. She was Sita, Sakuntala and Savitri who had to suffer for no fault of her own. She was subjected to self-immolation or Sati.

The Freedom Movement in India ameliorated the condition of Indian women. With the advent of many reformist movements, all the marginalized sections of society (women one such important section) raised their voice for their legal rights. Education facilities reached to the doors of women which uplifted their condition. It will be relevant here to quote a few lines from the ICSSR Report:

> "It was left to Mahatma Gandhi and the Freedom Movement to place the movement for women's emancipation in its proper perspective, as part of the larger movement for the removal of inequalities that oppressed all the weaker sections" (17-18).

A.S. Altekar's *The Position of Woman in Hindu Civilization* (1956) which was followed by Ananda Coomaraswamy's *The Dance of Shiva* (1957) presented a historical and a sociological survey respectively of the status of women in India. The freedom movement, independence and spread of education contributed a lot in uplifting the condition of women in India. All these multifaceted activities and movements left their indelible imprint on the pages of literature of Post-Independence era. Many men and women writers created such female figures who symbolized the ideal of Indian womanhood. The early Indian English novelists such as Mulk Raj Anand, R.K. Narayan and Raja Rao reflected sociological realism in their works and created the archetyped female protagonists to whom their husbands were gods and it was their duty to serve that god. After the Second World War, the women writers like Kamala Markandaya held mirror to the Indian villages where the husbands were worshipped like gods.

In the wake of feminist movement in India, themes like woman's search of identity, quest for selfhood, relocating the self, and awareness to seek a balance between tradition and modernity became popular in the works of male as well as female writers of the Post-Colonial Indian English Fiction. The Indian English Fiction resounded with the women's assertion of her individuality, social and economic freedom, freedom of mental make-up and also emotional independence.

The female writers like Ruth Prawer Jhabvala, Nayantara Sahgal, Nergis Dalal, Shashi Deshpande, Mahasweta Devi, Bharati Mukherjee, Rama Mehta, Shobha De and Arundhati Roy portray myriad faces of this new woman who gradually learnt to fight for her rights and lived not only as a wife, mother or daughter but also as an individual. These women give a tough fight against the established order and often come upon new concepts of morality, sometimes they fall rebellion and go too far against the accepted code of morality that they enter into extra-marital relationship and become lesbians.

The heroines of Nayantara Sahgal such as Saroj in *Storm in Chandigarh* and Simrit in *The Day in Shadow* strive to reach to their true self and are bold enough to overcome depression and dejection. About her women Nayantara Sahgal writes: "I try to create the virtuous woman, the modern Sita if you like. My women are strivers and aspirers toward freedom, toward goodness, toward a compassionate world. Their virtue is a quality of heart and mind and spirit, a kind of untouched innocence and integrity" (Qtd. in Jain, 145).

Sometimes this new woman succumbs to the present unfavourable circumstances and turns out neurotic. Anita Desai's *Cry the Peacock* and *Where Shall We Go This Summer?* Bharati Mukherjee's *Wife*, Kamala Markandaya's *A Silence of Desire*, Ruth Prawer Jhabvala's *Get Ready for Battle* portray such women who in their fight for their existence lose their equilibrium. In their struggle for existence the new women muster courage to cross all the boundaries of docility and like Ibsen's Nora desert their husbands and children. One such illustrious character is of Savitri in R.K. Narayan's *The Dark House*. The gusto of being a liberated self as prompted by this New Woman's shattered conjugal life manifests itself in a socially and ethically unapproved solution, *i.e.* her being a lesbian.

Astha and Pipeelika in Manju Kapur's novel *A Married Woman* are such new women who disillusioned by the male integrity become lesbian beloved and lesbian lover respectively. The women writers especially showed their concern for the plight of Indian woman. They depicted her journey through the stages of submissiveness and subservience to liberation and creativity. The present paper is going to study in depth the characters of Rukmani in Kamala Markandaya's novel *Nectar in a Sieve* and of Saru or Sarita in Shashi Deshpande's novel *The Dark Holds No Terrors*. While Rukmani represents a literate yet tradition bound, rustic Indian woman to whom life is a process of self-effacement, Deshpande's Saru represents a middle-class, sensitive, educated and urbanite professional woman to whom life is a process of self-realization.

Rukmani, the protagonist of Kamala Markandaya's maiden novel *Nectar in a Sieve*, is married to a tenant peasant, Nathan, who is far below her status. She enjoys her marital life with whatever her husband earns whether plenty or scanty due to draught. She belongs to a generation of self-sacrificing women for whom the happiness and satisfaction of husband is the "be all and end all" of life. Born in the family of rich farmer father, Rukmani after marriage learns how to remain happily despite all destitution. She concedes:

> "This, mud hut, nothing but mud and thatch was my home. My knees gave...and I sank down" [4].

She learns to be proud of her domestic space and enjoys her married life at all planes whether sexual, physical or psychological. She is uncomplaining and finally moulds herself thoroughly into the frame of a traditional figure who works from dawn to dusk for her family. Soon she becomes the mother of five sons and a daughter Ira. When the daughter was born, not only her husband but she too regretted over the birth of a female child. She is literate but her bias for a girl child is that of a conventional grandmother or great grandmother. She reacts sharply or rather sourly at the birth of Ira and sheds "tears of weakness and disappointment; for what woman wants a girl for her first born" (14). She wanted to give a male child to her husband because a son can "continue his line and walk beside him on the land." She was depressed for not having a son. She told Dr. Kenny:

> "I have no sons,...only one child, a girl...why should it be? What have we done that we must be punished? Am I not clean and healthy? Have I not borne a girl so fair, people turn to gaze when she passes?" (20).

Rukmani's image of a self-sacrificing woman and conceding to woman's subjugation with a spirit of nonchalance becomes evident when she comes to know of Nathan's extra-marital relationship with Kunti and quietly endures it. She married her daughter Ira to a peasant boy at the age of fourteen. But after five years of marriage, her son-in-law abandoned her for being barren.

"Mother-in-law" he said, "I intend no discourtesy but this is no ordinary visit. You gave me your daughter in marriage. I have brought her back to you. She is a barren woman" (50). Rukmani as well as her husband Nathan tolerate it with equanimity. Nathan blames his daughter Ira and supports the step taken by his son-in-law: "I do not blame him.... He is justified, for a man needs children. He has been patient" (50). Rukmani too like her husband did not protest but she behaved in a sensible way—once when she sought Dr. Kenny's medical assistance to bear a son and again when she took her daughter to Dr. Kenny to be treated for barrenness. This shows that despite of being deeply rooted in traditional Indian values, Rukmani was well aware of herself and sought herself within the orbit of family ties. She went to Dr. Kenny furtively since she knew that her husband would not like her going to a foreigner. In this protagonist of *Nectar in a Sieve,* we find a fusion of tradition and modernity. Since she lacked education, she was not so much aware of her rights as of her duties. She subjected herself to domestic servility and unlike western liberated women sought her identity in that enclosed space.

Ira, like her mother, presents the image of a self-sacrificing female and bears all complacently. She suffers a lot on account of this discrimination which our society observes between males and females. She adopts prostitution for feeding her younger brother Kuti. Her father resents her coming late at night. Actually it is his inflated male ego that gets hurt. But Rukmani endures it in a matter-of-fact way.

The establishment of the tannery dishabilitates Rukmani and Nathan. It is for a while that she exhibits the sparks of protest when she cries: "They may live in our midst but I can never accept them...." (28). Nathan and his wife Rukmani leave the village after being deprived of the land they till. Rukmani quite devotedly and submissively shares all misfortunes with Nathan till he dies. Thus the heroine of *Nectar in a Sieve* confines herself to the cage of familial bonds and prefers self-abnegation to keep up the harmony in marital relations. Though she is capable of realizing her self, she does not have the courage to list an objection to male oppression. She accepts her ignominious fate unprotestingly. To some extent the socio-economic forces including her economic dependence and also her belonging to the *second sex* are responsible for all the crises she bears. Had she been educated and self-sufficient, she would have been different and would have enjoyed different status. Rukmani, though literate, has orthodox and traditional mode of thinking. She is not well educated and is unable to judge her capacity. All these are the root causes which lead to the exploitation of the fair-sex. The female characters of Markandaya like Rukmani and Irawady adjust with complete withdrawal.

Nevertheless, Markandaya infuses her heroine with a bold spirit who patiently suffers a lot as the corroding poverty and misfortunes one after another cross her path. Of course some critics like Chaman Nahal consider Rukmani as a silent sufferer and find no quest for autonomy in her character. They consider her as a passive character who accepts all her misfortunes and calamities silently. It is her passivity which stops her from asking anything for her sake as she realizes. "Want is our companion from birth to death, familiar as the seasons or the earth, varying only in degree. What profit to bewail that which has always been and cannot change" (113). Grounded in Eastern cultural code, she, "*an acquiescent imbecile*" believes in sacrifice for it cleanses the soul.

Sarita or Saru, the protagonist in Shashi Deshpande's magnum opus *The Dark Holds No Terrors* represents the sensitive women of post-independence India who are introspective, self-aware, convent educated but tradition bound. Saru represents that new woman who while remaining confined to the familial bonds asserts her identity, struggles for her rights and eventually reaches to self-actualization. She represents a realistic picture of the contemporary middle class, educated, urban Indian woman who despite being educated and economically independent remained a victim of injustice within the family. The age-old belief is that she, as Manu declared, "must be kept in subordination to the males of the family: in childhood to the father, in youth to her husband, in old age to her sons" (qtd. in ICSSR Report, 13-14). Manu added, "Even though the husband be destitute of virtue and seeks pleasure elsewhere, he must be worshipped as god" (13-14). But Shashi Deshpande depicted such women who are liberated selves as they move on to discover themselves. Deshpande said, "...I strongly react against any kind of cruelty or oppression against women or any kind of denial of opportunities to women because they are women. We are all human beings and we should all have the rights to live our lives" (Interview Sree, 155).

The heroines of Shashi Deshpande whether Indu, Saru or Jaya are all intelligent and understanding women. Unlike the mythical figures as that of Sita and Savitri, they recognize the new roles which they want to perform in the new world. She deconstructs the myths like Sita as a perfect woman, or as a self-sacrificing woman since she believed that all these myths have been created by men. She created a new woman who is capable of self-analysis. While acting as a wife, mother, daughter etc. she tries to discover for herself new ways of living and also new ways of functioning. Since Deshpande claimed to write from real life and not from myths etc., hence she did not create the "self-sacrificing mothers and totally chaste wives." She portrayed them as human beings as they are in their real life.

When asked if she was a feminist, she spontaneously replied that she was a feminist but not a feminist writer since she did not believe in any propaganda. She believed that "a woman is also an individual like man with lot of capabilities and potentials. She has every right to develop all that. She should not be oppressed just because she is a female. Like man she also has her own qualities. She has every right to live her life, to develop her qualities, to take her decisions, to be independent and to take charge of her own destiny" (Interview Sree, 154-55).

All her women are liberated selves since liberation to Deshpande does not mean doing without the family or breaking off the familial ties. With this realization they move on and as Deshpande herself said that they are not revolutionaries and never walk out of the family. They do not escape the situations rather face them with the idea what they are. She defines liberation in the following words, "Liberation means you refuse to be oppressed, you refuse to give up your individuality, you refuse to do things which go against your conscience. You realize the potential you know what you are worth of. You know what is your value. You take that into account, and this is liberation" (Interview Sree, 147).

Saru, the heroine of *The Dark Holds No Terrors*, is educated, economically independent, middle-class working woman who as a girl was sensitive enough to realize her mother's attitude of discrimination on her being a girl. She recalls how she had been made to feel that she belonged to a different family and was an *amanat*. Only her brother Dhruva was the permanent member of the house. This discrimination led this teenager to be rebellious. She talked to her mother rudely:

> "Don't go out in the sun. You will get even darker."
> "Who cares?"
> "We have to care if you don't, we have to get you married."
> "I don't want to get married."
> "Will you live with us all your life?"
> "Why not?"
> "You can't"
> "And Dhruva?"
> "He is different. He's a boy..." (50).

She remembers her mother's favourtism how there had been *puja* on Dhruva's birthdays while her birthdays passed away unnoticed. She recalls the traumatic reminiscence of her childhood when her mother told her, "It rained heavily the day you were born. It was terrible" (169). But she felt, "And somehow, it seemed to me that it was my birth that was terrible to her not the rains" (169). Later Saru chose to study medicine and to marry Manohar, a low caste boy not because she loved him but it was to defy her mother because she believed, "No body likes me. Nobody cares for me. Nobody wants me" (83).

In other words, Sarita married Manu to secure her identity as an individual. As S.P. Swain writes: "Her marriage with Manu is an assertion on and affirmation of her feminine sensibility" (35-36).

Saru became successful doctor and her steady rise in status hurt the male-ego of Manu as no male (Indian especially) can ever like his wife to be superior to him. Soon Saru and Manu's marriage resulted into strained conjugal relationship. Manu's sense of male superiority could not tolerate that his wife "earns not only the butter but most of the bread as well" (200). To assert his masculinity, he became a rapist and sexually attacked his wife. Saru felt convinced that partners in marriage can never be equal. She once said: "A wife must be a few feet behind her husband. If she is an M.A., you should be B.A. If he is 5'4" tall, you should not be more than 5'3" tall. If he is earning five hundred rupees, you should never earn more than four hundred and ninety, if you want a happy marriage" (137).

Indu, Saru and Jaya—all in their search of liberation—leave their parental homes but later they come to their parents' house and there they (re) discover themselves. Saru goes back to her father's house after her mother's death and there she finds herself in the process of discovering herself. She feels how she has been cruel to her brother, mother, children and to her husband. She is involved in fighting her own battle. She is ready to face the situation audaciously. She regains her self-confidence as she clearly asserts:

> "All right, so I am alone. But so's everyone else. Human beings...they're going to fail you. But because there's just us, because there's no one else, we have to go on trying. If we can't believe in ourselves, we're sunk" (220).

The uncomplaining and undemanding, wordless partnership of her father and Madhav teaches her interdependence in life and also how to face the reality. She admits that it's one's own self which is real. She decides to talk to Manu because throughout her life she has been avoiding talking to him. Consequently, she has been confronting the problem. In the words of Deshpande, "She (Saru) realises that the problem has been herself. So she is going to change herself now" (Interview Sree, 145). She introspects and tries to change herself for she thinks, "It's not what he's done to me, but what I've done to him" (216). Thus, Saru, an educated and intelligent being, comes to self-analysis and self-discovery. Unlike Rukmani of Markandaya, she does not surrender before the negative social forces. She fights them back and emerges victorious. Markandaya as well as Deshpande portray the predicament of Indian woman who at times idealises the image of tradition-bound woman with the attributes such as submissiveness, gentleness, docility etc. and yet she is not merely a silent sufferer. While Markandaya's heroine, Rukmani, shows extraordinary patience and submissiveness, Deshpande's Saru reaches to the stage of self-actualization where she feels that she is not merely an appendage to man. But this is also true that she cannot live without the confines of familial bonds. This liberated woman ultimately resolves: "My life is my own...somehow she felt she had found it now, the connecting link. It means you are not a strutting, grimacing puppet, standing futilely on the stage for a brief while between areas of darkness" (20).

WORKS CITED

Deshpande, Shashi. *The Dark Holds No Terrors*. New Delhi: Penguin Books, 1980. All subsequent references of the text are from this edition.

ICSSR Report. *Status of Women in India*. New Delhi, 1975.

ICSSR Report. "The Manusmriti." *Status of Women in India*. New Delhi, 1975.

Markandaya, Kamala. *Nectar in a Sieve*. 1954; rpt. Bombay: Jaico Books, 1978. All subsequent references are from this edition.

Sree, S. Prasanee. "Interview with Shashi Deshpande." *Women in the Novels of Shashi Deshpande: A Study*. New Delhi, 2003.

Swain, S.P. "Shashi Deshpande's *The Dark Holds No Terrors*: Saru's Feminine Sensibility." *Indian Women Novelists*, ed. R.K. Dhawan. New Delhi: Prestige Books, 1990, Set I, Vol. 4.

16

Women in the Novels of Kamala Markandaya

V.K. Singhal

Kamala Markandaya has immortalised herself in the realm of Indo-Anglian Literature for thoroughly exploring the infinite varieties of the female world with its inexhaustible capacity of the greatest tolerance, fortitude, the spirit of sacrifice, sex-appeal, the element of love with all psychological complications, various recesses of beauty, the feelings of nationalism and internationalism and an immeasurable capacity for standing against the misfortunes of life. Uma Parameswaran has appreciated her position: "Kamala Markandaya is, undoubtedly, one of the major novelists on the Commonwealth scene" (89).

Stephen Ignatius Hemenway observes: "Markandaya is definitely one of the most productive, popular, and skilled Indo-Anglian novelists and a superb representative of the growing number of Indian women writing serious literature in English" (52). Kamala Markandaya having her limitations of range and vision, lacks the all-embracing attitude of Raja Rao but she has epic dimensions, and keen sociological aspects of Mulk Raj Anand. Her humanistic vision is conveyed through her women like Rukmani, Mirabai, Premala, Sarojini, Caroline, Bell, Nalini, Anasuya, Ellie and Annabel, Helen, Vasantha, Lalitha and Saroja etc.

Nectar in a Sieve, Kamala's first but epoch-making, realistic and poignant novel "deals with basically the tragic turmoils caused by socio-economic factors in the life of Rukmani—the narrator-heroine" (Prasad, 11). The novelist has delineated the character of her heroine in the most miserable Indian rural conditions before independence. She, youngest of the four daughters of a village Headman, is married at the age of twelve to a poor farmer Nathan but he has proved to be a very loving husband. Justifying the title, Rukmani always displays her rare qualities of adjustment, accommodation, fortitude and forbearance. She undergoes all penury, lives in a self-built hut in a very miserable condition and bears her husband children. All types of problems occur before her—like hunger, starvation, i.e. natural as well as man-made problems. Madhusudan Prasad observes: "Rukmani consequently experiences one misery after another. Her husband becomes unfaithful. Her daughter Ira resorts to prostitution to save the family from starvation. Kuti, the youngest child of Rukmani, dies of starvation. Her two sons, Arjun and Thumbi, leave for Ceylon for work, and Raja, the third son, dies in a quarrel and finally, they are evicted from their land" [Introduction (iii)].

Rukmani and Nathan have to go to their son Murugan only to find that their son has gone away after deserting his wife and children in very sorrowful and precarious condition. Rukmani undergoes all the ordeals of life, they became stone breakers, while returning to the village, Nathan dies. She displays her exemplary courage and fortitude, people ask her: "Have you no sons to help? She replies with the greatest hesitation: "Yes, no, not here" (185). Without giving up hopes Rukmani perseveres against all adverse circumstances and stands like a firm rock. She takes the adopted child Puli with her and starts looking to future afresh with her greater energies and sharper understanding of life. Selvan gives the greatest assurance to her mother: "Do not worry. We shall manage" (189). Noticing the shadow of her husband in her children, she is elevated to go through the struggle for existence. Rukmani emerges as a greater *Karamyogi* than her husband

Nathan for she has displayed all her optimistic view of life against all the odds of life. Iyenger has rightly pointed out:

> "Calm after storm, spring after winter—such is the unending cycle, one must hope and one must persevere even if one is engaged only in trying to discover 'nectar in a sieve'" (439).

Iyenger has further appreciated Rukmani as 'a mother of sorrows,' because her life has been full of several tragic happenings such as 'failures of harvest, the deaths of Raja and Kuti, the departure of her sons for city and for Ceylon, the desertion of Ira by her husband, because of her failure to give birth to a child and then the birth of an illegitimate son, the withdrawal of Selwam from agriculture, the deprivation of their land due to tannery....' (Srivastava, 3). Her son Murugan goes away leaving his wife in the lurch who ultimately becomes a prostitute to keep her body and soul together. She has discovered that life is still more tragic in the city than in the village. Finally, there is a bolt from the blue in the form of her husband's death.

Rukmani presents a marked contrast with Kunthi in her approach to life and total understanding of life. Kunthi is pleased by the installation of tannery in the village while Rukmani holds the view that industrialization will rob the village of its original and natural charm. She comments: "Somehow I had felt the tannery would, eventually, be our undoing" (135). Actually, Rukmani is an incarnation of the qualities of "simplicity, honesty, perseverance, selflessness, spirit of co-operation, faith in God and man and absence of jealousy and temptation" (Srivastava, 10). She feels a great sense of restlessness and deprivation after losing her land: "In it we had lain together, and our children had been born. This hut with all its memories was to be taken from us, for it stood on land that belonged to another" (137). Meena Shirwadkar has appreciated Rukmani, "In her mute suffering [she] resembles Maurya in Synge's *Riders to the Sea*."

In another novel *Some Inner Fury*, Kamala Markandaya has dramatised the East-West Conflict in a tragic manner laying stress on the themes of love and death. Two wonderful women—Mirabai and Premala shine up representing diverse qualities of love and understanding: "The personal relationships operate on memory levels—between Mira, an Indian girl, and Richard an English man; between Kit Samy, a westernized husband and Premala, a typical Indian wife" (Srivastava, 61). The novelist has depicted the theme of love in the backdrop of India's Revolution for Independence. The love between Mira and Richard is based on all caution and carefulness, while the love between Premala and Kit is cold. Mira loves the Englishman Richard from the core of her heart, but "her inner fury is completely quenched when her love for Richard results in an ecstatic experience of the sweep and surge of love..." (Krishna Rao, 48). The love between them grows in different stages, she first receives him at the railway station, calls him at her house, provides him a *dhoti* and a pair of *chappals* joyfully, then visits clubs with him, love is enkindled and they think of solemnising their love in the shape of marriage, then they visit Kanniyakumari, where she is melted observing him taking his bath naked. They are, therefore, tempted to enjoy the sexual act and finally the tragic end, Richard is mercilessly killed by Indian revolutionaries and Mira is in the state of total disappointment. Thus, she sublimates her love to the national love and patriotism.

Premala is destined to lead a different sort of life, she is deprived of love within marriage. Being a perfect Indian girl, she symbolises all Indian traditions, culture and other characteristics like tolerance, the spirit of sacrifice and selfless love. Unfortunately, her husband Kit fails to reciprocate her sentiments, so, her love is suppressed and she ultimately sublimates it in the form of social service. She becomes a helping partner of an English missionary Hickey in maintaining a village school. A revolutionary Govind loves her sincerely, and she also responds to it from the core of the heart, but it is not matured and she is burnt up within the school by the Indian revolutionaries. Her husband Kit is transformed, he repents tremendously but it is all in vain. Mira is never convinced that Premala is no more: "But I could not believe she was dead. The feeling would not come then. I looked at her and she had always been beautiful and she was beautiful now" (*Some Inner Fury*, 133).

R.K. Srivastava points out a remarkable difference among the women characters of *Nectar in a Sieve*, and *Some Inner Fury*: Markandaya's female characters in *Nectar in a Sieve* are uneducated and remain passive recipients of loving or cruel treatment of their husbands; In *Some Inner Fury*, they are educated and assert their individualities—Premala by adopting a child against Kit's wishes and Mira by loving Richard against Govind's and her parents' wishes" (69). Madhusudan Prasad mentions: "Markandaya's third novel *A Silence of Desire* explores the theme of clash between traditionalism and modernism, between faith and reason represented by Sarojini and Dandekar who form a married couple in the novel" (V). Sarojini is the central figure of the novel, she wrote story, novels round about her. She is a God-fearing, religious-minded and very caring wife, while her husband Dandekar, a government servant is always opposing her with his modernism and a western attitude to life.

Sarojini in *A Silence of Desire* symbolises all traditionalism and religious-mindedness, while her husband Dandekar stands for the changing modern times. R.K. Srivastava observes: "Sarojini—represents the segment of stable society which has been highly religious-minded to the point of blind worship for thousands of years" (93). Kamala Markandaya has portrayed a typical Indian woman who is fundamentally religious, but at the same time is aware of the changing trends of the modern society: Sarojini dislikes to be called superstitious although she has no faith in hospitals but trusts in faith-cure. Her cousin Rajan and aunt Sita also belong to this category having an implicit faith in God. She makes fun of her husband Dandekar for his ignorance of the significance of religion and the power of faith: "You with your western notions, your superior talk of ignorance and superstitions, when all it means is that you don't know what lies beyond reason and you prefer not to find out" (97).

According to Meenakshi Mukherjee, Sarojini possesses her own personality, she can stick to her principles challenging her husband and the deaths of her mother and grandmother in hospitals have confirmed her faith in God. Many a time her wayward husband Dandekar is saved by her strong character; he suffers from the tortures of conscience when he sleeps with a prostitute. "The pangs of conscience arise because his waywardness is contrasted with her stability and fidelity." (Srivastava, 99). Actually, Sarojini being a perfect housewife, becomes an integral part of the life of Dandekar, she is the *Griha Lakshmi* or the kitchen queen and her presence imparts life to her family. Kamala Markandaya has beautifully shown that both faith and doubt or science co-exist in India. R.K. Srivastava aptly observes: "Markandaya has portrayed these bi-polar worlds through a cluster of images which while gravitating to either one side or the other end up many times in the middle—a neutral territory" (109-110). Faith is further symbolised by *Tulasi* plant. R.K. Srivastava further mentioned: "Taken together, both the Tulasi tree and Sarojini represent faith and as such are on the opposite pole from Dandekar who ostensibly represents reason but which is all tainted and twisted with his male ego and muddleheadedness" (110-111).

In another novel *Possession*, also, Kamala Markandaya has given us a variety of women. The central figure of the novel Caroline Bell—a youthful, sophisticated divorcee comes to India in the quest of pleasure, comes across a fourteen year old rustic boy Valmiki—a talented painter—who needs all patronage and every kind of assistance for being extremely poor and needy. Therefore, she takes him to London, his talents are flowered up and he acquires all name and fame as an excellent painter. Both enjoy a lot, she enjoys his youth for her physical pleasures and he every kind of comfort and luxury, both move abroad enjoying a free life. Suddenly Valmiki starts feeling tortured within that his talents are going in vain. At this time Caroline shows him a letter from Swamy, his friend in India, in order to inspire him. Thus being inspired, he starts painting again and an exhibition of his paintings is arranged by her. He enjoys sex with his housekeeper

Ellie and makes her pregnant but Caroline brings about a separation between them very cunningly.

Valmiki is further disillusioned, he starts living with another woman Annabel, but Caroline poisoned her mind that Ellie has committed suicide out of frustration. Thus, getting discarded by both Caroline and Annabel, Valmiki begins to live in a separate apartment in the most rejected manner. In this state of crisis Anasuya comes to his rescue, and makes arrangement for his journey, back to India by selling one of his paintings. Valmiki has returned to India, to his old environments and to Swamy and for never going back to the possessive Caroline, who is different from other women of Kamala. Rukmani in *Nectar in a Sieve* and Nalini in *A Handful of Rice* represent female qualities like gentility and grace, Caroline symbolises patriarchal traditions and the British dominion over India. R.K. Srivastava again mentioned: "In the character of Lady Caroline Bell, Markandaya has transformed the patriarchal suppressed woman into a domineering and tyrannical possessor and an active victimizer of an adolescent male" (126). Anasuya is a typical Indian woman possessing all feminine traits like docility, passivity, non-aggressiveness and loving as well self-sacrificing. In *A Handful of Rice*, Kamala Markandaya has presented her heroine Nalini in the background of social injustice and economic inequality.

Once, while avoiding the clutches of the police, Ravi goes into the house of a tailor whose name is Apu. Apu's wife punishes him badly in the night, in the morning. When he confesses, she forgives him, gives him food and allows him to go back. Things take a different shape, being fascinated by Apu's daughter Nalini; he stays back, marries and starts leading a new life under the love of Nalini. Many ups and downs came into life. When Apu dies, he becomes the head of the family, he becomes violent. He wants to join Damodar for earning a lot by unfair means, he also wants to join the mob with a stone in his hand but drops it because there is a tremendous impact of Nalini in his life. She symbolises domestic happiness, a clean, healthy and traditional life. "She promises sweet life but demands hard and honest labour" (Krishna Rao, 14).

Thus, Nalini plays a very dominant role "in the life of Ravi, he turns into a respectable householder, a decent citizen with a decent job and a wife to support" (*A Handful of Rice,* 108). She sustains him all through his struggles as a wife, guide, friend and philosopher. Kamala Markandaya again observes: "All he had for his comfort was the sound of her, the wish of her sari, as she whisked about the place at her mother's bidding, or a glimpse of her sitting cross-legged like an inaccessible goddess in one of the inner rooms" (*A Handful of Rice*, 34). Both Ravi and Nalini present the contrasts of life, he avoids the vicissitudes of life while she faces them bravely. "She confronts things, whereas, Ravi evades, delays or faces clumsily" (Srivastava, 187).

Kamala Markandaya has portrayed different kinds of women in *The Coffer Dams*. Helen, the young wife of Haward Clinton, the owner of a large British Engineering Firm in India with Mackendrick has been presented with the greatest focus of attention. With her sense of sympathy for the poor workers, a spirit of adventure and a tremendous love for Indian culture, traditions, customs and even tribesmen, she is fascinated by an Indian tribesman, Bashiam for his sincerity, integrity and honesty. R.K. Srivastava maintains: "What keeps Helen humanized is that she shows no interest in the work-site, the machines, or even the non-human Clinton, but visits settlements of the tribesmen" (Srivastava, 195).

In another novel *The Nowhere Man*, Kamala Markandaya has dealt with the problems of identity and elderly Indian immigrants. Srinivas and his wife Vasantha find it simply impossible to create their own identity in England. Vasantha is always an Indian lady even on a foreign land symbolising Indian rules and regulations. She ultimately dies of despair leaving her husband in the greatest despair of life. Mrs. Redcliffe also comes in the life of Srinivas but she is no match to Vasantha. Kamala Markandaya observes: "But she cannot fill the gap left by Vasantha because the affection between Srinivas and Vasantha is the product of an Indian marriage, the union of two souls. Mrs. Pickering can care for his creature, comforts but she cannot become his *Sahadharma-charini*. This spiritual loneliness nags Srinivas' mind much more than his physical solitude" (196).

Kamala Markandaya has presented two types of village virgins—Lalitha and Saroja in *Two Virgins*. Lalitha being more beautiful and more ambitious than Saroja falls a victim to the temptations of life. A film director Gupta tempts her, enjoys her and makes her pregnant. She attempts to commit suicide, Saroja checks her but ultimately Lalitha leaves her house. A.K. Bhatnagar observes: "Lalitha's life is a living example of the tragedy of the modern woman particularly in India" (89).

In The *Golden Honeycomb*, written in a political and patriotic background, Kamala Markandaya has glorified the character of Mohini who is superior to Manjula, Vatsala, Vimala and Usha. Margaret P. Joseph appreciates her: "She is self-willed, and outspoken, vivacious and volatile, shrewd and intelligent, sensual and loving, absolutely feminine in her caprices, her sense of humour and her independence" (154).

Thus, in the words of A.V. Krishna Rao, Kamala Markandaya has shown "the creative release of the feminine sensibility in India" (50). Her women are more positive towards life and its problems than those of Anita Desai. Margaret P. Joseph aptly maintains: "The depiction of the tragic has a positive value, it stresses the necessity for the removal of conditions that can cause tragedy" (211). Women characters like Rukmani, Mira, Sarojini, Nalini, Caroline, Anasuya, Vasantha, Lalitha, Mohini etc. symbolise not only her great tragic vision of life; but also all happiness, contentment, charm and solace in human life. A.K. Bhatnagar aptly concludes: "It is her genuine concern for the suffering humanity and a message of love and fraternity that she is regarded a champion for the cause of humanity" (138).

WORKS CITED

Bhatnagar, A.K. *Kamala Markandaya: A Thematic Study*. New Delhi: Sarup and Sons, 1995.

Hemenway, Stephen Ignatius. "The Novels of India." *The Indo-Anglian Novel*. Calcutta Writers' Workshop, 1975, Vol. II.

Iyengar, K.R. Srinivasa. *Indian Writing in English*. Bombay: Asia Publishing House, 1973.

Joseph, Margaret P. *Kamala Markandaya*. Liverpool: Lucas Publication, 1988.

Markandaya, Kamala. *Nectar in a Sieve*. New York: Penguin Putnam Inc., 1995.

— *Some Inner Fury*. London: Putnam and Co., 1955.

— *A Silence of Desire*. London: Four Square Books, 1966.

— *The Nowhere Man*. 1972; rpt. Bombay: Orient Longman, 1975.

Parameswaran, Uma. *A Study of Representative Indo-English Novelists*. New Delhi: Vikas Publications, 1976.

Prasad, Madhusudan. (Ed.), *Perspectives on Kamala Markandaya*. Ghaziabad: Vimal Prakashan, 1984.

Rao, A.V. Krishna. "Continuity and Change in the Novels of Kamala Markandaya." *Perspective on Kamala Markandaya*. (Ed.) Madhusudan Prasad. Ghaziabad: Vimal Prakashan, 1984.

Shirwadkar, Meena. *Image of Women in the Indo-Anglian Novel*. New Delhi: Sterling Publishers, 1979.

Srivastava, R.K. *The Novels of Kamala Markandaya*. Amritsar: Guru Nanak Dev University, 1988.

17

The Evil Effects of Industrialization in Kamala Markandaya's *Nectar in a Sieve*

Sharda Jain

India needs to industrialize itself quickly and rapidly in order to overcome poverty and to march ahead on the path of progress. However, India must recoil from blindly following the West because it would make us false and faithless to the insights deeply ingrained by our rich tradition. East-West encounter manifests itself in Kamala Markandaya's first novel *Nectar in a Sieve* (1955) in the form of conflict between the human values and the industrial pattern of life.

Nectar in a Sieve embodies mainly rural economy on the verge of urbanization and industrialization. The novel ultimately deals with the exploitation of the poor by the rich and the evil effects of industrialization. Set in a South Indian village, *Nectar in a Sieve* presents the story of the rural people. The village unchanged for a long time is suddenly invaded by industry and technology in the shape of tannery which leads to sinister consequences. The cardinal problem of the novel is that of the deteriorating influence of the industrialization on human lives. Dr. A.V. Krishna Rao rightly observes:

> "In *Nectar in a Sieve,* Markandaya dramatises the tragedy of a traditional Indian village and a peasant family assaulted by Industrialization" (Rao, 1972, 56).

The novel, in fact, portrays the hardships and tragedy faced by the peasant folk in a traditional village under the invasion of tremendous change introduced by industrialization. It depicts the hunger, toil and torture, suffering and anguish of the peasants—the worst victims of the process of modernization and industrialization.

The novel delineates the story of human degradation and debasement wrought about by the impact of industrialization. In the novel the author portrays the simple lives of the peasants who grow and live, suffer and endure and emerge, more dignified and more humane. The novel brings to the fore the conflict between the agrarian values and the industrial systems of society. Rukmani, the narrator heroine, nostalgically broods over her past life and depicts her life story beginning with her marriage in such a way as to depict simultaneously the agony of the Indian farmers and their best efforts to survive not only the vagaries of nature, but also the disturbances caused by the tannery, recently established in the outskirt of their village. Before the advent of tannery, the life of Rukmani with her family was simply peaceful. A wave of pride surged in the heart of Rukmani as a spiritual reaction to the love and care of her husband who was poor in everything except in love for his wife. Rukmani needed nothing else, no wealth, no further pleasures.

Though village life offers no luxuries to Rukmani and Nathan, yet they lead a calm and peaceful life. They struggle hard to survive the relentless strokes of nature and society. However, the placid and traditional life in the village suddenly begins to change under the impact of industrialization, and peace and tranquility of their life is destroyed by the process of modernization, i.e. by the establishment of a tannery by an Englishman. The building of the tannery is the beginning of this change in the life of Rukmani and her village as she records:

> "But the change that now came into my life, into all our lives, blasting its way into all our village, seemed wrought in the twinkling of an eye" (25).

We note that from the very beginning Rukmani opposes the advent of tannery, the symbol of modernity and industrialization which spoils the natural beauty of the countryside. The calm and serene life 'far from the madding crowd' is invaded by din and bustle, filth and dirt, meanness and selfishness. Rukmani gloomily observes:

> "Already my children hold their noses when they go by, and all is shouting and disturbance and crowds wherever you go. Even the birds have forgotten to sing, or else their calls are lost to us" (29).

The loss of natural beauty and human virtues is the unavoidable result of industry. The sweet peace and tranquility of the village fade away giving rise to the urban squalor and vice. The mischief flourishes in such an atmosphere. Kunthi, the evil beauty of the village, regards tannery as a boon and feels elated at her village growing into a town.

Symbolising the traditional sweetness of life, Rukmani revolts emphatically against the encroachment of the Western industrial values on rural life. The evils of industrialism—inflation, vice and ugliness crop up and create havoc in their lives. Materialism grows relentlessly, animals are butchered and used commercially, the land of villagers is swallowed gradually. The simple rural human values are replaced by those of materialism and industrialism. The villagers become the mute spectators to this horrible spectacle while the tannery flourishes. The reflection of Rukmani suggests this havoc in her life:

> "Somehow, I had always felt the tannery would eventually be our undoing.... It had changed the face of our village beyond recognition" (133-134).

The village obviously stands at the periphery of urban civilization. The two elder sons of Rukmani, Arjun and Thambi, join the tannery. Another son Murugan leaves the village and goes to the city in search of a job. While working in the tannery Arjun and Thambi experience the impact of new tendencies on the traditional ties. Both actively participate in the meetings of workers, their protests and strikes, demanding an increase in their wages.

Rukmani and Nathan are in the grip of harrowing poverty and terrible drought leading to the death of their younger son Raja. Another son grows weaker and weaker day by day. Revolting against the false norms of traditional society and unable to bear the starvation of her family any more, their daughter Ira takes recourse to prostitution, specifically to feed her younger brother. For, under the impact of modernity and industrialism, she regards the preservation of life more pious than the observation of a so-called morality. Tannery is indeed the root cause of tragedy in the lives of Rukmani and Nathan, Arjun and Thambi, Ira and Raja. However, having no other alternative to save her child from starvation, Rukmani herself is compelled to accept the situation of Ira's prostitution. Kai Nicholson rightly observes:

> "Nature may have brought upon hardships, but the tannery had socially degraded them" (Nicholson, 1972, 119).

Time and again the novel suggests that the spirit of resignation and stoicism strengthens one like Rukmani in times of suffering. After shedding the spirit of acceptance one is ruined. For instance, Rukmani's son refuses to accept the working conditions in the factory and his rebellion results in his death, wrought about by the evil impact of industrialization. However, in the case of Rukmani, the spirit of Oriental stoicism never breaks down.

In general, the advent of tannery has resulted in the loss of traditional values, in social degradation and has become a source of inflation, vice and moral debasement. Kamala Markandaya presents a realistic and vivid account of the dislocation and disintegration of a family by the octopus of industrialism. The establishment of the tannery also results in the eviction of Nathan's family from the land they have farmed for thirty years, leading them to utter destitution and despair, insecurity and privation. Rukmani voices the disgust of a thousand dispossessed families saying 'while there was land, there was hope.'

The theme of the novel is not only the calamities wrought about by nature but also by man and the clash between the traditional values and the forces of material and industrial progress. Markandaya has presented a strong criticism of industrialism and its intrusion upon the placid rhythm and serene beauty of rustic life. The encroachment of industry causes the decay of human values, creates havoc in village economy and brings in social degradation of human beings.

The novel clearly brings out the clash between the agrarian and industrial systems of society. Industrialization in general, and tannery in particular, pollutes completely the serene atmosphere of the village with its smells and clamour, and corrupts the values of people dehumanizing them.

The main target of Markandaya's attack is the evils brought about by the industrialization which no doubt enriches the people but not without its poisonous side effects. For instance, it results in greater commercialization of life, an alien population, labour unrest and the consequent death of Rukmani's son. This urban and industrial culture is in conflict with the naturalistic conception of human dignity. The tannery remains a sinister presence throughout the novel.

However, Rukmani, unstung by the bug of industrialism, displays her faith in human dignity by assimilating the destitute leper boy Puli into the nectar of her love and warmth and gets him cured of his disease and infuses meaning into his life. The central theme of the novel is the rural society assaulted by industrialism and its intrusion upon the placid rhythm of their life. Kamala Markandaya recreates the evil and negative impact of industrialization on their lives in a touching manner.

Thus the novel concentrates on the conflict between the traditional values of India and industrial and material values of the west. Industrialization and technology are productive of men's well being and prosperity, yet they threaten the very fundamental human values. In the industrialized society, humanity and human values are dead and people prey on each other like vultures. The industrialization exercises a malevolent effect on people. The moral decay permeates the life of those dazzeled by industrialization. To quote the words of K. Meera Bai:

"The novel reflects Kamala Markandaya's concern with the effect of industrialization on the agrarian Indian society and the consequent social and economic upheaval" (Bai, 1991, 192).

As the evils of industrialization and urbanization still loom large over our life and the erosion of human values continues unabated, the voice of Kamala Markandaya heard in her *Nectar in a Sieve* is still relevant.

WORKS CITED

Bai, K. Meera. "Method and Narrative Techniques in Kamala Markandaya's *Nectar in a Sieve.*" *Indian Women Novelists,* Set I: Vol. I, ed. by R.K. Dhawan. Prestige Books: New Delhi, 1991.

Markandaya, Kamala. *Nectar in a Sieve.* Bombay: Jaico Publishing House, 1955.

Nicholson, Kai. *Social Problems in Indo-Anglian and the Anglo-Indian Novels.* Bombay: Jaico Publishing House, 1972.

Rao, A.V. Krishna. *The Indo-Anglian Novel and the Changing Tradition.* Mysore: Rao and Raghavan, 1972.

18 Treatment of Conjugal Love in Kamala Markandaya's *Nectar in a Sieve*

Alka Rani

The novel, *Nectar in a Sieve,* deals with the desolate life of an Indian peasant, Nathan. Kamala Markandaya's first hero, "is defeated by rain, fleeced by the moneylender, and evicted by the landlord, and yet he does not give up working and hoping for a better future" (Chauhan, 136). However, the novelist does not say anything about the predicament of Nathan's parents. The only thing that the novelist points out about Nathan's life before his marriage with Rukmani is that Rukmani's father could not find a rich husband for her, and married her "to a tenant farmer who was poor in everything but love and care for his wife, whom he took at the age of twelve" (*Nectar in a Sieve,* 2). The very first instance of Nathan's love and care for his wife is seen in his treatment of wife just after the marriage. At the time of departure from his father's house, Rukmani wept, but it was Nathan who soothed and calmed her. For six hours they rode on and on along the dusty road, passing several villages on the way to theirs, which was a good distance away. Half way there they stopped and ate meal: boiled rice, *dhal*, vegetables and curds. Rukmani says, "A whole coconut apiece too, in which my husband nicked a hole with this scythe for me so that I might drink the clear milk" (3).

I

Nathan, right from the time of his birth to the time of his death, has been groping after a comfortable life, but his fortunes have always been in a sharp descent. Rukmani, just after her marriage with Nathan, realised that poverty did not disturb the easy pace of their life. "Peace and quiet were ours" (7), she remarks, and the feeling of want and poverty runs like an undercurrent: "How well I recall it, how grateful I am that not all the clamour which invaded our lives later could subdue the memory or still the longing for it. Rather, it has strengthened it: had there not been what has been, I might never have known how blessed we were" (7). Rukmani points to the role of Nathan in the novel when she observes: "True, my husband did not own the land he tilled, as my father had done; yet the possibility was there that he might one day do so. We owned our own ploughing bullocks; we kept a milch goat. From each harvest we saved, and had gunny-sacks full of the husked rice stored away in our small stone-lined granary" (7).

So there was food in plenty for two people, and Nathan hoped that he would own the land he tilled. He was quite sanguine of his labour, but he was ignorant of the cruel hands of destiny. Another feature of Nathan's character during the early phase of his life is hinted at by Rukmani: "What patience indeed my husband must have had, to put up with me uncomplainingly during those early days of our married life. Not one cross word or impatient look, and praise for whatever small success I achieved" (8). Nathan praised his wife for those little duties which fell beyond her experience before marriage: "when Nathan saw it he was full of admiration, and made much of this one fruit—he who was used to harvesting a field at a time" (8). To this extent Nathan and Rukmani lived happily, but what was to follow changed their taste of life.

Rukmani was on her way to motherhood; and therefore, Nathan wanted her to stoop as little as possible. "Now that I did not work in the fields," says Rukmani, "I spent most of my time tending my small garden" (12). Nathan's wife knew how to read and write. She spent most of her leisure time in reading and writing, and Nathan's joy knew no bounds to see his wife in doing so. "I think," says Rukmani, "it cost him a good deal to say what he did, and he never varied his attitude once. That was typical of my husband: when he had worked things out for himself he would follow his conclusions at whatever cost to himself. I am sure it could not have been easy for him to see his wife more learned than he himself was, for Nathan alas could not even write his name; yet not once did he assert his rights and forbid me my pleasure, as lesser men might have done" (12). Nathan could not bear with his wife's uneasiness.

The months which consumed outnumbered the hands that produced: Ira was born; and after a gap of some seven years, five more children were born: Arjun, Thambi, Murugan, Raja, and Selvam. When Ira was born, Nathan was not as worried as Rukmani: "Only Nathan did not say it to me, for he was worried too, and knew better. We did not talk about it, it was always with us: a chill fear that Ira was to be our only child" (18). When Arjun was born, Nathan was "overjoyed at the arrival of a son" (20). On the tenth day from the birth of the son, Nathan invited everybody to feast and rejoiced with them in their good fortune. However, with six children to feed Nathan could no longer afford to eat all the vegetables he grew. Once a week he would cut and pack his garden produce, selecting the best and leaving the spoilt or bruised vegetables for his family, cover the basket with leaves and set off for the village. Stringency tempted him to fall in the net of Biswas, the moneylender.

The tannery came into existence, and it further made life more and more difficult for Nathan who unlike others believed that "they will be back; for you may be sure they did not take so much trouble only to leave a shell in our midst. Therefore it is as well to accept these things" (28). However, misery began to weave its web round his life: "Our children had not seen us so serious, so vehement, before. Three of my sons huddled together in a corner staring at us with wide eyes, the two youngest lay asleep, one in Ira's arms, the other leaning heavily against her; and she herself sagged against the wall with their weight as she sat there on the floor. There was a look on her lovely soft face that pierced me" (28). Now Ira was thirteen, and Rukmani implored Nathan to get her a husband. Anxiety began to plough the visage of a man like Nathan: the questions of Ira's marriage as well as of food for eight members of the family occupied his mind.

To add fuel to the fire, the Zamindar sent Sivaji to realise the rent of the land, which could not be paid owing to the failure of the crop. One year it rained beyond limits, and the following year there was no rain. Once Nathan said to his wife, "It is a bad season. The rains have destroyed much of our work; there will be little eating done this year" (39). To save his family from starvation, Nathan went to break the dams. His wife and children were with him. They could gather a huge number of fishes. Rukmani remarks: "We ate, finding it difficult to believe we did so. The good food lay rich, if uneasy, in our starved bellies" (45). The Zamindar's man, Sivaji, demanded the rent, and this time he was a bit severe in his attitude to Nathan; therefore, Nathan sold "the pots and pans, the food and the bullocks" (76). The money was pooled and counted—there was in all one hundred and twenty-five rupees, not even the half he had to pay. For the rest, Sivaji agreed to wait.

Nathan passed his hard time tossing between hope and fear. In this connection, Rukmani observes: "Hope and fear. Twin forces that tugged at us first in one direction and then in another, and which was the stronger no one could say. Of the latter we never spoke, but it was always with us. Fear, constant companion of the peasant. Hunger, ever at hand to jog his elbow should he relax. Despair, ready to engulf him should he falter. Fear; fear of the dark future; fear of the sharpness of hunger; fear of the blackness of death" (79). Nathan married Ira with hopes, but despair followed the marriage; he welcomed five sons, but they posed the problem of food; and he worked hard on land in expectation of storing grain for food, but heavy rains and then drought crushed his hopes. He was forced to send two of his sons to the tannery, but a strike in the tannery put him again in the hands of want and hunger.

Then came death: Raja was dead, he was caught stealing calf-skin from the yard of the tannery, and he was beaten to death. Kuti too died: he was the last child, conceived in happiness at a time when the river of Rukmani and Nathan's life ran gently. Then came disintegration: Nathan was deprived of the land which was the course of his livelihood; his one son (Murugan) already settled in a town some hundred miles away, and the other one (Selvam) was now an assistant to Dr. Kenny. Ira and her illegitimate son (Sacrabani) were left to the care of Selvam. Nathan and Rukmani were to go to Murugan: "We were to go and that our children and grandchildren were to stay" (138). At last they were at the centre of the city; but Koil Street where their son lived was some six miles away. "Nathan was very tired; the heat and the noise, the bustle of the city, had taken their toll. He was walking sluggishly, now and again he stumbled" (143). They were, therefore, forced to take some rest in this unknown place.

Bad luck brought Nathan and his wife to the temple where beggars were given food. Both Nathan and Rukmani were hungry. Though their conscience did not allow them to be beggars, yet hunger made them what they hate to be. While satisfying their hunger, they lost their bundles—their only possessions. Rukmani recounts the calamity: "We had left them (bundles) propped against one of the carved stone pillars in the long corridor leading to the assembly hall. We went to it, but the bundles had vanished" (148). Then Nathan and his wife reached the destination, but they came to know that Murugan worked for the collector of Chamundi Hill. Even when Nathan and Rukmani reached the place where Murugan and his wife lived, they were shocked to know from Murugan's wife, Ammu, that "He left me. He has been gone nearly two years" (61). Nathan and his wife had to leave the place in sheer disappointment.

Nathan and Rukmani were compelled to bear with the company of beggars at the temple. "Many a time," says Rukmani, "my husband stood aside unable to face the fray: If I had not reproached him his distaste of the whole procedure would have led him to starvation" (166). Nathan did not like this way of life: "Better to starve where we were bred than live here. Whatever happens, whatever awaits us, we must return." But the questions before them were beyond solution: "For where shall a man turn who has no money? Where can he go?" (167). Nathan wants to go to his village, but there is no money; he wants to work hard, but there is no vigour in his body; and he wants to earn his honest bread, but he has lost his health. "Whether from its fumes or from the blighting of our hopes, my husband began to suffer again from rheumatism, and at the same time the old bouts of fever began" (167).

With Puli, the orphan, Nathan and Rukmani worked on the quarry; but breaking stone in old age and shattered health is not suitable for the two. Nevertheless, Nathan has the satisfaction of earning his own bread. Further, he is serious about saving money for going back to his village. But what Rukmani says about Puli is a nuance of bitter truth: "In the short time Puli had spent with us we had come to be curiously dependent on the boy, respecting his independent spirit as much as his considerable knowledge of the city and its many kinds of people. Yet I thought, what I did not wish to think, of the time when the disease that had claimed his fingers would creep up eating away his limbs—or attack some other part, his feet or his eyes, what then of this bright fearless child who boasted that he stood alone? There is a limit to the achievements of human courage" (168). And then follows Nathan's death: he dies like a beggar, like an orphan, like a no man's man.

II

Nathan is blessed with the power of patience, perseverance, and tolerance; as such, his relations with his relatives, neighbours, and acquaintances are by and large cordial and harmonious. Though there are some characters who fall beyond Nathan's liking for them, he is seldom at enmity with them. For instance, the building of tannery is cursed and condemned by one and all, but Nathan does not see any harm in it. He tells his wife: "And did you not benefit from their stay, selling your pumpkins and plantains for better prices than you did before" (28). Or when Rukmani tells Nathan that Ira should be married soon, as she has begun to show signs of youth in her body, the patient Nathan retorts, "My daughter is no wanton. Not only men but women look at her, for she is beautiful" (30). Nathan's view of things and persons is moderate.

Nathan loves his wife, Rukmani. He does not want her to exert and strain against hard work. Rukmani is surprised to feel how affectionate has been her husband: "What patience indeed my husband must have had, to put up with me uncomplainingly during those early days of our married lives. Not one cross word or impatient look, and praise for whatever small success I achieved" (8). Even the easy flow of life comes to an end, Nathan does not speak a word that may wound his wife's sensibility. The two successive failures of crops owing to heavy rains and drought have caused irreparable losses to Nathan's economy. Nevertheless, his dealing with his wife has not changed in tone and temper. Nathan's love for his wife is at the front when he "seized me and swung me high up, in front of all those people. Several of the women were laughing at him indulgently, the children were twittering with pleasure" (57).

Nathan never ignored the sexual urges of his wife. Though it appears that Rukmani, as Kunthi holds, had sex with Doctor Kenny, yet a careful study of the novel shows that Rukmani is just obliged to Doctor Kenny for his missionary zeal. The light-heartedness that came in the wake of Deepavali made Nathan feel how spirited his wife was; so he came abruptly towards his wife: "In the straining darkness I felt his body moving with desire, his hands on me were trembling, and I felt my senses opening like a flower to his urgency, I closed my eyes and waited, waited in the darkness while my being filled with a wild, ecstatic fluttering, waited for him to come to me" (57). Nathan honoured the sentiments and feeling of his wife; and he seldom did anything contrary to the wishes of his wife. He was happy in her happiness, and he shared her cares and anxieties. He favourably responded to the demands of her body, mind and heart.

When Nathan has come on the verge of ruin, his wife wants that they should go to Murugan leaving Ira and her child in the care of Salvam, he is not willing to do so. But just to please his wife he decides to go to Murugan. Rukmani says in this connection: "I closed my eyes and felt his hands on my temples where the pulses beat, gently stroking, soothing me in the only way he could. He suffered for me, not so much for himself" (137). And even Nathan held that "There are some things that cannot be sacrificed...besides I would never be happy. Certainly your mother would not let me rest" (137). While uttering these words, a little smile spurted on his face. The man who has lived in the village right from his birth can hardly be happy in the town. But Nathan consents to go to the town where Murugan has been living: "We were to go and that our children and grandchildren were to stay" (138).

III

Nathan-Rukmani relationship symbolises the traditional intimacy, cooperation, tolerance and patience of Indian husband and wife. Nathan's love for his wife, and her devotion to her husband are indicative of Kamala Markandaya's deep insight into the Indian psyche and social atmosphere. Although Rukmani seems to be dominating in the novel, she never underestimates the qualities and position of her husband, Nathan. Both face misfortunes and enjoy the happy moments of their married life together without pride or grudge. However, there are certain instances when they could have fallen out with each other, but their common sense, mutual understanding, sense of responsibility and duty towards the family keep them united till the end of Nathan's life. Although able to read and write, Rukmani never shows any superiority over her illiterate husband. Nathan, out of his love for her, ignores her weakness, if any. This understanding of each other's feelings and sentiments projects them as ideal husband and wife in Indian English fiction.

WORKS CITED

Chauhan, P.S. "Kamala Markandaya: Sense and Sensibility." *The Literary Criterion*, XII, 1976.

Markandaya, Kamala. *Nectar in a Sieve*. Bombay: Jaico Publishing House, 1955.

19 From Demand to Denial: The Enigmatic Journey of an Unclaimed Parcel

Gunjan Chaturvedi and *Ranjana Mehrotra*

> "Wipe out the paints, unmould the clay
> Let nothing remain of that yesterday."
>
> (Das, *My Story*: 111)

Thus cried out Kamala Das in her very first poem. She exhibited an exceptional courage in giving words to the harrowing situations of feminine experiences and in making efforts to subvert the established order that supports the imbalance of power between sexes. She articulated her innermost passions, desires and ambitions with absolute frankness and became "a voice for the 'silences' who could not speak beyond whispers even among themselves" (Kaur: Preface). A creative woman, vocal in defining her identity and in revolting against the sexist culture's effort to exploit, passivise and marginalize women, Kamala Das contributed a large share in creating an environment in which the artists of the future like Gauri Deshpande, Mamta Kalia, Tara Patel, Imtiaz Dharker, Charmayne D'Souza, Menka Shivdasani, Adarsh Mishra etc. could flourish. As Rajlukshmee Debee Bhattacharya rightly puts it: "they are rooted in her and linked with her, sharing the same ambience and the same concerns...the same wine seems to be poured from so many bottles" (161). Ms. Das felt disgusted with the kind of gender arrangements that treat women as slaves and thwart their desire to seek freedom and equality, to seek a right to exist as independent human beings. She raised a voice of protest against sexual politics that assigns the status of the colonized to the woman and expects her to conform to her man-made 'Angel in the House' image—a passive, submissive, docile, self-negating, self-crippling, self-denying, self-annihilating being, ready to force herself into the male-sanctioned moulds:

"I am the sinner,
I am a saint. I am the beloved and the betrayed,
I have no joys which are not yours, no
Aches which are not yours. I too call myself I."

(An Introduction)

Through her autobiography, poetic compositions, novels, short-stories, essays, interviews etc. she gave a clarion call to all her sisters, cowering beneath the monstrous ego of males to rise and flutter female wings, to develop faith in their own powers, to dethrone the myth of femininity, to refuse and reject victim-positions and to aspire for the subject-positions. She chided the yielding, self-surrendering maids and said:

"Woman, is this happiness, this lying buried
Beneath a man? It's time again to come alive.
The world extends a lot beyond his six foot frame."

(The Conflagration)

She felt suffocated in the world of discriminative value-systems, hypocrisies and prejudiced laws and felt like a prisoner entrapped in a suffocating environment:

"As the convict studies
His prison's geography
I study the trappings
Of your body, dear love,
For I must some day find
An escape from its snare."

(The Prisoner)

She resented that:

"...the boundaries of
Paradise had shrunk to a mere
Six feet two..."

(The Invitation)

She provided Indian English literature with a new discourse of woman's body language from the point of view of a woman. She exhorted women to assert their individuality and to aspire for and be ready for the freedom that they deserve:

"Getting a man to love you is easy,
Only be honest about your wants as
Woman...."

(The Looking Glass)

When her autobiographical work *My Story* was first published about three decades ago, *Women's Liberation Movement* in India was yet in its infancy. The work "gave a rude jolt to the complacent and conformity ridden Indian society and its patriarchal values." Kamala Das shocked the world with her uninhibited phrasing that scandalized the conservative people. She stunned the conventional minds with her erotically titillating allusions, celebrated "femininity, woman's body to be more specific, and in the process" proved "herself to be a feminist of the most radical kind" (Mittapalli and Piciucco: Preface). The autobiography was, in fact, a record of a flamboyant, volatile rebellion against a male-oriented universe. It was an attempt to move from margin to center. According to Kamala Das' own testimony, she wrote the book because "(she) needed to disturb society out of its complacence.... (She) wanted to make women of.... (her) generation feel that if men could do something wrong, they could do it themselves too.... (She) wanted to remove gender difference..... (She) wanted to see that something happened to society which had strong inhibitions and which only told lies in the public" (Das, 'It is Animal Lust'). Her several short-story collections also weave a web of feminine experiences in all their variegated hues and "form a holistic social framework of woman as victim, as mother, as goddess, as emotion, as intellect and a host of other images in relation to man" (Begum, 39). When sporadically she ventured into the realm of fiction writing, there also she evinced the same concern and restlessness with the traditional positioning of women. Her poetry, however, voices the sense of protest most strongly. Her anger and disgust expressed there are directly the progeny of an old social set-up oriented towards the total annihilation of the feminine personality:

"You planned to tame a swallow, to hold her
In the long summer of your love so that she would forget,
Not the raw seasons alone, and the homes left behind, but
Also her nature, the urge to fly and the endless
Pathways of the sky."

(*The Old Play-House*)

The image of the lady that gets conjured up before our mind's eye after reading her compositions is that of a woman totally unencumbered by the conventional falsifying colours, of a lady who promises to break the shackles and fly away freely into the limitless skies:

"I shall someday leave, leave the cocoon,
You built around me with morning tea,
Love-words flung from doorways and of course,
Your tired lust. I shall someday take
Wings, fly around, as often petals
Do when free in air."

(*The Old Play-House*)

Hers was effort that instilled courage and confidence among the ladies of her generation to confront life boldly and to assert their identity. Today, however, she appears to have undergone a metamorphosis, to have taken a complete U-turn, to have given up her quest for emancipation from traditional role-expectations and to have been transformed into a woman pining for restraints and revelling in her circumscribed existence. The lady who had once vigorously demanded freedom and independence from the masculine yoke, now denies it and says, "I don't want freedom. I had enough of it thrust on me. Freedom had become a burden for me.... I want a master to protect me. I want protection and not freedom. Before I was the rebellious type, I used to move around a lot, involve myself in various activities; most of the time taking risks and living dangerously. Now I have changed. I have become a virtuous, clean woman. A puritan in all senses, who prays daily, wears white clothes and is conservative in thinking. I want guidelines to regulate and discipline my life. I want a master to protect me.... My husband died seven years ago and I am now a lonely widow who is 67 years old. When he was there, he provided me with protection. I had not to bother about getting tickets, passport, visas and such other things. I just had to follow him" (Das, *The Times of India,* 1999). The 'Queen of Erotica' (as she was once described) whose earlier work had been a vehicle for voicing an "inner privacy," had been a protest against the senseless restrictions which force a sensitive woman to lead an insipid life, has now been fascinated by the "orthodox" lifestyle of the Muslim women and has embraced Islam. 'Burqa' a constant eyesore, mind sore and heart sore for the feminists, has to her become a symbol of protection—"I feel burkha can sometimes serve as a bullet-proof dress. It protects a woman against the piercing eyes of men. You are so safe inside a burkha. No one dares trouble you" (Das, 'I Needed to Disturb Society': 1992). Though she claims that she wears a 'Burqa' out of her own wish and would certainly dislike it, if it were forced on her, still the fact remains that she has accepted this restraint wholeheartedly and even endorses its use. Hinduism, she says, had given her too much of freedom. She found it "too lenient" and what she wants is restraint. Her conversion has antagonized many who have gone to the extent of seeking judicial redressal in the matter. Nabeesa Ummal, a retired Professor and CPI (M) activist, has, in a belligerent mood, flung a challenge in her direction to write a book like *My Story* now. "She" says Nebeesa, "will face the same fatwa and fate as Bangladeshi writer Taslima Nasreen" (*India Today:* Dec. 1999). Even Keralites among whom Kamala Das has spent a major portion of her life, were taken aback by this decision of hers and were made to retort, "It hurts the pride of the layman and the literate alike; we nurtured a rebel of sorts in our midst for so long, and look how she rejects us for the aliens" (Qtd. in Sodhi, 61). Perhaps despite all the claims of flexibility and tolerance of Hinduism, its followers are not broadminded enough to accept the conversion of a woman's libber.

The religious matters are, however, outside the jurisdiction of the topic under consideration. Let us leave them aside. Still no one can gainsay the fact that for the supporters of Women's Liberation Movement the remarks made by Kamala Das (now Bibi Suraiya) are certainly shocking, frustrating and to a large extent, damaging to the cause. One definitely has every right to rediscover or reinvent oneself at any point of time in one's life but when after contributing so much to awaken females out of their age-old slumber, after retaliating so vehemently against the worn-out social values and traditions which hinder and retard the emotional as well as intellectual development of a woman's personality, when Kamala Das goes to the extent of repudiating her autobiography, as she did in an interview with Suma Jossan (published in *The Sunday Observer,* Nov 8, 1987), when she claims that it does not project her real self at all, when she says that she wrote the book only to pay her hospital-bills and made it "hot" only on the advice of her husband so that it sold better, when she asserts that she would not have written such a book if she had been affluent, when she even claims that she has entered social service to 'atone' for having written the book, it is really disillusioning coming from a female who had once been widely acclaimed as "the unofficial spokesman of the Indian counterpart of the Women's Liberation Movement in the West" (Kohli, 27).

In an interview given to *The Hindu,* while talking about the reasons behind embracing Islam, Kamala emphasized her need to belong somewhere. "How long," she moaned, "can I remain an unclaimed parcel with the address stamped on me. There should be someone to claim me" (Das, *The Hindu*). Actually the need to be claimed (by a male) has always been a part of Kamala's psyche. The woman who lamented the hollow prescriptions of society:

> "An ideal woman, they said, was but
> a masochist. Trained from infancy
> to wear the flannels of cowardice
> next to her skin, trained to be inert
> under a male committed by vows to
> feed her, clothe her and buy for her the

1000 sq.ft. flat with a loft
for storing the debris of passing years."

(*A Feminist's Lament*)

seems to have been, in a mildly masochistic way, in love with the very stifling conditions against which she rebelled. Devindra Kohli aptly says that Kamala Das, "seems to have a good deal of the conventional woman in her make up, so that...(she) can not help...expressing an ambivalence proceeding from her own duality, proceeding from, that is, the combination in herself of a need for domestic security and the desire for an independence, an independence consistent with a non-domestic mode of living" (27). Bruce King has also expressed a somewhat similar opinion about her. "The interest of Das' poetry," says he, "is...the instability of her feelings, the way they rapidly shift and assume new postures, new attitudes of defence, attack, explanation and celebration. Her poems...are...involved with the self and its varied, often conflicting, emotions ranging from the desire for security and intimacy to the assertion of the ego, self-dramatization and feeling of shame and depression" (150).

Beneath the rebellious facade of Kamala Das lurks a personality—timid, withdrawn, sensitive, needing a "man for construction and destruction" (*The Invitation*). Even in her *My Story,* after attacking so furiously the mores of a society that thrives on the silence of women, she chooses to return home to Nalapat from Bombay, which is certainly symbolic of an acceptance of the patriarchal power. "I should never have walked out of my red-tiled home in Malabar," she mused, "...The process of change, the imitation of the city—type was itself a long illness, a nausea in the brain" (Das, 'She-Mouse Returns Home'). In an interview with Iqbal Kaur she confessed, "I really turned traditional at least externally. But inside," she insisted, "I was the same rebel" (Das, 'I Needed to Disturb Society'). But I would say that throughout she has remained traditional from inside too. She used to obey the commands of her husband "like a computer" (Kaur, 160). She may give any number of excuses but the fact is that despite claiming that marriage nauseates her because it legitimizes violence on women and gives men a legal control on women's bodies, she could never dare break off her ties with her "cruel" husband. An Indian wife, she said, is an "Olympic call-girl" and Indian marriages are no better than rapes, but now she plans to get married again, at the age of about 70, and desires to be completely possessed by a man though the name of the prospective suitor has been kept in the dark.

In her literary compositions this vein of traditionalism comes forth absolutely and clearly. The amazon who candidly talked about her emotions sans hypocrisy, had courage to seek fulfillment outside marriage, if it was not forthcoming within it and who did not at all hesitate to give words to her experiences in extra-marital relationships frankly, as she has accepted at the end of one of her poems:

"I am a freak. It's only
To save my face, I flaunt at
Times, a grand, flamboyant lust."

(*The Freaks*)

Her poem 'Jaisurya' about the birth of a son is, to quote Dushyanti Mendis, "an anti-feminist poem" (133). Amar Kr. Singh has called the composer of the poem an "archetypal mother happy in giving birth to a son" (126). In the poem she gives vent to a sense of pride and repeatedly asserts that the son has liberated her by bringing light in her life. "It is clear," says Dushyanti Mendis, "that Das, the woman, lives in darkness and that her son, although born out of her womb, must be kept separate from this darkness. The question is, if Das' child had been a daughter, would she too have been equated with light, or would she have been a part of this darkness?" "The last four lines," Mendis goes on to assert, "sound the death-knell for feminism" (133). These lines equate the son with "the right" and the "Sun-drenched golden day," while the mother has been equated with "the wrong" and the darkness in unequivocal terms:

"Out of the mire of a moonless night was
He born, Jaisurya, my son, out of the
Wrong is born the right and out of night
The Sun-drenched golden day."

(*Jaisurya*)

Even her love for Krishna, the divine lover, shows her dependence upon males. In her *My Story* she openly admits that she was dissatisfied with her marital rel-tionship and committed adultery because "I needed security, I needed permanence. I needed two strong arms around my shoulders..." (194). When she was "free from the last of human bondage", her quest for the security of the arms of some male made her turn to Krishna who, she felt, had come to "claim" her (Das, *My Story,* 195). In her poems of divine love the devotion described by her is generally in connection with Krishna's pursuit of Radha but it is more the devotion of the self-negating Mira Bai's than that of Radha whose love relationship was based more or less on terms of equality. In talking about the 'Radha-Krishna' myth Kamala Das did not have to fight against religion because the concept of sexual freedom is rooted in it but the language in these poems remains the language of the prisoner:

"Your body is my prison, Krishna,
I cannot see beyond it,
Your darkness blinds me,
Your love-words shut out the wise world's din."

(Krishna)

By becoming a votary of Krishna, says Manju Jaidka, "she indirectly turns her back on herself as a responsible, free-thinking adult and opts for childhood once more, going back to the legends that the grown up world used to feed her on. Ironically, she is once again defining herself in terms of values and traditions handed down to her by the patriarchal set-up, thus conceding the superiority of their world and the inadequacy of her own." "At this point," asserts Ms. Jaidka, "it becomes interesting to ponder what exactly Kamala Das has achieved by turning away from one form of love (the husband's, the lover's) to another (Krishna's). Has she not cast off one kind of bondage only to take on another?" (Jaidka, 97). The answer to these questions is certainly going to be in the affirmative.

It is, in fact, really difficult to fight for the dignity and true emancipation of women because the values and attitudes which one has to struggle against are usually deep rooted not only in the minds of men but also in the consciousness of women. When this struggle passes through a transitional phase, it usually manifests contradictory patterns and results in the subjugation and the emergence of new forms of bondage. This is exactly what seems to have happened in the case of Kamala Das. She refused to surrender in front of males but secretly cherished their admiring eyes and protective presence in her life. Therefore, she first tamely accepted the superiority of Krishna and now has become subservient to Allah. As a woman she has always embodied an opposition between what she feels she should be and what she feels she is. She revolted against the stifling influences of the patriarchal society but her revolt has failed because "while rejecting one set of male values, she inadvertently opts for another which, paradoxically is equally male-oriented, equally humiliating to women.... Kamala Das could have been a torch-bearer, the Indian counterpart of someone like Adrienne Rich. But she never really understood what the feminist movement was all about..." (Jaidka, 98). The lady who felt disgusted with the idea of fitting into a predefined lot:

> "Dress in saris, be girl,
> Be wife, they said, be embroiderer, be cook,
> Be a quarreler with servants.
> Fit, in oh,
> Belong, cried the categorizers...."
>
> (An Introduction)

has also been guilty of making irresponsible statements like the one given below—"Off and on I too toy with idea of joining the Women's Lib Movement, if only to have fun of walking around with no bra on. Such a delicious pleasure! But you must do it only when there are several men around to throw admiring glances to your full blown beauty. Otherwise you might as well wear the wretched thing and forget about the movement" (Das, *Blitz*, 1977).

Some say that the dissolution of the feminist perspective in her later life is the "result of the maturing vision of Das as an artist" (Mohanty, 52); some others opine that perhaps it is only a participatory research undertaken by her to comprehend the real condition of the ladies reeling underneath the great burden of conventions and restrictions; to some it is only a reaction of the exceedingly Bohemian life led by her in her youth, while many regard it only as a publicity gimmick "prompted by a desire for public spotlight that had for long been her companion but was slowly shifting allegiance" (Chakrabarti, 53). The fact, however, is that today she appears to have completely buckled under pressure and gone back on the rebellion she had initiated. It is sad that instead of putting only one step forward and becoming a staunch feminist, she has taken several steps backward and accepted a position, apparently willingly, against which she once raised a strong voice of protest.

Kamala Das once declared, "I want to bring variety into my life, to be in ten different *avatars* in one life. Be this, be that, change, blossom like a flower and each petal different from the other" (I Needed to Disturb Society). We can only hope that the present stand of Kamala Das is only one of her many *avatars* with at least one more remaining to follow. In the patriarchal culture of India, even today, everything seems to be polarized in opposing pairs. Women, here, are still "left wandering forever in the sterile desert that stretches at the bottom of the pyramid" (Pande, 159-160). We wish that the next *avatar* takes Kamala closer to the question of the equality and freedom of females because our country needs creative artists like her who can correct the warp in the sexually biased culture and can falsify the myths that tend to restrict the freedom of the 'fair-sex'.

WORKS CITED

Begum, Jameela. "Female Consciousness and the Short-Story Form: Uncertainties and Diversifications in Kamala Das's Stories." *Perspectives on Kamala Das's Prose,* ed. Iqbal Kaur. New Delhi: Intellectual Publishing House, 1995.

Bhattacharya, Rajlukshmee Debee. "A New Generation of Indo-English Women Poets." *Poetry Chronicle,* Vol. 3, Nos. 5-6, 1991.

Chakrabarti, Piyas. "Kamala Das: The Voice Within." *Re-Markings,* Vol. 3, No. 1, March, 2004.

Das Kamala. "The She-Mouse Returns Home," An interview. *Imprint,* Oct. 1973, 19.

— *My* Story. New Delhi: Sterling Paperbacks, 1937.

— *Blitz.* March 12, 1977.

— "'It is Animal Lust': An. interview with Iqbal Kaur." *The Tribune,* 19th Jan., 1992.

— "'I Needed to Disturb Society': An interview with Iqbal Kaur," Dt. 18th Aug. 1992, *Perspectives on Kamala Das's Poetry,* 160.

— "Kamala Das Embraces Islam." *The Hindu,* online edition on Indiaserver.com, 12th Dec., 1999.

— www.timesofindia.com /19 12 99 /19 conim3.htm

Jaidka, Manju. *From Slant to Straight: Recent Trends in Women's Poetry.* New Delhi: Prestige, 2000.

Kaur, Iqbal. (Ed.) *Perspectives on Kamala Das's Poetry.* New Delhi: Intellectual Publishing House, 1995.

King, Bruce. *Modern Indian Poetry in English.* Oxford University Press, 1987.

Kohli, Devendra. *Kamala Das.* Arnold Heinemann, 1975.

Mendis, Dushyanti. "Structures of Feeling: The Poetry of Kamala Das." *Modern Indian Poetry in English Critical Studies.* Creative New Literature Series 42, (Eds.) Nil, Shah and Pramod K. Nayar. New Delhi: Creative Books, 2000.

Mittapalli, Rajeshwar and Piciucco Pier Paolo (Eds.) *Kamala Das: A Critical Spectrum.* New Delhi: Atlantic Publishers and Distributors (P) Ltd, 2001.

Mohant, Niranjan. "Feminist Perspective on Kamala Das' Poetry." *Perspectives on Kamala Das's Poetry,* (Ed.) Iqbal Kaur, 1995.

Pande, Mrinal. *The Subject is Woman.* New Delhi: Sanchar Publishing House, 1991.

Singh, Amar Kumar. *Enlightening Studies in Indian English Poetry.* New Delhi: Manak Publications, 1993.

Sodhi Meena. "Kamala Das: Reinventing Self in *Points of View.*" Vol. IX, No. 1, Summer, 2002.

Ummal, Nabeesa. *India Today,* 27th Dec. 1999.

20

Voice of Protest and Self-assertion in the Poetry of Kamala Das

Arun Kumar Mishra

Voices in Pre-independence Indian English poetry are found to be changing in different periods. We hear the early voice of identity in the poetry of Henry Louis Vivian Derozio (1809-31) *et al,* the rising voice of Indian modernity in the poetry of Michael Madhusudan Dutt (1824-73) *et al*, and the strong voice of assertion of Indian life in the poetry of Toru Dutt (1856-77), Sarojini Naidu (1879-1950) *et al.* In British India, Indian English poets had virtually no freedom in the use of language but after independence, Indian English Poetry bloomed like a flower and had a significant output. Though Indian women poetry in English has developed along the same literary and linguistic lines as that of men's, the Indian women poets in English speak in a different voice because they tend to speak in their own voice. This trend has been duly acknowledged by Arlene Zide, the editor of the Penguine anthology of contemporary Indian women poets, *In Their Own Voices.*

Kamala Das, a poet, novelist and short-story writer appeared on the post-independence Indian literary horizon in the 1960s when the voice of the Third World countries in English was gaining prominence over that of the British writers. She has been a "mover and shaker' not only as a poet but also as a person. Born in 1934 in a high caste Nayar family of renowned Nalpat clan, she has converted to Islam and become Kamala

Surayya. She loves to court controversy and sensationalism, often caused by her forceful assertion and dazzling frankness. It has always been a part of her intent, need and strategy to jolt a complacent patriarchy and orthodoxy. Yet personal idiosyncrasies never outweigh the public concerns of her art, which assumes greater significance through its rich sub-texts. Among the thirty Indian women poets in English having many collections to their credit, Kamala Das possesses the individuality and verse power of her own. She has lent a new voice to Indian women's poetry in English—a voice of protest and self-assertion. What gives her poetry a unique dimension is the wide range of her personal experiences. Her poetry is intensely autobiographical and she is considered to be bolder than any other woman writer of English in India in opposing the 'dreary dead habits' of society. Dr. Laksmishree Banerjee makes an important observation in this context when she says:

> "Kamala Das's poetry, for the first time, evinces an articulately brave, confessional mode of writing; she does this with self-confidence and deliberation. She proclaims her total outrage against meaningless social norms and bindings for the Indian woman" (13).

Issues concerning women are the recurring themes in the poetry of Kamala Das. Women's social deprivation in respect of education and career, sexual desire and frustration, suffocation of a caged loveless marriage, numerous affairs, the futility of lust, the shame and sorrow of not finding love after repeated attempts, the loneliness and neurosis that stalks women especially and such other things which were not spoken of candidly are powerfully dealt with for the first time in her poetry. Those who say that theme in the poetry of Kamala Das is love and for Kamala Das love hardly goes beyond sex and lust do not do justice to her as they tend to ignore the seriousness of purpose in her poetry. Prof. Bruce King rejects such views when he writes:

> "The interest of Kamala Das's poetry is not the story of sex outside marriage but of new postures, new attitudes of defence, attack or celebration...Das opens area in which previously forbidden or ignored emotions can be expressed

in ways which reflect the true voice of feelings; she has shown how an Indian woman can create a space for herself in the public world" (20).

Kamala Das protests against the marginalization of women and social injustices and communicates a powerful female sensibility in her poetry. Her voice of protest and self-assertion is heard loud and clear in her *An Introduction* (1965) in which she speaks in the guise of a sixteen-year-old girl who rebels against the norms of patriarchal society to defend and secure her identity. Her defence against patriarchal dictation of "Don't write in English" (52) presents a passionate defence not only for writing in English but also for writing in Indian English—the English one is comfortable with. She clamours for artistic and personal freedom of expression in the matters of language, form, subject and style:

"Why not let me speak in
Any language I like?" (52).

As language parameter is a kind of cage which makes one unable to convey true emotions and feelings, one needs to choose a language of one's choice for self-expression. Naturally there is rising voice of frustration and anger against any control or restriction imposed on her. She speaks firmly and confidently: "....The language I speak,

Becomes mine, its distortions, its queerness
All mine, mine alone. It is half-English, half-
Indian, funny perhaps, but it is honest,
It is as human as I am human, don't
You see?" (52).

Her protest against the 'British snobberies' and the infatuation of Indian elite with 'British English' and her assertion of human right to speak in the language of her own choice, in her own natural voice are appreciated by Bruce King who finds that Kamala Das uses English unselfconsciously, unaffectedly and naturally without the concern for correctness and precision which characterized most earlier modern verse.

As the poet proceeds further, she transforms her protest against language imposition into protest against the imposition of marriage, sex and other social norms. She becomes the champion of women who have been oppressed for centuries. She breaks the patriarchal stronghold and tells loudly and boldly what women suffer silently—the story of her quick growth into puberty, her sudden marriage, her first sexual encounter in a closed room on the wedding night, etc. She attacks the institutions of marriage which gives a man a legal right to commit marital rape on his teenage bride. She rebels impulsively and defies the gender code. She dresses herself in a shirt and trousers, cuts hair short and sits on walls. She refuses to fit in the constructed role of "a girl," "a wife." She does, wish to become a woman by wearing *saris.* Like her own language, she chooses her own man. The poem ends with a strong note of self-assertion: "I too call myself I" (53), an assertion of her individual-self, her independent-self and her integral-self. She refuses to be weak and passive and self-less, self-denying, sacrificing and compliant angel under a masculine value system. The use of the first person pronouns 'I' for 30 times, 'my' for 10 limes and 'me' for 8 times in comparison to the use of the second person pronouns for 5 times and the third person pronouns for 9 times marks strong note of self-assertion in her poems. Dr. Laksmisree Banerjee who sees a post-modem trend in the poetry of Kamala Das, writes:

> "A study of the poetry of Kamala Das and her compeers in the late 1960s and 1970s shows that post-modernism has already become a perceptible force with the increasing dilemma and perplexities of modern life gaining ground through the universal and esoteric fluency of the Indian English language" (13).

Kamala Das speaks against all forms of dominance and asserts the need of sanity in human relation which is the only mode of preservation of human existence on this planet. Her poem *The Sunshine Cat* shows how an attractive, sensitive and creative woman caught in a loveless marriage suffers a nervous break down and becomes a cold, half dead woman now of no use at all to men. To her the tragedy of life is not that 'man dies' but 'love dies.' She opposes all gender bias which distances men from women and discriminates between them. In her poem *The Doubts* she asks the feminists as well as the anti-feminists:

"When a man is dead, or a woman
We call the corpse not 'he'
Or 'she' but 'it' Does it
Not mean that we believe
That only the souls have sex and that
Sex is invisible?"

To her masculinity and feminity are the traits of one's personality which transcends gender barriers based on biological and social identity. She asks again:

"[...] Is she
A male who with frail hands
Clasps me to her breast, while
The silence in her sick room, turning
Eloquent, accuses
Me of ingratitude?
And is he female who
After love, smoothes out the bed sheets with
Finicky hand and plucks
From pillows strands of hair?"

However, she does not reject her feminity, her womanhood, her biological identity. Rather she expresses her endless female hunger when she says:

"[...] I am sinner,
I am saint, I am the beloved, and the
Betrayed. I have no joys which are not yours, no
Aches which are not yours. I too call myself I" (53).

She remains the eternal Eve proudly celebrating her essential feminity lest she should be thoroughly anchorless. Like Eve she is opposed to 'the forbidden fruits' and the idea of the woman led by the man. Like Adam and Eve in Milton's *Paradise Lost,* she wishes to walk hand in hand with her man because woman is not made from man's head to be above him, nor from his foot to be stamped by him, but from his side to be equal to him and from near his heart to be loved by him. Her voice is the voice of her-assertion of womanhood sagging under the pressure of patriarchy.

WORKS CITED

Banerjee, L. "Modern English Poetry by Women: A Critical Survey in the Context of Feminism and Commonwealth Literature." *Journal of English Studies,* Vol. 1, No. 1 (Summer, 1995), Ranchi University, Ranchi.

Das, Kamala. "*An Introduction, The Sunshine Cat,* and *The Doubt.*" *An Anthology of Indian English Poetry*. New Delhi: Orient Longman, 1989.

King, Bruce. "Women's Voice." *Modern Indian Poetry in English*. New Delhi: OUP.

Zide, Arlene. "Introduction." *In Their Own Voice*. New Delhi: Penguin India, 1993.

21 Post-Colonial Argument in the Poetry of Kamala Das

Shilpi Saxena

In the last few decades postcolonialism has taken its place with theories such as post-structuralism, and feminism as a major critical discourse in the humanities. The literature of the Postcolonial Era represents the urge for freedom and the awareness of independent identity of the oppressed and subalterns who maintain their silence because of the centralization of power in the hands of imperialists. A productive area of collaboration between post-colonialism and feminism presents itself in the possibility of a combined offence against the aggressive myth of both imperialist and national masculinity. In 1985 Gayatri Spivak raised the question of the identity of subaltern and threw a challenge to the race and class blindness of the western academy, "Can the subaltern speak?" (271-313). By "subaltern" Spivak meant the oppressed subject or more generally those 'of inferior rank,' and her question followed on the work begun in the early 1980s by a group of intellectuals now known as the subaltern studies group. The subaltern is expressed in terms of class, caste, age, gender or any other way. The question "Can the subaltern speak?" (271-313) circulates around the self conscious scene of Post-colonial texts and theories. Post-colonial studies have come to represent a confusing and often unpleasant label of subaltern voices.

Said's intervention urges postcolonialism to reconsider the significance of all those other liberationist activities in the colonized world such as those of the women's movement which forcefully interrupt the triumphant and complacent rhetoric of the anti-colonial nation state. He laments:

> "Students of post-colonial politics have not looked enough at ideas that minimize orthodoxy and authoritarian or patriarchal thought that take a severe view of the coercive nature of identity politics" (264).

Bill Ashcroft is of the view that feminist and postcolonial theory have followed 'a path of convergent evolution.' [249] Both bodies of thought have concerned themselves with the study and defence of marginalized 'Others' within repressive structures of domination and in so doing, both have followed a remarkably similar theoretical trajectory. Leela Gandhi expresses her view:

> "Feminist and postcolonial theory alike began with an attempt to simply invert prevailing hierarchies of gender/culture/race, and they have each progressively welcomed the post-structuralism invitation to refuse the binary oppositions upon which patriarchal/colonial authority constructs itself" (83).

It is only in the last few decades or so, however, that these two parallel projects have finally come together. A feminist movement has been a well-organized movement activating a new awareness among the fair sex. It has been a silent by product of the female reaction—a natural one, to the dictatorial relationship imposed on women by a society dominated by men. Religion and politics failed to liberate them, and even literature could not rescue them from their plight, caged and battered they remained helpless for centuries. Constrained by the "fear of flying" they made an occasional flutter, till a few of them in twentieth century burst the cage open and sailed into regions from which sometimes a return seems to be impossible. Erica Jong's fear of flying is, in essence, her experience as a woman who, through the character of Isadora, expresses her fear and all the tragic moments related to that.

Doris Lessing's Anna disintegrates herself in the process of her urge to become a free woman.

Among the noted female writers of the century Kamala Das occupies a central place by seeking to liberate female sex from the attitudes of the conventions ridden patriarchal society. She expresses her resentment against sexual colonialism that refers to a relationship between the sexes which is a relationship of dominance and subservience. Men are the colonizers, the women are colonized as Simon de Beauvoir admits:

> "The position that women occupy in the society is comparable in many respects to that of racial minorities in spite of the fact that women constitute numerically at least half of the human race" (Qtd. in Preface, Parshley 7).

Kamala Das in many of her poems expresses her protest against women's socialization into an unquestioning acceptance of their destiny in terms of inferiority, passivity, submissiveness and dependence. She protests against the rigid gender divisions that sexist culture wishes to establish—divisions according to which men are superior, God like while women are inferior, inert, afflicted with a natural defectiveness.

Kamala Das expresses her desire to demolish the concept of male domination and his egoistical superiority over her. In the poem entitled *A Losing Battle* she condemns the attitude of male towards innocent females. In this poem she says that men are worthless and that to trap them women should also try to become selfish. Men always treat women only as an object or a play-thing but women being sentimental love them with full devotion. She protested against the passivity of Indian women and showed them a way how to save themselves from the lust of men. She suggested that women should also make a show of love but should not fall in love with men. Love for women is sacrifice and devotion but for men love is only lust. She asserts that a woman should use not love but the cheapest bait of all. Her protest is reflected in the lines:

> "How can my love hold him when the other
> Flaunts a gaudy lust and is lioness
> To be Beast. Men are worthless, to trap them

Use the cheapest bait of all, but never
Love, which in a woman must mean tears
And a silence in the blood"
("A Losing Battle," *Only the Soul Knows How to Sing,* 48).

This pleading for women's liberation from male domination is even more aggressive and uninhibited in a poem entitled *The Conflagration.* Here Kamala Das tries to make women conscious of their rights. She says that women should come out from the four walls of the house and break all the barriers which bound and suppress them. Kamala Das asks women if to lie beneath a man in bed constitutes happiness. She urges women to come to life by asserting their independence because this world extends a lot beyond a lover's or a husband's six foot frame. To quote:

"Woman, is the happiness, this lying buried
Beneath a man? It's time again to come alive
The world extends a lot beyond this six foot frame."
("The Conflagration," *The Descendents,* 20)

The artificiality of man-woman relationship in the society is a recurring theme in the poetry of Kamala Das. She is particularly obsessed with the fact that woman had been trivialized and marginalized. She gets disturbed to see that even the matriarchs had accepted their biology as destiny and did not revolt against their colonization by men. In the poem entitled *The Old Playhouse* she expresses her miserable life after marriage. She was forced to perform all the domestic duties of a wife. She used to put saccharine tablets into her husband's tea and give him the vitamins at the fixed time. She compares herself to a "swallow" and her husband to a "captor" who wanted to tame her and keep her fully under his control. He was a hard task master and he was so conceited and egoistical that in course of time, she lost her identity because of her feeling of slavery to his whims and wishes. Her resentment against the way the ruling sex tries to control the subordinate sex is visible in expression like:

"You called me a wife,
I was taught to break saccharine into your tea and

> to offer at the right moment the vitamins.
> Cowering beneath your monstrous ego I ate the magic loaf and became a dwarf. I lost my will and reason."
>
> ("The Old Playhouse," *The Old Playhouse and Other Poems,* 1)

Such type of man and woman relationship is not based on the equal response but it is based on the concept of domination and subordination. Iqbal Kaur called it a "sexual colonialism in its 'most overpowering form'. It does not let women feel that they are being victimized" [202]. There is a colonization not only in terms of social existence but also in terms of sexual domination. Man seems to possess every right to satisfy himself while a woman is supposed to make mute and positive response only. When she declares, "You called me a wife" is a challenge to the traditional code of morality thrusted on woman in male dominated society. The excessive domination compels a woman to do only what is decided and expected by her husband. The dignity of self-respect, freedom and independent judgment comes to an end in such type of mechanical relationship.

Kamala Das' real contribution is in the depiction of the female journey from victimization to consciousness. There is a call to all sisters "cowering beneath your monstrous ego" to rise and flatter the female wings. Kamala Das condemns the gender division created by the male dominated society and pities the lot of women because there have been losses in the war of the sexes. The male desire to relegate women to margins suffocated her. She writes:

> "Even the air-conditioner helps so little, all pervasive is the male scent of your breath. The cut flowers in the vases have begun to smell of human sweat. There is no more singing, no more dance, my mind is an old playhouse with all its lights put out" ("The Old Playhouse," *The Old Playhouse and Other Poems,* 1).

Kamala Das finds it difficult to reconcile with man-woman relationship as a relationship in which man is the 'subject', the 'Absolute' and woman is the 'object,' 'the other.'

She voices her restlessness with the fetters of feminity in most of her poems. In one of her poems entitled *Suicide* she writes:

"I must pose
I must pretend
I must act the role
Of happy woman
Happy wife."
("Suicide," *The Old Playhouse and Other Poems,* 34)

Thus, the male governed society leaves a woman no choice so far as acting her satisfaction with her position as the inessential is concerned. In the society to which Kamala Das belongs it was impossible for a woman to rebel against the masculine yoke, against a male's overwhelming sense of superiority because a male she was given to understand, was no less than God.

Kamala Das through her poems shows her exceptional courage to challenge the long established social system and to preach "a new kind of morality." She did display tremendous courage in revolting against the sexual colonialism and providing hope and confidence to women that they can refuse and reject the victim position. She has presented an uninhibited critique of the male-dominated society and has wished to shatter the traditional image of woman as an 'Angel in the House', a passive docile, self-annihilating creature. She has tried to provide courage as well as hope to women that, in spite of the masculine nature of our culture, they can still transcend the existing reality and can refuse victimization at the hands of men. They can manage to develop inner strength and can realize their potential to come out of the margins and to occupy the 'Subject Positions.'

WORKS CITED

Asheroft, B. (Ed.). *The Postcolonial Studies Reader.* London: Routledge, 1995.

Gandhi, Leela. *Postcolonial Theory: A Critical Introduction.* Oxford University Press, 1998.

Kaur, Iqbal. *Protest against Sexual Colonialism, Gender and Literature.* New Delhi: B.R. Publishing Corporation, 1992.

Parshley, H.M. "Translator's Preface to Simon De Beavouir's *The Second Sex*." Penguin Books, 1972.

Spivak, G. *Can the Subaltern Speak?* Reprinted in *Marxist Interpretations of Culture*, eds. Cary Nelson & Lawrence Grossberg. Basingstoke: Macmillan Education.

Said, E. *Culture and Imperialism*. London: Chatto & Windus, 1993.

22 The Agony of Discrimination in Arundhati Roy's *The God of Small Things*

Sunanda Mukesh

Feminism, the talk about women's stride, is not new but it is painful that with the growth of nation the problems of women are increasing and the situation is worsening. Discrimination is writ large against them. She does whatever she can, sacrifices whatsoever she has, worries her little head for every little thing and is full of anxiety. She gets withered, frail or dies but who is going to believe or respect, consider or regard the feminine genuity, sincerity and devotion to her family. Finally, she is held responsible for every disorder, for every ill-luck or misfortune. Emotionally crippled, sexually harassed, and suffering from domestic violence, shattered, shorn and bruised, the modern woman is struggling hard to pave her path, to search her identity, to find an equilibrium between house and the advancing world around. Many women writers are voicing the pangs, problems and fears of the weaker sex. They study minutely their inner psyche, the glooming depression and isolation, leading to nervous break down and suicide.

Strangely enough, women are like Dalits. Both voice their emancipating demands, claim their rights, and assert their existence as both are the have-nots of society. The little done, the undone vast. This article is a study in the causes of the agony of discrimination that are loudly pronounced in Indian literature written in English. It has been and will ever be a prominent theme of post-independence writings.

The flourishing women studies all over the world start from Simone de Beauvoir's *The Second Sex* (1949). Mary Wollstonecraft's initial document *Vindication of the Rights of Women* is an important milestone in the stressful journey of a woman. It is highly contended that society is and always has been in the hands of men. Socialized to accept an inferior status and role, she may find that she cannot gain acceptance in her new culture. She has been subjected to different roles by home, school and society. She has to face contradictory expectations. She is a victim to emerging clash between the old and the new identities. She reacts violently against the old identification. She becomes moody, depressed, irritated and even irrational by assertive and excessive aggressiveness. She is forced to feel 'inferior,' 'marginalised.' This new woman finds no 'space' or 'a room of her own' but feels 'isolated,' 'lonely' or 'out of place.'

Dr. V. Belok comments, "The type of marginal personality is very often found in fictional portraits of academic women. Many women fit in very well with the new identity but those who cannot suffer most. They hate themselves and get angry and self-annoyed."

I quote a little story from Graciela Hierro's article 'Women Alone':

> "Two girls playing at being adults ask one another:
> 'And what are you going to be when you grow up?'
> 'I'm going to be a mom.'
> 'No, you can't be that alone.
> You must be something more.'
> The question is, what is this something more?
> Something more than a wife-mother image?" (77).

Graciela Hierro answers emphatically, "By 'woman alone' I mean a woman with a consciousness of gender, who is usually educated, predominantly professional, independent, autonomous, economically self-sufficient, who may or may not have been married, have had children or not, but who lives alone, without a steady partner, or without a partner at all. This type of woman is characterised by the fact that she has a job, a view of life, and pursues activities which do not fit into the traditional system of feminine values..." (77).

(In the patriarchal, masculine world, a subjective concrete personality of the lonely woman enjoys a 'gender consciousness'). There is an underlying, inherent self-contradiction in the new woman. She has to be honest, sincere, and loyal to the patriarchal monopoly yet she explores a language and 'gender identity.' She, now, has a voice of her own, though hardly noticed. She has an existence which stands her on no footing. She is alone because she has protested against the male dominion or sexual harassment. She is standing on a burning lake, like Satan of *Paradise Lost* exclaiming, "What though the field be lost; All is not lost; the unconquerable will...." She moves out of her Eden garden, her Paradise because she has tasted the mortal fruit, the forbidden fruit of knowledge or wisdom. Yet she tries to build a 'Pandimonium' of her own because 'Better to reign in hell than to serve in heaven' (Milton, Line 260).

Modern woman exercises her choice and breaks away from her traumatic experiences. Women are now free, liberated and assertive. It is this question of self-realisation or identity which permeates the new Indian fiction written in English. It may be 'Ammu' of Arundhati Roy's *The God of Small Things*, Devi of Gita Hariharan's *The Thousand Faces of Night* or Anuradha of Arun Joshi's *The Lost Labyrinth* or the heroines of Anita Desai or Sarita in Shashi Deshpande's *The Dark Holds No Terrors* who feels, "Everything in a girl's life was shaped to that single purpose of pleasing a male" (Deshpande, 163). In fact, there has been no marked change in man's attitude to women. A woman has no right to aspire to become anybody other than a full-time housewife. A man does not understand or rather ignores her concerns, interests and ambitions. Even marriage is a traditional destiny forced upon her. Shobha De's *Second Thoughts* describes Maya, confined to her house, marginalised in her existence, frustrated with hopeless emptiness, ruthlessly seduced by the neighbour, Nitin, yet feeling superior to her husband, avenging against him. Simultaneously, in Nayantara Sehgal's *The Day in Shadow*, Simrit is victimised by a selfish husband, Som. Obviously, tortured beyond tolerance she turns to Raj, who is understanding and sympathetic.

Manju Kapur's first novel *Difficult Daughters* is a story in the background of partition. She describes the traumas of her female protagonists. She resonates with her feminine assertion, hatred for violence, blood, death and ill feeling in the name of God. Like *Difficult Daughters*, *A Married Woman* is a true confession of a woman's personality, her discontentment in marriage, her defiance and restlessness. Her anxiety, discomfort, loneliness and isolation do not encourage her to give voice to her unhappiness over her troubled relationship. The Babri-Maszid episode creates a great political stir. She wants to have a break from 'dependence syndrome.' Manju Kapur expresses her concern for women with a missionary zeal. A woman is not only a wife, mother but something more. "Dealing with religion, politics and social values Kapur realizes India as socially cosmopolitan, politically egalitarian and religiously sectarian. The age old themes of marriage and politics are coupled with lesbian relationship" (Nayak, 137).

It is very important that a woman should be able to understand and determine her position in the traditional family structure as well as her intellectual demand, economic status and freedom in sexual relations. Strangely enough, if she transgresses the established order, she suffers from an uncanny feeling of 'guilt' but when she is capable of unquestioning obedience to the authority, the patriarchal autonomy, when she is manipulating well as a mother, a wife; why then she should not be allowed to reconcile with her 'new woman's image' to her present circumstances. She now enjoys a new position in the family due to her autonomous economic status.

Women face another problem of 'marginalisation' or 'Glass Ceiling' syndrome (quoted by Graciela Hierro). As they go out in public world they share ruptured or estranged relations with their husband. Moreover, they suffer from a feeling of 'guilt' towards their children, 'Did I devote enough time to my children?' According to psychologists, like Freud 'fathers are not directly responsible for the mental health of their offsprings.' The patriarchal system always held mothers responsible to look after children. Then? Should not a woman be educated? Should she stick to the age old patriarchal hierarchy? Was she not happy in the Victorian era when Tennyson specified the role of man and woman in his poem 'The Princess':

"Man for the field and woman for the hearth
Man for the sword and for the needle she
Man from the head, woman from the heart
Man to command, woman to obey;
All else confusion."

The Indian fiction writing in English between 1950 to 1980 shows the Indian woman—passive or aggressive, traditional or modern—reflecting a sense of isolation, fear, bewilderment and emotional vulnerability. To quote J.K. Dodiya and K.V. Surendran, "Men have attained the status of colonizers and women the colonized" (Preface). Woman was the first human being who tasted bondage. "Woman was a slave before slave existed," said August Bebel in his text on 'Women under Socialism.'

The Indian woman today is rarely considered as an individual. Instead she is viewed in her roles of daughter, wife or mother. To quote Heather T. Frazer, "Since she is thought to be lacking any internalized norms or self-discipline, it is imperative that her father, husband and sons protect her from herself and the outside world. This submissive position is reinforced by institutions of caste, religion, joint family and village. A woman who abdicates her traditionally sanctioned roles is liable to experience severe censure" (109).

Arundhati Roy's novel *The God of Small Things* gives vent to the agony of Ammu, Margaret, Baby Kochamma and Rahel. All these take decisions which culminate in disaster and death. It is important to understand the cause of their agony. It is primarily 'discrimination' from society which impels them to act differently. It is difficult to diagnose the cause of suffering.

The theme of agony of discrimination is very well established in Arundhati Roy's *The God of Small Things*. The novel is set in a small place Ayemenem near Kottyam in Kerela. It is a story of a Syrian Orthodox Christian family. The action of the novel moves as a flashback of Rahel's memory. Four major women characters represent puzzling problems. Ammu, Margaret, Rahel and Baby Kochamma take decisions but they fail miserably and disastrously. G.D. Barche in his article rightly questions, "What fails their choices? What defeats their decisions? Is it fate or frivolity, i.e. the triffling habit or nature? or is it social tyranny?" (107).

Baby Kochamma, i.e. Navomi Ipe is the eldest woman character of the novel. She was the daughter of Rev. E. John Ipe. She fell in love with the Irish monk Father Mulligan. She almost seduced him "with a trembling, kissable mouth and blazing, coal black eyes" (23) but he left her bruised and broken. She became a Catholic. Finally her father withdrew her from the convent and brought her back to home. She did a diploma in Environmental Gardening in America and she settled as an unmarried, ex-nun, though at heart still loving Father Mulligan. She loved TV. She did not trust anyone except her maid Kochu Maria. She was harsh, cruel and avenging against everyone, specially Ammu and her twins. Even at the age of eighty- three, she was living like a girl of 16, wearing make-up and putting on expensive sarees. She called Estha abnormal. She was uncomfortable with every person who disturbed her secluded life. She turned almost abnormal, while writing in her diary: "I love you. I love you." Thus, the early heart break almost changed her and she became a living torture and cruelty to everyone around her. What an outcome of the deprivation of her personal joys!

Next woman character is Margaret Kochamma, "The bushy eye browed Waitress," the Ex-wife of Chacko. Like a rebel she escaped from her parents but her life was full of misery and turbulence. She suffers from various misfortunes. She is alone, separated from her first husband, losing the second husband and her daughter Sophiya Mol. When she first met Chacko she did not know anything about him. But she was drawn towards him and they got married. Margaret kept on serving and Chacko kept house filthy and dirty. The daughter, Sophie Mol was a relief to them. But very soon Margaret realised her mistake. Chacko went to India and they got separated. She was very well looked after by Joe, but his sudden accident broke her though she posed to be hard and stoic. For Sophie, she decided to go to India and meet Chacko. They were very happy. The cousins Estha, Rahel and Sophie played together. Chacko and Margaret returned from Cochin to find their daughter dead, drowned. "When Margaret Kochamma saw her little daughter's body, shock swelled in her like phantom applause in an empty auditorium. It overflowed in a wave of vomit and left her mute and empty eyed" (263). She mourned two deaths, not one. With the loss of Sophie, Joe died again, "She had come to Ayemenem to heal her wounded world, and had lost all of it instead. She shattered like glass" (263). The loss of her daughter made her hysterical and she was reduced to nothingness. So she is a woman who has high hopes and dreams but her wrong choice of husband or fate's harshness makes her miserable.

The most important character is Ammu, the daughter of Bennan Ipe, who made her suffer in her early years. He felt that college education was unneccesary for a young girl. There was nothing more for Ammu than to wait for marriage proposals but her father had no dowry. She grew desperate and went to Calcutta to meet an aunt. There she was proposed to and got married, "She thought that anything, anyone at all, would be better than returning to Ayemenem." "She made a mistake. She married a wrong man." Ammu was beautiful but her husband lost his job due to his 'alcoholic stupor.' His manager Mr. Hollick suggested that Ammu be sent to his bungalow to be 'looked after.' When she said nothing, "He grew uncomfortable and then infuriated by her silence. Suddenly he lunged at her, grabbed her hair, punched her..." (42). Ammu too hit him hard. He started 'badgering', "This fell into a pattern. Drunken violence followed by post-drunken badgering..." (42). Ammu could not tolerate the filthy foul smell of vomiting and violence on children. So she left for the father's house with her twins. She returned "to everything that she had fled from only a few years ago" (42).

Later on, she was attracted to Velutha, a young Paravan. They were together for thirteen nights. Velutha was brutally killed in the police custody. Fate or fault, but Ammu certainly suffered as a woman for no mistake. The treatment given by her husband was unmanly, brutish and cruel. She left him for the sake of her children. Her attraction towards Velutha was just natural, an instinct that seeks fulfillment and gratification. But society could not forgive them. The police registered a case of rape and abduction and Ammu was called *Veshya*. Finally she died in her lodge. The lonely woman meets the tragic end because she cannot withstand the public humiliation. She was left for herself when she died. She was thirty-one, "Not old, not young, but a viable, die-able age" (3). She was taken to electric crematorium. She became a Receipt No. 2498673.

Another woman character that suffers the agony of a deprived lot is Rahel, the twin sister of Estha. "They were two-egg twins. 'Dizygotic' doctors called them" (2). The story is a flashback in Rahel's memory. Estha was sent to their father whom Ammu (their mother) had divorced for his drunken frivolity. After Ammu's death, Rahel was sent to Nazareth Convent from where she was expelled for her 'moral perversion' because 'she didn't know how to be a girl.' Obviously, she was neglected. "Rahel grew up without a brief. Without anybody to arrange a marriage for her. Without anybody who would pay her a dowry and therefore without an obligatory husband looming on her horizon" (17). She got admission into a mediocre college of Architecture in Delhi. She was avoided by all. However, she met Larry McCaslin, a research scholar. 'Rahel drifted into marriage like a passenger drifts towards an unoccupied chair in an airport lounge' (18). She went to Boston with him but when they made love he was offended by her eyes as if they belonged to someone else. He could not understand "that the emptiness in one twin was only a version of the quietness in the other" (20). They were divorced. She worked as a waitress, then a night-clerk for several years. She returns to Ayemenem to meet Estha. They love each other. They are very close. "They lay like that for a long time. Awake in the dark. Quietness and Emptiness. Not Old. Not Young. But a viable die-able age. They were strangers who had met in a chance encounter. They had known each other before Life began" (327).

Thus, it is an endless journey in a woman's psyche. The Indian traditions do not support her at all during her struggle to redefine herself. The new voices of India, the new feminists, the women writers echo the inner turmoil, the seething anger and the pant up depression. Finally to conclude in words of Bhagabat Nayak, "A group of Indian women novelists in their in-betweenness, hybridity of thought and multi-cultural and multi-religious social dimensions have contextualized the women problems in general and middle-class and upper-class women in particular" (124). The woman has to work for her liberation without resigning herself to her destiny. Yet everyone has some moment of joy, which make 'her' the 'god of small things' but the ultimate agony of discrimination and deprivation turns her to be 'The God of Loss.'

WORKS CITED

Belok, Michael V. "Introduction." *Women an International Perspective.* Meerut: Anu Books, 1997.

Barche, G.D. "Women in *The God of Small Things* Victims of Fate and Frivolity." *Indian Women Writers*, eds., J.K. Dodiya and K.V. Surendran. New Delhi: Sarup & Sons, 1999.

Deshpande, Shashi. *The Dark Holds No Terrors.* New Delhi: Penguin Books, 1980, 1990.

Dodiya, J.K. & K.V. Surendran. "Preface." *Indian Women Writers: Critical Perspective.* New Delhi: Sarup & Sons, 1999.

Frazer, H.T. "Female Power in Changing India: Myth or Reality?" *Women an International Perspective*, ed. Michael V. Belok. Meerut: Anu Books, 1977.

Hierro, Garciels. "Women Alone: Towards a Feminist Ethic of Pleasure." *Woman: A Global Perspective*, eds. Lucy Forsyth, Townsend and Gaby Wiener. Meerut: Anu Books, 2001.

Milton, John. *Paradise Lost Book I.* New Delhi: Macmillan & Co., 2001.

Nayak, Bhahabat. "Feminine Assertions in Manju Kapur's *A Married Woman: A Socio-Ethical Perspective.*" *Indian Journal of English Studies*, Vol. XLI, 2003-04.

Roy, Arundhati. *The God of Small Things*. India Ink., 1997.

Tennyson, A. *The Princess*.

23

Midnight's Children in the Light of *Vakrokti*

Ajai Sharma

Kuntaka established *vakrokti* as the soul of literature and gave a detailed analysis of *vakrokti* in his book *Vakrokti-kavya-jivitam*. The very title of the book suggests that Kuntaka considers *vakrokti* to be the life of literature. Kuntaka defines *vakrokti* as engaging description that is different from traditional statement. This type of description gives pleasure to the reader. According to Kuntaka, *vakrokti* is the result of amalgam of word and its meaning. Kuntaka divides *vakrokti* in six categories:

(1) *varnvinyas vakrata,*

(2) *padpurvardh vakrata,*

(3) *padparardh vakrata,*

(4) *vakya vakrata,*

(5) *prakaran vakrata,* and

(6) *prabandh vakrata*

Vakrokti is usually translated as deviation in English. *Prakran vakrata* and *prabandh vakrata* make it problematic and it comes nearer to Victor Shklovolaky concept of defamiliarization as propounded in his essay "Art as Technique" than simple lexical and sentential deviation. Still better, *vakrokti* should be understood as deviation-defamiliarization. Since English is not an inflectional language like Sanskrit, all the categories and sub-categories and sub-sub-categories of *vakrokti* as propounded by Kuntaka cannot be found in English language and literature. However, the concept of *vakrokti* remains a powerful tool in the hands of a critic to evaluate any literature, including English. Since it would require voluminous thesis to study *Midnight's Children* completely in the light *of vakrokti*, I shall confine myself to the study of first chapter in general and first paragraph in particular of the novel.

The *Midnight's Children* begins with a typical example of *vakrokti*. "(1) I was born in the city of Bombay... once upon a time. (2) No, that won't do, there is no getting away from the date. (3) I was born in doctor Narlikar's Nursing Home on August 15th, 1947. (4) And the time? (5) The time matters too. (6) Well then: at night... (7) No, It's important to be more... (8) On the stroke of midnight, as a matter of fact. (9) Clock-*hands* joined palms in respectful greetings as I came. (10) Oh, spell it out, spell it out: at the precise instant of India's arrival at independence, I tumbled forth into the world. (11) There were gasps. (12) And outside the window, fireworks and crowds. (13) A few seconds later, my father broke his big toe; but his accident was a mere trifle when set beside what had befallen me in that benighted moment, because thanks to the occult tyrannies of those blandly saluting clocks. (14) I had been mysteriously handcuffed to history, my destinies indissolubly chained to those of my country. (15) For the next three decades, there was to be no escape. (16) Soothsayers had prophesied me, newspapers celebrated my arrival, politicos ratified my authenticity. (17) I was left entirely without a say in the matter. (18) I, Saleem Sinai, later variously called Snotnose, Stainface, Baldy, Sniffer, Budha and even Piece-of-the-Moon had become heavily embroiled in Fate—at the best of times a dangerous sort of involvement. (19) And I couldn't even wipe my own nose at the time" (*MC*, 9).

At the surface level, the novelist inverts the position of adverbial by placing it at the end of the first sentence. This late placing of the adverbial "once upon a time" is very engaging/

wonderful or *chamatkarik* as Kuntaka would like to call it because it seriously questions the assumption created in the mind of the reader by the preceding part of the first sentence that the reader is reading an autobiography. The adverbial locates the story in the hoary past. Since the adverbial is preceded by three dots, the idea that it is a tale about hoary past is reinforced. The reader is forced to reread the first sentence so that he may correct his basic assumption about the nature of the book. The first part and the second part of the first sentence create two types of contradictory assumptions. How can one be so old that one was born once upon a time? Moreover, the city of Bombay did not exist in the hoary past. The second sentence challenges the very idea of reading a book. The conversational style creates the impression that the reader is either a listener himself/herself or listening to a vocalized monologue or overhearing a story being told. Even after multiple readings, the reader is not any wiser about the above assumptions. The novelist reveals the information very grudgingly as if trying more to hide than to tell. The reader begins to wonder why should the novelist at all write a novel if he is so unwilling to part with the information. Sentence 10 challenges the assumption created by sentence 1 that it is either an autobiography or a fairy tale. Sentence 10 leads one to believe that it is a historical novel set against the backdrop of the mega event of Indian independence. The reader begins to expect the description of momentous political events. Again *vakrokti* intervenes with the description of such insignificant event as hurting the toes in sentence 13. The reader is surprised by the information that Saleem cannot wipe his own nose despite the fact that most of his aliases refer to his prominent nose. Yes, nobody can ever expect a new born baby to be able to wipe its nose but the very fact that it is written makes it an example of *vakrokti*. Saleem is given all types of derogatory names in sentence 18. Saleem is surprised that he is called Piece-of-the-Moon. Saleem's surprise surprises the reader because Piece-of-the-Moon is very common way of communicating endearment to the baby in India, however ugly the baby might be. Sentence 1 is a good example of what Kuntaka calls

Visheshan vakrata a sub-category of *padpurvardh vakrata.* Rushdie leaves sentence 7 incomplete as if to give the impression that he is unable to find appropriate word, or the word is so simple that the novelist need not waste his time completing the sentence. It can be classed as *Samvriti Vakrata,* a sub-category of *padpurvarh vakrata* where ineffable is described. Here the novelist has simply left it unnamed. Sentences 10, 14 and 16 are good examples of *kriya vaichitraya vakrata,* a sub-category of *padpurvardh vakrata.* Sentence 18 can be cited as *vriti vakrata*, a sub-category of *padpurvardh vakrata.*

Describing Kashmir of the spring of 1915, the novelist uses *upachar vakrata*, a sub-category of *padpurvardh vakrata* in order to give life to the valley. In *upachar vakrata*, the qualities of one realm are transferred to another realm. The novelist writes: "The world was new again. After a winter's gestation in its eggshell of ice, the valley had beaked its way out into the open, moist and yellow. The new grass bided its time underground; the mountains were retreating to their hill-stations for the warm season." (*MC,* 10) The verbs like 'beak,' 'bide' and 'retreat' and the noun like 'gestation' give the whole description of a human dimension. The novelist later on describes the eyes of his grandfather, Aadam Aziz with the help of *sahajvastu vakrata* that is a sub-category of *vakya vakrata. Sahajvastu vakrata* lies in literal description. In it the obvious is presented in such a way that even the literal description becomes *chamatkarik.* "In those days travellers were not shot as spies if they took photographs of bridges, and apart from the Englishmen's houseboats on the lake, the valley had hardly changed since the Mughal Empire, for all its springtime renewals, but my grandfather's eyes—which were, like the rest of him, twenty-five years old—saw things differently...and his nose had started to itch" (*MC*, 10).

The novelist uses a very telling example of *vishisht prakaran ki atiranjana*, a sub-category of *prakaran vakrata* by telling one incident twice but from slightly different perspective in chapter one itself. The simple incident is that Dr. Aziz bows to pray to God and in the process hits the ground and his nose begins to bleed. In the first instance the novelist writes, "One

Kashmiri morning in the early spring of 1915, my grandfather Aadam Aziz hit his nose against a frost-hardened tussock of earth while attempting to pray. Three drops of blood plopped out of his left nostril, hardened instantly in the brittle air and lay before his eyes on the prayer-mat transformed into rubies" (*MC*, 10). In the second narration of the same incident, it is the valley that struck Aadam Aziz on the nose and thus uses *upachar vakrata*, a sub-category of *padpurvardh vakrata*. The novelist writes, "On the morning when the valley, gloved in a prayer-mat, pouched him on the nose, he had been trying, absurdly, to pretend that nothing had changed. So he had risen in the bitter cold of four-fifteen, washed himself in the prescribed fashion, dressed and put on his father's astrakhan cap; after which he had carried the rolled cheroot of the prayer-mat into the small lakeside garden in front of their old dark house and unrolled it over the waiting tussock.... Forward he bent, and the earth, prayer-mat-covered, curved up towards him. And now it was the tussock's time. At one and the same time a rebuke from Ilse-Oskar-Ingrid-Heidelberg as well as valley-and-God, it smote him upon the point of the nose. Three drops fell" (*MC*, 10-11). The novelist uses *samvriti vakrata,* a sub-category of *padpurvardh vakrata* in the description of beautiful eyes of his grandfather. The novelist simply writes, "His sky-eyes you know about" (*MC*, 13). A *rudivaichitraya vakrata*, a sub-category of *padpurvardh vakrata* is found in the description of nose on different faces. The novelist writes, "On Aadam Aziz, the nose assumed a patriarchal aspect. On my mother, it looked noble and a liltle long-suffering; on my aunt Emerald, snobbish; on my aunt Alia, intellectual; on the uncle Hanif it was the organ of an unsuccessful genius; my uncle Mustapha made it a second-rater sniffer; the Brass Monkey escaped it completely, but on me—on me it was something else again" (*MC*, 14).

A very good example of *varnvinyas vakrata* is found in the comment of Ingrid on the nose of Dr. Aziz. "Ingrid announced, 'You could cross a river on that nose' (Its bride was to wide)" (*MC*, 13). Another example of *varnavinyas vakrata* occurs when the novelist calls Tai "a watery Caliban" (*MC*, 15) or when a fisherman's tales are referred to as "fishy tales" (*MC*, 15) or when Aadam Aziz's friendship with Tai is said to land Aziz in hot waters because Aziz's mother gives him a hot water bath in order to kill the lice that may have traveled to Aziz from the unwashed body of Tai.

The novel jumps back in time to the childhood of Saleem's grandfather, Aadam Aziz. Aadam once had temerity to ask about the age of Tai who has always been old. Tai points to Kashmiri Mountains and claims that he is as old as mountains or even older than the mountains. "'I have watched the mountains being born; I have seen emperors die. Listen, Listen, nakkoo...'—the brandy bottle again, followed by brandy-voice, and words more intoxicating than booze— '...I saw that Isa, that Christ, when he came to Kashmir'" (*MC*, 16). Tai continues his monologue, "'Nakkoo, listen, listen. I have seen plenty. Yara, you should've seen that Isa when he came, beard down to his balls, bald as an egg on his head. He was old and fagged-out but he knew his manners. 'Your first, Taiji,' he'd say, and 'Please do sit;' always a respectful tongue, he never called me crackpot, never called me *to* either. Always *Aap*. Polite, see? And what an appetite! Such a hunger, I would catch my ears in fright. Saint or devil, I swear he could eat a whole kid in one go. And so what? I told him, eat, fill your hole, a man comes to Kashmir to enjoy life, or to end it, *or* both" (*MC*, 16). It is a good example to *prakaran vakrata*. Tai keeps mixing geological time with historical time with his claim that he is as old as mountains. His Christ eats a child in one go. The whole monologue of Tai is simply *avidyaman ki kalpana*. What is important about Tai is that he believes what he claims and wants that Aadam Aziz should also believe him. There is a good example of *visheshan vakrata*, a sub-category of *padpurvardh vakrata* in the phrase 'brandy-voice and words more intoxicating than booze.'

At another place the novelist uses *kalvaichitrya vakrata*, a sub-category of *padparardh vakrata*. The novelist writes, "In the brandy bottle of the boatman Tai I see, foretold, my own father's possession by djinns...and there will be another bald foreigner...and Tai's gas prophesies of another kind, which was the consolation of my grandmother's old age, and taught her stories too...and pie-dogs are not far away...Enough" (*MC,* 17). All the incidents described here took place in past but the author sees them in future and uses present tense in order to communicate the future time of the incidents. Interestingly, in the sentence, the son foretells his own father's future. Another example of *kalvaichitrya vakrata,* a sub-category of *padparardh vakrata* occurs when Tai brings the news that Naseem, the daughter of Ghani, the landowner, is ill:

> '"Ohe! Doctor Sahib! Ghani the landowner's daughter is sick.'
>
> The message, delivered curtly, shouted unceremoniously across the surface of the lake although boatman and pupil have not met for half a decade, mouthed by woman's lips that are not smiling in long-time-no-see greeting, sends time into a speeding whirlgig, blurry fluster of excitement....
>
> '...Just think, son,' Aadam's mother is saying as she sips fresh limewaler, reclining on a takht in an attitude of resigned exhaustion, 'how life does turn out. For so many years even my ankles were a secret, and now I must be stared at by strange persons who are not even family members.'
>
> ...While Ghani the landowner stands beneath a large oil painting of Diana the Huntress, framed in squiggly gold. He wears thick dark glasses and his famous poisonous smile, and discussed art. 'I purchased it from an Englishman down on his luck, Doctor Sahib. Five hundred rupees only—and I did not trouble to beat him down. What are five hundred chips? You see, I am a lover of culture'" (*MC*, 18).

In the above quotation, the novelist has used present tense consistently though the incidents happened at different times in the past. Dr. Aziz is thrilled on getting the news that Ghani's daughter is sick. The novelist writes, "But the young Doctor has entered the throes of a most unhippocratic excitement at the boatman's cry, and shouts, 'I'm coming just now! Just let me bring my things!'" It is an example of *rudivaichitrya vakrata*, a sub-category of *padpurvardh vakrata*. Here a proper name is used as an adjective by adding a negative prefix to it. Another simple example of *rudivaichitrya vakrata* is found in "Doctori-attache" (*MC*, 19), an expression used by the mother of Aziz, referring to the handbag in which Aziz keeps his medical instruments. There is a good instance of *upachar vakrata*, a sub-category of *padpurvardh vakrata* in which animate qualities are transferred to the inanimate. The boatman Tai disapproves of everything modern. He does not like the handbag of Dr. Aziz because he sees the bag as a symbol of modern medical science. He abuses bag like anything. The Heidelberg bag quakes under the torrent of abuse. "Sistersleeping pigskin bag from Abroad full of foreigner's tricks. Big-shot bag.... That bag should fry in Hell with the testicles of the ungodly" (*MC*, 20). Here Tai transfers human characteristics and human fate to the bag. Ghani's appreciation for European paintings becomes *vakrokti* in the light of the fact that Ghani is blind and uses dark glasses. Towards the end of the chapter, Doctor Aziz confronts a classic example of *vakrokti* in the form of a perforated sheet through which he is asked to diagnose the ailment of Ghani's daughter and prescribe medicine.

WORK CITED

Rushdie, Salman. *Midnight's Children*. London: Vintage, 1995.

24 Narayan's *The Guide* in the Light of Rasa Theory

Kshama Gupta

The theory of *Rasa* was postulated by Bharata. He talks of the emotional delight that we get in literature and says that there are various emotions like love, humour, anger, etc. Aristotle's theory of Katharsis deals with the purging away of the painful elements of pity and fear. But this theory cannot express the process of true literary enjoyment because there are not just two emotions. There are many other emotions which are as necessary as these two. Indian theorists pay appropriate attention to these emotions. According to *Rasa* theory these feelings or emotions lie as instincts in the heart in shape of *Sthayi Bhavas* and are evoked unconsciously through literary presentation. The empathy with the emotions of characters when the material layers of individuality vanish giving rise to the pure consciousness causes *Rasa Ananda*.

Rasa theory was postulated by Bharata for *natak* or drama only. But it can be applied to novels also. Drama and novel are two different branches of literature but have close similarity. The novel is the most popular branch of literature in the modern times. Like poetry it has established itself as the major vehicle of human emotions in the field of literature. Besides it, the aim of novel is also delightful teaching like drama. Thus the theory of *Rasa* can be applied to novel also.

The Guide is the most widely read of Narayan's novels. It was first published in 1958. It has been translated in many languages of Europe and India. It won Sahitya Academy Award in 1961. The story of this novel is narrated at two levels—the flash back and flash on—the past is recounted by Raju to Velan and the present as narrated by omniscient author. The story opens at a point in Raju's career when his role as guide, lover, impresario and prisoner has already ended. He is about to assume the role of a sage. His past is unrolled through retrospection. *The Guide* successfully portrays the intensity of various emotions. These emotions stir up the emotions of the readers and develop into a state of great pleasure. Emotions like love, humour, pathos, anger, *veer* and *santa* can be traced in the story of *The Guide*.

The sentiment of love has been given the supreme place in literature and has been called *Rasa-Raj*. It can be said to be the noblest frailty of mind and it is as old as humanity itself. The arrival of Marco and Rosie marks a turning point in Raju's life. Overwhelmed by the beauty of Rosie, he falls in love with her at the first sight.

> "She did have a figure, a slight and slender one, beautifully fashioned, eyes that sparkled, a complexion not white but dusky, which made her only half visible—as if you saw her through a film of tender coconut juice" (*The Guide,* 65).

At the snake dance show Raju watches her most insistently. He is immensely delighted to see the performance. She "swayed her whole body to the rhythm" (68) and that was sufficient to tell Raju that his dream girl was "the greatest dancer of the century" (68). Raju is always haunted by that image and is over-conscious of her presence. "I ate my food in silence, trying to revive in my mind the girl's scent filled presence" (69).

With his experience of life Raju takes no time to judge the loveless wedlock of Marco and Rosie. They are two souls with clashing instincts and discordant interests, which fate has joined together. Rosie is young, joy and fun loving woman with an irrepressible fascination for dance, while Marco is an old cold serious scholar obsessed with archeological pursuits. Soft springs of love have dried in him. "Anything that interested her seemed to irritate him" (76).

Sitting on the verandah of the Peak House, Raju is overwhelmed by her perfume. They are there to see some fierce animal that night.

Bright eyes shone amidst the foliage, she pulled my sleeve and whispered excitedly:

> "'Something, what can it be'?
>
> 'Probably a panther,' I said to keep up the conversation. Oh the whisper, the stars and the darkness—I began to breathe heavily with excitement'" (79).

Here Rosie and Raju are the object and alamban. Whisper, the stars and the darkness are the excitants. Heavy breathing is the consequent and excitement is the transitory feeling.

Raju tells Rosie much as soon as he has the occasion to speak to her in private. "All night I didn't sleep.... The way you danced your form and figure haunted me whole night" (72). And further "life is so blank without your presence" (73). Discerning Rosie's passion for dance, he feigns great interest in this art and wins her favour by flattering her. "I spoke out my love but sandwiched it conveniently between my appreciations of her art" (84). Raju cleverly and slyly made his way into Rosie's heart by giving her what her husband always denied—the delight of life. While Marco stays at the Peak House to study the Memphi Caves nearby, Raju and Rosie came down to the town and have an exciting time together. The starving girl Rosie has the real taste of life. In her madness of ecstasy she surrenders to Raju:

> "'Shall I go away?' I asked in a whisper.
> 'Yes, Good night', she said feebly.
> 'May I not come in?' I asked.
> 'No, no go away,' she said. But on an impulse I gently pushed her out of the way, and stepped in and locked the door on the world" (89).

The sexual union is thus consummated. The whole scene has been presented with extreme delicacy. The language takes on the flavour of lived experience.

Narayan projects the mental state of a man deeply in love with a girl. Raju "was obsessed with the thoughts of Rosie." (115). He admits, "The only reality in my life and consciousness was Rosie" (118). This is not one sided love affair as is the case with Chandran in *The Bachelor of Arts*. Rosie also begins to take interest in Raju. Her love for Raju finds expression in various ways. At the dinner table she snatches the dish from Raju's hand and gives him the pleasure of her touch:

> "She suddenly darted forward and forcibly snatched it away from my hand. O that touch made my head reel for a moment. I didn't see anything clearly. Everything disappeared into a sweet, dark haze as under chloroform" (77).

When Raju is watching her performance, he is so rapt that he forgot his surroundings. He is watching her with open mouthed wonder. "Suddenly she stopped and flung her whole weight on me with 'What a darling you are giving me a new lease of life'" (125).

When lovers are separated they become gloomy and dreamy. They desire for each other's company. They lose vitality and charm in life. Their only wish is to see the object of their love. Rosie is sad on her quarrels with Marco on the issue of her taking up the career of a dancer. In her agony Rosie asks Raju to leave them in an insulting tone. Forty-eight hours ago she was in the arms of Raju and her behaviour now was quite unexpected for him. He left them and the coming days were very miserable for him. He had "no taste for food, no sound sleep, no stability...no peace of mind, no sweetness of temper or speech...." (136). He looked forlorn and was uninterested in everything. He was never at peace. His mind was troubled all the time. He plunged in a world of gloom. He admits, "I felt bored and terrified by the boredom of normal life. So much had I got used to a glamorous romantic existence" (139). All the time he was thinking of Rosie. He sulks and mopes about a month. Here he is oppressed by grief at separateness. Memories play the role of excitant. Sulkiness of behaviour is consequent. His detachment from everything and his curiosity, concern and worry for Rosie are the transitory feelings.

Anger is the dominant emotion of the sentiment of fury or *Raudra Rasa*. When a person looks at his enemy or at somebody who is harming others, his anger is aroused. When Marco learns from Rosie herself that he has been cuckolded by Raju, he flies into fury. He condemns her for ever. To Rosie's plea, "I want you to forget everything. I want you to forgive me" (151), he gives a rather cold reply "yes I am trying to forget—even the earlier fact that I ever took a wife" (152). He coldly disowns her—"You are not my wife. You are a woman who will go to bed with anyone that flatters your antics" (152). Here Rosie herself is object, her affair with Raju is the excitant. Her husband abandoned her consequently. Agitation, pride and wrath of her husband are the transitory feelings.

Another example of the sentiment of fury can be seen when a terrible draught hits the village Mangla. The rains failed, the summer was scorching, plants were withering, animals had no fodder, the rivers shrank, the wells dried up. Cattle stopped yielding milk. More cattle were found dead, prices shot up. There were violent fights over food in the village. The peace loving village turned into a veritable battleground. When the village shopman demanded higher price, a customer lost his temper and slapped his face. The shopman attacked the customer with a chopper. As a result many villagers invaded the shop. Shopman's relatives attacked the other group at night.

> "Velan and his man also picked up axes and knives and started out for the battle. Shrieks and cries and imprecations filled the air. The little hay that was left was set on fire and the dark night was ablaze" (96).

In the incident the clashing groups are objects. Their actions using force etc. and the insulting comments are the excitants. Raising of the arms and weapons to strike one another are the consequents. Their agitation, wrath, pride, arrogance are the transitory feelings.

Abandoned by her husband, Rosie returned to Raju. He took it as a heaven sent blessing. He lodged her in his house. In spite of his mother's repeated warning he continued his flirtation with Rosie. His railway shop was taken away from him on the charges of neglect and mismanagement. He was desperate and angry. He slapped the boy who used to manage his shop. The porter, boy's father, protested his behaviour. The new shopman was also watching the scene curiously. It was disliked by Raju and he cried to him that he would face the same situation some day:

> "He twirled his whiskers and said, 'How can everyone hope for the same luck as yours?' He winked mischievously, at which I completely lost my temper and flew at him. He repelled me...and I fell back and knocked against my mother...." (157).

Due to Rosie, Raju neglected his business, ran into debts, involved himself in litigations and brought himself almost to the brink of ruin. His mother called her brother who was very angry with Raju. He pulled him down by the collar of his shirt and asked:

> "What has come over you? You think yourself a big man? I can't be frightened of scapegraces like you. Do you know what we do when we get an intractable bull calf? We castrate it. We will do that to you, if you don't behave" (167).

After the exchange of hot words between them his uncle examined Rosie and asked her to leave. Rosie began to sob and Raju was completely maddened by it. He flew at his uncle and knocked the cup out of his hand and shouted at him to get out. Seeing all this his mother came out of the kitchen, with tears in her eyes and flew at sobbing Rosie:

> "Are you now satisfied with your handiwork, you she-devil, you demon, where have you dropped on us from? Everything was so good and quiet—until you came; you

came in like a viper.... What a fine boy he used to be! The moment he set his eyes on you, he was gone" (170).

His maternal uncle shouted, reprimanded, bullied and ordered but the result of this noisy encounter was that Raju became more stubborn not to drive Rosie out. In this furious episode Raju and Rosie are the objects, their illegal relationship is the excitant, use of abusive language, to raise their arms to strike one another are the consequents. Their wrath, arrogance etc. are the transitory feelings.

Rosie excites the pity of the reader. Her relationship with her husband is quite weak. There is no love between them. The fault lies more in her husband. Rosie is deprived of the experience of a husband in a proper sense. Her husband has so far been able to intensify only the sense of futility of her life. Due to his cold behaviour Marco is unable to understand the claims of his young and beautiful wife. In the room of hotel where Rosie has had one of their usual rows with her husband, she herself has shut up the door of her room as if on the whole world and is feeling terribly pent up, lost and dejected. When she opens the door "She looked, disheveled, her eyes were red with recent tears, and she wore a faded cotton *saree*, no paint no perfume" (72).

Rosie belonged to the family as dancers, traditionally dedicated to the temples. She has the instincts and urges of a dancer in her blood. She has Master's degree in Economics and married Marco for status and respectability. Marco looks down upon dancing as cheap acrobatics. He is interested in painting and old art and things like that and not in the living things. Raju feels sorry for her, "I sighed deeply, overcome with the sadness of her life" (86). He was very unhappy to think of her.

Raju trains Rosie as a good dancer and launches her on a career as a public dancer. Rosie who is reborn as Nalini, soon becomes the dancing sensation. There is a phenomenal rise in the fortunes of Raju. A new fantastic world of showmanship replaces the old world of romantic love making. He is, no doubt, successful as an impresario but his motives are questionable. He scarcely cares for her personal feelings. His eyes are only on the cheques that Rosie brings. He makes her work like a machine and allows her no time even for a little sight seeing. He becomes possessive and jealous. He confesses—"I had a monopoly of her and no body had anything to do with her.... She was my property. This idea was beginning to take root in my mind" (186) and "I liked her to be happy but only in my company" (190). Some strange weariness seemed to be coming over Rosie. She asks wearily:

> "All day long and all through the week you are collecting cheques more and more often. But when is the time coming when we can enjoy the use of those cheques" (194).

Just as Raju goes on leading a reckless life, drinking and gambling and squandering money, weariness descends on Rosie gradually. She says,

> "Do you know the bulls yoked to an oil-crusher. They keep going round and round, in a circle, without a beginning or an end" (194).

She realizes that she has become the prisoner of her ambition. She feels sick and laments, "I feel like one of those parrots in a cage taken around village fairs, or a performing monkey, as he used to say" (203).

The intoxication and enthusiasm generating from the success gradually starts fading away. Rosie becomes painfully conscious of the fact that despite her success she has not got anything substantial. She begins to realize that the craving of her inner being was not simply the realization of her ambition. Raju ate, slept and lived with her without least understanding her mind. He failed to understand her inner needs. To her Raju appears no better than Marco. In her disillusionment she suffers from a sense of repentance. Her grief awakens the same dominant emotion in the heart of the readers and it is excited by her words and miserable condition to be transformed into pathetic sentiment.

Sentiment of humour is as important for life as sentiment of pathos. It is primarily as a comic writer that Narayan excels. The absurd and the incongruous in life do not annoy him, it only amuses him. Narayan employs all the effective methods of humour—traditional as well as innovative. His novels are rich in situation, full of comedy, comic characterization and subtle shades of irony. His humour is genial.

The Guide belongs to the genre of serious comedy. Its theme is full of philosophical profundity but the treatment bears the characteristic comic strain of the author's art. His humour is noticeable in the tone and style of narration and characterization. The note of humour is struck right in the beginning when Raju is enjoying the memories of his school—the typical village school on the broad verandah of the village headman's house. The school master who addressed his pupils as donkeys, the short clumsy youngsters always fumbling and shuffling, getting on his nerves, the school master entering his house for a moment's nap or many other domestic calls leaving the boys on the verandah to fight and scratch, bleat and yell or invade his secrecy and peep in to find him sitting before the oven baking something excite our laughter.

A drain flowed beneath the pyol. The boys floated their paper boats down the drain and then laid on their bellies and watched the boats float away. The warning of their teacher is humorous, "If you fall off into the gutter, you will find yourself in the Sarayu river, remember, and I shall have to tell your father to go out and look for you there" (27).

Laughter is the dominant emotion of sentiment of humour. Here the master and his pupils are the objects. Their actions—the master's language, the use of donkey etc. for the boys and the behaviour of boys are the excitants of the sentiment of humour.

The grotesque in appearance as usual provides him with his comic material. Raju christens Rosie's husband Marco because:

> "I have not met a more grotesque creature in my life. Instead of calling herself Rosie, she could have more logically have called him Marco Polo. He dressed like a

> man about to undertake an expedition with his thick coloured glasses, thick jacket, and a thick helmet over which was perpetually stretched a green, shiny waterproof cover, giving him the appearance of a space traveler (9-10).

There are many other comic characters. The Sait is one such character—"The profound solemnity of this puny man with his ledger clutched under his arm and his multi-coloured turban" (161) will not cease to tickle us. Velan's brother is also an amusing character. This witless youngman becomes the cause of Raju's penance to bring down rains:

> "He had hardly anyone to speak except his cattle the whole day and he spoke to them on equal terms and abused them and their geneology unreservedly" (98).

He is so frightened by Raju that, when villagers asked him, he blabbers incoherently and lands Raju in the role of a saviour.

The portrayal of the 'adjournment expert' and the star lawyer from Madras are unsurpassable. The star lawyer with 'his long coat, his dhoti and turban and over it all his black gown' amuses us:

> "A case in his hands was like a dough, he could knead, draw it up and down. He split a case into minute bits and demanded as many days for microscopic examination" (223-224).

Even in the atmosphere of mounting tension Narayan's comic sense remains unimpaired. The telegraph master of Mangla becomes comical in his harried nervousness at the deluge of press telegrams. The press reporters rushing their hour to hour stories to their papers all over the world were all very aggressive. The little telegraph master was scared of them. "He had spent a fairly peaceful life until then, and the present strain tore at his nerves" (241). James J. Malone—the film maker from California—also provides comic relief in a tense situation.

Raju has been mistaken for a saint by the simple and credulous villagers. They thrust a fast upon him. Since it was difficult enough to find knee deep water, the villagers had made an artificial basin in sand and fetched water from distant wells to fill it. Despite the irony of situation, the stupidity of villagers excite laughter. Narayan's sunny temper wouldn't miss the incongruity of a situation however sacrilegious. We are told about Raju's craving for Bonda:

> "While discoursing on Bhagwad Geeta to his audience the other evening, Raju had a sudden craving to try this out himself he was now equipped with a charcoal stove and frying pan, and what could be more musical than well-kneaded dough dropping into boiling oil?" (104-105).

Narayan's perceptive eye discerns the comic in the common place, for example when Raju gave a banana to the boy. "The boy peeled the plantain, swallowed it whole and started munching the peel also" (35). When Raju said that it would make him sick he replied in negative.

All these incidents and characters account for the sentiment of humour in *The Guide*. *Hasya* is the dominant emotion of this sentiment. The persons who excite laughter are the objects. Their behaviour, comic and unusual dresses are excitants. The movements of eyes, lips, nose, cheeks while laughing are the consequents. Sleep, indolence etc. are the transitory feelings.

Affectionate and caring attitude of Raju's mother for him can be placed in the category of *Vatsalya Rasa*. In her nourishing, caring, loving and protective aspects as a mother, she has left many a fond memory in the mind of Raju. Recounting one of these experiences of his early childhood, Raju tells us:

> "Her presence gave me a feeling of inexplicable cosiness. I felt I ought to put her proximity to good use, and complained, 'Something is bothering my hair,' and she ran her fingers through my hair and scratched the nape of my neck" (20).

Her motherly concern can be seen when she dressed the child in the morning to send to school. She warns Raju that through his association with Rosie he would come to grief and it happened so. It is her concern for the boy that she says to Rosie, "What a fine boy he used to be! The moment he sets his eyes on you, he was gone" (170). Again, when she is leaving the home of her husband with her brother she is worried for Raju even in her anger against him. Before going she says—"Be careful with your health" [175]. Dominant emotion of *Vatsalya Rasa* is a natural love of parents for their children. Here Raju is the object. His behaviour and actions are the excitants. Worry, pride and concern for his well being are the transitory feelings.

The sentiment of fear can be seen when the village is hit by a drought. Rivers were shrinking, cattle were unable to yield milk. They lacked the energy to drag the plough through the furrows, the bones of sheep were sticking out. The people were fearful:

> "The wells in the villages were drying up. Huge concourses of woman with pitchers arrived at the river, which was fast narrowing from morning to night they come in waves and took the water.... They quarreled at the water-hole for priorities, and there were fear, desperation and lamentation in their voices" (93).

Cholera broke out in the next village causing the death of thousands of people. They were much terrified. They were losing their heads. Sentiment of fear is based on the dominant emotion of fear. Here drought is the object of fear. Shrinking rivers and drying wells, loss of fodder for the cattle, death of human beings and cattle are the excitants. Destruction of mental and physical activity and trembling of villagers and their becoming pale are the consequents. Fright, doubt and agitation of villagers are the transitory feelings.

Heroic sentiment is based upon the dominant emotion of enthusiasm or *Utsah*. There are four kinds of heroic persons: *Yudhveer*—a person who fights bravely in the battlefield, *Danveer* is a person who gives alms to the poor, *Dharmveer* who believes in good works and *Dayaveer* who is sympathetic towards the people who are helpless. The objects of this sentiment are enemies during war etc. A heroic moral transformation into sainthood encloses the story of Raju's degeneration. Raju takes his first step to the ultimate goal of

Hinduism by beginning to conquer self and act disinterestedly. His heart is filled with the feelings of love and compassion. He muses:

> "If by avoiding food I should help the trees bloom, and the grass grow, why not do it thoroughly? For the first time in his life he was making an earnest effort; for the first time he was learning the thrill of full application, outside money and love; for the first time he was doing a thing in which he was not personally interested" (237-238).

Now he has no exasperation for Velan showing so much faith in him. The barrier of ego has been transcended. In this twelfth day, the last day of his fast, he is ready to perform the ritual despite a precarious physical state. Raju can be placed in the category of *Dharmveer*. Doing good work is the consequent and his patience, wisdom, pride are the transitory feelings.

After his resolve to go through the fast honestly, he feels new strength in himself. He also acquires the peace of mind. Here we have the *Santa Rasa* or the sentiment of peace. Here the object is Raju's moral duty not to insult the faith of villagers. The villagers' faith in him is the excitant. Raju's resolution to take up his fast honestly is the consequent. His detachment and joy that he feels are the transitory feelings.

WORK CITED

Narayan, R.K. *The Guide*. Mysore: Indian Thought Publications, 1994.

25

Image of Indian Woman in the Fictional Works of Bhabani Bhattacharya with a Particular Reference to *Music for Mohini*

Gunjan Mittal

Women have traditionally played a complex and striking role in Indian society. A brief glimpse of Indian woman makes it obvious that Indian women have been showing their worth in each and every sphere whether it is history, scriptures or literature. In the modern time, women are on the path of progress without any full-stop and have been exposing their mettle as well as spirit in every field and haply for better than the male. In recent time woman is not a puppet in the hands of man but she has developed her true identity in every walk of life. In Indian English literature Kamala Markandaya, Shashi Deshpande, Ruth Prawer Jhabvala, Arundhati Roy, Anita Desai, Shobha De, Bharati Mukherjee and Manju Kapur and many more female novelists have left their indelible imprint on the Indian readers. Their vast contribution to English literature is not only remarkable but excellent too.

Modern era has brought an entire change in women's existence. Although they have always been the heart of family life because they play various roles as wife, mother, daughter, sister, companion, mother-in-law, daughter-in-law and always live for the continuance of family values and make efforts to maintain its unity, but now at present time with the national movement and other subsequent political events, "Women have thought more in terms of nationalism than men, and they have a great sense of service to their country" (Cormack, 169).

Freedom for Indian women meant freedom not only from the hands of British rulers and their cruelty but actually their release from centuries of male-domination as well as social and cultural norms. Now woman is not enclosed within four walls but she is trying to effect a slow but sure change within her own home.

In earlier fiction women were represented in a single-dimension—a responsible daughter or all sacrificing mother, an obedient wife or beloved and a virgin. Earlier they were considered weak, emotional and only confined to the household works. But today women have achieved a separate identity as well as a distinguished place in fiction, due to their awareness in every field whatever—political, social, cultural or individual. The novelists through their writings have tried to bring freedom to the female from their age long subjugation by men.

A general analysis of Bhabani Bhattacharya's novels makes one thing clear that this most significant aspect of womanhood is clearly visible in his works. From *So Many Hungers!* to *Shadow from Ladakh* women play an important role in his novels.

Either they are the central figures or play equally important roles or sometimes they are the source of inspiration from which male character derives courage and strength. Being a great humanist, Bhabani Bhattacharya has dealt with the human fate and man's struggle against those problems which he has to face for his survival throughout his life in the world. His protagonist, whether male or female, is eternally engaged in struggling and fighting against the injustice that he or she faces in various walks of life. Sometime his female character comes forward and raises active step to come out of her sufferings. As Marlene Fisher marks out:

> "Dr. Bhattacharya's female characters represent the triumph of the human spirit over famine and starvation and their

accompanying degradation and over the inevitable crises that arise when old and new values clash" (68).

Various aspects of womanhood find ample space in the novels of Bhabani Bhattacharya because he tried to paint an ideal picture of Indian woman. As Kajoli in *So Many Hungers!* suffers a lot during famine but she knows how to live majestically at the crucial time and gets strength during the moments of weakness and despair.

In *He who Rides a Tiger* Chandralekha is true to her name in features and actions. When she finds that it is impossible for Kalo to dismount from the tiger's back, she is found ready to sacrifice her own life.

A Goddess Named Gold is the evidence of those courageous women who participate in freedom struggle. Meera, a girl of sixteen is the symbol of womanhood and buoyant spirit. Her old and spirited grandmother also encourages the rebellious women of the village to fight for their rights. As B. Shyamla Rao comments:

> "Bhattacharya's fourth novel *A Goddess Named Gold* may be termed a women's novel. In essence it is a feminist novel as the liberation of the country from the clutches of the Sethji is accomplished by women only" (58).

This novel may be considered as a true replica of courage of the women of Sonamitti that helps them to liberate themselves from Seth Samsundarji.

Suruchi in *Shadow from Ladakh* is really an incarnation of womanhood who proves an ideal wife, mother as well as a perfect woman. Though she surrenders herself to her husband completely, she emerges as a full and a mature woman who doesn't lose her true identification. Marlene Fisher pointedly states:

> "Although the novels of Bhattcharya tend to be centered around his female characters, their themes touch broadly upon some of the most vital aspects of men and women alike—particularly men and women as members of society" (95-108).

It appears that through the portrayal of feminine characters in his novels, Bhabani wants to bring into limelight the significant role played by women. The female characters in his novels are elevated to a higher state. Loftiness, grandeur, dignity and nobleness are richly found in these leading ladies. Mohini has beauty and playfulness, Kajoli is innocent. Chandralekha has her compassion and attraction, Meera has simplicity and honesty so Suruchi has her strong sense of identity. They are worthy enough to serve as model. Bhattacharya's attitude towards woman character is that of respect and sympathy too. Neither he believes in revolutionary changes for women's liberation nor he advocates to confine them to the boundaries of traditions. Each woman character of Bhabani has a definite touch of idealism. In chronological order Bhabani Bhattacharya's second novel *Music for Mohini* is partly autobiographical because its hero Jayadev is shy and reserved like Bhabani himself while Mohini is modeled on the nature of Salila. In fact this novel of Bhattacharya is really a different one because it's first and foremost a novel of character and the only novel of Bhattacharya in which the name of the chief protagonist appears in its title. Actually Mohini is a medium to express Bhabani's innermost feeling to portray the Indian woman who in her life plays various roles as that of a mother, companion, daughter or a wife. Mohini upholds the true ideal image of an Indian woman because Bhabani Bhattacharya has brilliantly presented a beautiful synthesis of the old and the new in the character of Mohini. He reveals the finest values of Indian womanhood in Mohini's character. In the words of Rashmi Gaur:

> "Bhattacharya has portrayed Mohini as a representative of his image of the new woman who is to act as a bastion against the corrupting influence of the west and protect the traditional values of personal and social life from any sudden or violent change" (56).

Mohini proves a perfect woman at all the stages of womanhood. From the very early stage of the novel we observe that Bhattacharya has presented her something of a tomboy, climbing a tree, singing and dancing with gay lying to her father that she was reading Ancient Indian History while she was enjoying a Bengali novel, *The Poisoned Kiss*.

In relationship with her brother Heeralal, there is melody of friendship. Heeralal is like a companion of Mohini as both share their every secret with each other. She behaves, protects and gives tenderness to him of an elder sister. She was so close to her brother Heeralal that he goes with her to her husband's house so that she would not feel alone and adjust conveniently in her new environment. This beautiful aspect of sister and brother relationship and companionship runs through her vein so deeply that in the absence of Heeralal in her husband's house she develops a friendly relationship with a motherless child Ranjan and imparts her love, protection and blessing to him. Mohini also provides him precious knowledge from the *Ramayana*, *Mahabaharata* and such other legendary tales. Ranjan also has same kindly feeling for Mohini and worships her like an elder sister. Ranjan on his turn introduces her to dozen of little brothers—his friends and brings Ashu, Rabi, Montu and Gopal etc. to her garden. In this way due to her loving and affectionate nature Mohini finds various little brothers in the village of Behula. Her relationship with Rooplekha, Jayadev's sister is also of a friend. It is Rooplekha who encourages aptly and that's why in a short while they both become good friends. She not only plays the role of sister of younger ones but she is also superior in the role of a Bau-sister, that is, elder sister to her husband's friend Harindra. When she cleverly speculates the attraction of Harindra for Sudha, the Saturn's Eyesore, she makes promise to Harindra that she would definitely bring the two together after her return to Behula from her father's home.

This facet of her behaviour portrays that Mohini is also aware of all her liabilities towards her father and grand-mother. Despite being a motherless child she is a very responsible daughter. Her father provides her convent education yet notwithstanding there is a perfect blend of tradition and modernity in the personality of Mohini. Her character is shaped by the modern influence of her father which is partially based on his traditional and cultural values. She is not only against the bride showing system but also opposes her grand mother's insistence on her old and orthodox ways:

> "Never had she been so angry with Old Mother. Why must she, who was of another age, have her way against all reason? Why must her antiquated outlook prevail against even Father's judgment? With her fixed ideas, her iron prejudice against modernism, how could she expect to know, to feel, to understand the new generation?" (44).

However, the widening gap between the Old Mother and Mohini is abridged when Mohini's marriage is finally settled with Jayadev by a bangle-seller and the horoscopes are matched. Though Mohini's father was not willing in marrying his daughter in a village, but being a responsible daughter Mohini persuades her father and assures him that she will be quite happy and satisfied in the village. Sashikala Singh rightly observes:

> "Mohini's willingness to settle in a rural atmosphere reveals the first change in her attitude to life. There are signs of a true Indian woman in her. There is a Mohini in every Indian girl with all her contradictions and the ultimate reconciliation to things Indian" (47).

Mohini's marriage brings a great change in the personality of this young and lovely girl. She encounters her dominating mother-in-law who is extremely tradition bound while on the other hand she comes across with the indifference of her husband Jayadev who is a research scholar as well as a social reformer. His only goal is to make his village Behula a model village and therefore, to fulfil his mission he fights against the superstitions, untouchability and caste system etc. along with young reformer Harindra. Mohini's life takes a turn, she has to make an adjustment with her husband Jayadev and her stubborn mother-in-law. If we estimate the character of Mohini as a daughter-in-law, we find that she is able to stand the test of time.

Being a modern sophisticated girl Mohini, like other girls, expects a lot from her husband Jayadev. Her heart is full of love for Jayadev and she also expects to be admired and loved by him in turn. But Jayadev grew up under the shadow of exaggerated various expectations as he is the only heir of the family. His spiritually fanatic mother who was widowed early in marriage brought him up with so much tenderness that neither he had a carefree childhood nor a bold exploring youth. The environment in which he grew up affects the personal relationship of Jayadev and Mohini. Jayadev expects Mohini as Matiyri or Gargi that's why on his nuptial night he provides her abstruse statement on the purity and holiness of the marriage bond instead of responding to her physically:

> "Bonds interminable holds us in sacred relation, more sacred than any on earth," he began and then paused, for he felt his words sounded hollow" (90).

It seems absurd to Mohini because she believes in the warmth of love and compassion which she fails to get from her husband while Jayadev considers that spiritual love and physical love should be kept apart. He expects Mohini to be his partner in his scholarly pursuits. Mohini's marriage fails to provide the promised happiness and bliss. In marrying a woman, a traditional husband obliges her "to give herself entirely to him; but he does not assume the corresponding obligation, which is to accept this gift and its consequences." Gradually Mohini suppresses her human desires and makes attempt to adjust herself with the new way of life. She loved to live a free life while in Behula she is always considered the mistress of the Big House. Jayadev had already made Mohini aware of the fact that she would have to mould herself to the stern traditional life pattern of the Big House imposed on the ladies and thus Big House makes heavy demands on Mohini. Mohini's mother-in-law is extremely tradition bound who lives only to keep alive the tradition of the Big House. Rooplekha, Jayadev's sister describes Mohini about the various facts of the Big House, including her mother and brother. As Rooplekha describes about the firmness of her mother:

> "My mother is the usual orthodox Hindu woman, only she is more intense than other, and all her faith is pinned to family tradition. No deviation for her, not one inch. Stern-willed, though tender at heart, she is a simple soul,

with singleness of purpose, a one-eyed mind. She exists for the Big House; she wouldn't have it changed the least way" (94).

This statement of Rooplekha reveals the firmness of a woman who can do anything. Like Mohini, Rooplekha has to adjust herself in a city because born and bred in the village, she was unable to adopt herself to the modern city life after her marriage but she tries her best to make an adjustment with new life. It is a well-known fact that an Indian woman faces an entire change in her life after marriage because she has to adopt the culture, tradition and customs of her spouse's family. Rooplekha expresses her feelings in such words:

> "You are city-bred, village-wed. I am village-bred, city-wed. We share one common lot: we have been pulled up by the roots. A city has as little mercy for an alien as the country, no more, no less. Years it was before I could fit in, Mohini, hard years" (92).

In the beginning, life was not easy for Mohini because she feels suffocated and lovelorn and finds life unbearable in the Big House. Her mother-in-law imposes a number of restrictions upon her. It is indecorous for women to have a meal along with the men. They are not allowed to move out of the house on foot, if they want to go anywhere they have to use either a palanquin or a bullock-cart. Being a radio artist, Mohini is fond of singing and music but in Big House music is tolerated only if it is used for worshipping. Mohini falls into a torturous state of loneliness and isolation. Yet she shows great fortitude and prepares herself to make adjustment with the stern rules and traditions of the Big House. Iyenger comments on Mohini's transformation:

> "She throws herself into new tasks, and she strikes roots into the soil of Behula. The strain is nothing, what matters is the sense of fulfilment alone. She is thus able to establish rapport with her husband readily furthering the causes so dear to him" (415).

It shows how Mohini endured all with great fortitude which is a characteristic trait of Indian woman. Gradually

Mohini starts learning Sanskrit from Jayadev and soon his belief has been proved wrong that there is nothing of the scholar in her. But he is impressed to find that Mohini starts to educate the village women by imparting them some elementary general education. Now husband and wife seem to ascend to a common pedestal. They develop a common interest which brings them closer to each other. She collects small village children in the garden whom she treats as her younger brothers and provides them precious knowledge so that she could assist her husband in his social duties. According to Indian mythological beliefs, woman is the other half, i.e. *ardhangini* of her husband. She is supposed to discharge at least half of the duties of her husband. Mohini judged from this perspective, proves an ideal Indian wife. She does not lag behind in discharging her social duties or rather the duties that she owes towards her husband. But soon she realizes that she is ignoring the dignity and authority of the Big House as its mistress. Progressively she begins to give importance to the traditions of Big House and prepares herself for living in an old world. Perhaps a suitable balance of old and new in her character helps her to negotiate the hostile situation in her life. As Shantha Krishanaswamy rightly observes:

> "...through her, the author aims at interlinking polarities, at connecting culture with culture, tradition with modernity, the individual and society" (61).

She not only complies with her mother-in-law to drop the singing of secular songs but also wears only cotton sarees and gold bangles instead of lovely and fashionable bangles. She realized that she has to learn and grow as well as she will have to modify her stand and make adjustment if she is to play the role of a good wife. It is really amazing that an impulsive girl like Mohini is transformed into an understanding and complacent housewife. As Bhattacharya comments:

> "Yes, the young mistress of the Big House took deeper colour from her new life everyday. Slowly she fitted herself to the rural design. Her sprightliness, her quick girlish laugh, she easily subdued. The mother was a ruthless teacher" (130).

Jayadev's mother wants Mohini to play the role of a mother in the kitchen, serve the farmhands as a sort of *Anupurna*, as well as to become the mother of Jayadev's child. Mohini also feels depressed, she questions her own credulity and becomes restless when her mother-in-law judges her every month. She swings between the traditional and orthodox mode of life and the enlightened and modern way of living. She thinks that perhaps she is needed only to bear a son for the Big House. Her existence in the Big House is only for the heir which she can give. In order to become pregnant Mohini drinks cold milk while looking at the moon. Really it shows the assertion and craving of a woman for children. It is considered that the primary object of marriage is to beget children. It is significantly described by Bhattacharya in the quotation from the marriage mantra with which the seventh chapter closes:

> "O Indra, kind of all the gods, let this lady be the mother of heroic sons" (63).

But a crisis arises when Jayadev approaches the age of twenty-eight, as it has been predicted by an astrologer that Jayadev will die an untimely death at this age unless a child is born to him. That's why mother of Jayadev was anxious that Mohini should become mother that would prevent the misfortune of Jayadev's death. About two years after the marriage, when mother finds no news of pregnancy from Mohini, she advises Mohini to cut the skin of her bosom and offer blood to the goddess in a lotus-leaf bowl in order to save the family. At this critical juncture Jayadev is bitten by a non-poisonous snake, which arises consternation in the mind of the mother who considers it as a warning for Jayadev's death. Mohini, frightened by this incident, becomes ready for sacrifice. But she is saved from this ceremonial offering of blood when in the nick of time Jayadev arrives and asks Mohini not to bow to superstition by complying with his mother's wish. This step of sacrifice which is raised by Mohini to save the family integrity does not define her as a victim but portrays her as a devoted woman. Shashikala Singh aptly remarks:

> "Bhabani Bhattacharya thus successfully presents in Mohini the typical Indian woman. She is not a synthesis of the tradition and modernity nor a 'battered victim,' but a new woman. She absorbs tradition only to give new direction to the concept of Indian womanhood" (51).

Though Jayadev's bold step against his mother's orthodoxy saves Mohini but one thing is remarkable that Mohini, at last, prepares to adjust herself with the Big House even she was ready to accept Sudha as a second wife only to save Jayadev. But fortunately, it is known that Mohini is already pregnant. It removes her fear of being replaced by Sudha. Thus life becomes a music for her once again. She makes struggle to reshape her mental values and revise her expectations, as well as to make the required adjustment to married life and to be the mistress of Jayadev's large village household.

Bhattacharya in his novels, especially in *Music for Mohini,* refers to the pivotal role played by his woman character. The novelist presents woman in myriad roles such as: Mother which is represented by Old Mother and Mother of Rooplekha, harsh mother-in-law by Jayadev's mother, connecting two different cultures through Mohini and Rooplekha, companion and sister by Mohini and Heeralal and at last wife and beloved with unspoken demands represented by Mohini. It describes the theme of uncertainty, alienation and communication in the married life of a woman. It is really the most artistic piece of Bhattacharya which deals with the ways in which Mohini a city-bred girl, given a modern education, solves the problems of her married life and adopts the lifestyle and tradition of Behula village, where she goes with so many dreams to live with her scholar husband. The two major female characters Mohini and Rooplekha feel uprooted after marriage. Mohini is city-bred and village-wed while Rooplekha, born and bred in the village, is unable to adapt herself to the modern city life after marriage. Rooplekha discloses her innermost feeling to Mohini:

> "We who're so wed, serve some real purpose. It's as though we made a bridge between two banks of a river.

We connect culture with culture, Mohini, over old Eastern view of life with the new semi-western outlook" (93-94).

Though in both the situations Mohini and Rooplekha have to suffer but the only difference is that former would feel much more disillusioned. Besides, Indian woman tries her best to make the situation favourable by her understanding and perseverance. Mohini also tries her best as remarked by Shashikala Singh:

> "As in the case of every Indian woman, Mohini's life too revolves round her family. Though an image of modernity, she also possesses all that is good about the tradition. Her immense respect for elders, her love and faithfulness toward her husband, and her commitment to the village people exemplify the characteristics of typical Indian woman" (52).

Thus *Music for Mohini* shows the status of woman in Indian society and in the home before marriage and after marriage. It is the destiny of every Indian woman to make adjustment with her life after marriage in order to enjoy the bliss of marital life. Old Mother in *Music for Mohini* while describing true meaning of marriage for a woman comments:

> "You will brighten another house, child. What use is a lamp, golden and filled with oil, if it has no wick. The house is the lamp, man is like oil, the woman is the wick, Mohini, and happiness the living flame" (39).

Hindu woman always worships her husband. Marriage brings an entire change in a girl's attitude because then she doesn't think of herself but prepares herself to make the necessary sacrifices as her situation and conditions demand. As Bhabani asserts in *Music for Mohini*:

> "A hundred thousand Hindu maids on each bridal day of the year give their hearts to their unknown husbands, asking nothing in return but approval" (63).

It clearly indicates the development of Mohini from her girlhood to the position of a wife as well as the mistress of the Big House. Progressively Mohini is transformed into an understanding and a competent housewife. As a heroine of

Bhabani Bhattacharya's novel, she possesses all the traits of a heroine and gives the mini-glimpse of all the aspects of Indian womanhood.

WORKS CITED

Bhattacharya, Bhabani. *Music for Mohini.* Delhi: Hind Pocket Books, 1952. All citations from the novel are from this edition followed by page numbers in parentheses.

Beauvoir, Simon de. *The Second Sex.* Tr. H.M. Parshley. Vintage, 1977.

Cormack, Margaret. *The Hindu Woman.* Bureau of Publishers, Teachers College, Columbia University.

Fisher, Marlene. "The Women in Bhattacharya's Novels." *Perspectives on Bhabani Bhattacharya*, ed. Ramesh K. Srivastava. Ghaziabad: Vimal Prakashan, 1982.

—— "The Women in Bhattacharya's Novels." *World Literature Written in English,* Vol. II, No. 1, April 1972.

Gaur, Rashmi. "Denial of Music to Mohini: A Critique of Bhabani Bhattacharya's Music for Mohini." *The Novels of Bhabani Bhattacharya,* ed. Monika Gupta. New Delhi: Atlantic Publishers and Distributors (P) Ltd., 2002.

Iyengar, K.R. Srinivasa. *Indian Writing in English.* New Delhi: Sterling, 1962.

Krishnaswamy, Shantha. "Bhabani Bhattacharya: The Pure Woman as Victim." *The Woman in Indian Fiction in English.* New Delhi: Ashish Publishing House, 1984.

Rao, B. Shyamala. *Bhabani Bhattacharya and His Works.* Bareilly: Student Store.

Singh, Shashikala. "The Image of Modern Indian Woman in Bhattacharya's Music for Mohini." *The Novels of Bhabani Bhattacharya,* ed. Monika Gupta. New Delhi: Atlantic Publishers and Distributors (P) Ltd., 2002.

26

The Condition of Married Woman in Bhabani Bhattacharya's *Music for Mohini*

Manjusha Kaushik

In our Vedas and Puranas woman is considered the incarnation of Goddess Lakshmi, Durga. She is more powerful and stronger than man. But in a modern perspective woman has lost that dignity and respect. Although she is progressing in every sphere of life but in her family life she feels helpless, because our society is male dominated.

Different critics have interpreted the status of woman in different perspectives here as "R.K. Narayan and Bhabani Bhattacharya explore the ethical and attitudinal dimension of women. Mulk Raj Anand and Nayantara Sehgal probe the economic, legal and institutional ramification of the problem unlike Raja Rao, who idealizes womanhood in spiritual, metaphysical sense. All these four novelists portray women as role performers, aspiring, suffering, protesting and reconciling as mothers, wives, sisters and mistresses" (Kaushik, 139).

According to the novelist the condition of a married woman is critical in a new house due to the change in ideology, way of talking, work attitude, routine, etc. A woman suffers too much to settle down in new circumstances, because everything, even her husband is new to her. There is no one who can understand her problems, she feels lonely and desolate in a new house where she is living as a foreigner.

There is a famous saying that marriages are decided in the heaven but are performed on earth. Before marriage, no one can forecast the future life of a girl, whether she would get better or not. According to old customs of our Indian society, marriage can be decided only on the basis of telling of the horoscope. There is a critical remark here that the pandit can prepare a horoscope though he is not God, hence how can he precept the luck of a man. How can we say that marriage which is based on horoscope will always be successful?

After marriage so many serious problems arise. Everybody in the new house expects from a newly wed bride to do everything for him. Everybody has the desire that she should be ever ready for the service of others. Nobody cares for her comfort and relief but demands only service from her. Jayadev dreams that his future wife should be like Maitreyi, as paragon of Vedic womanhood.

> "His heart warmed to Mohini...out of the mist of the past the Vedic woman took form, the woman who had been the spiritual partner of the greatest thinker of his age. It came on him, then, that this fusion of personalities was symbolic of the deeper fusion, then, that this fusion of which he dreamed, a profound union of today with yesterday."
>
> (*Music for Mohini,* 106)

It is the strength of Mohini's character that she easily overcame her dejection. She tries to rise up to the expectation of her husband. She realizes that her married life can be peaceful and meaningful only if she adjusts herself according to the wishes of her husband.

Another problem she faced is that a girl has no permission of doing the desired things just as we can see that Mohini, despite of being a radio singer and having good voice, cannot make use of it. It shows that there is a great distinction between man and woman. If a man has intelligence he can use it any time but woman cannot, because it is a male dominated society.

In the beginning of the novel Mohini is unaffected by any difficulty or worry and therefore she is happy. Life is a bed of roses for her. Here a question can be raised: What is the necessity of marriage in the life of a girl? Can't she live without a husband or is she only the subject of labour? The main aim of the novelist is to present the image of an ideal woman. Two women characters are in the novel—Mohini and Rooplekha. Both are uprooted and lost their individuality after marriage. But the Indian woman has strength and power to adjust herself in the most unfavorable circumstances. The adaptability to the changed atmosphere is praiseworthy in Mohini. She suffers a lot while making balance between the two cultures.

Mohini is considered as a selfless woman, she does not neglect the old but whatever the good and relevant is there she accepts. The main problem for Mohini in the Big House is that of her mental adjustment. Even when hardly two or three days had passed of her marriage, she realized that Jayadev is not what she had desired her husband to be. The very first night, Jayadev speaks to Mohini about the lofty conception of the relationship between husband and wife.

> "Bonds interminable hold as in sacred relation, more sacred than any on earth, he began and then paused, for the left his words sounded hollow" (12).

What is the reason that a girl is always ready to adjust herself in her husband's family. The answer is, only for her husband's sake. Even if a husband speaks only once to his wife in a day she feels satisfied and thinks it her precious possession. This is a famous proverb: *Behind the success of everyman there is a woman.*

Mohini's character is the best example of the theory of positivism. She does not try to leave the path of truthfulness. She realises that one day she would get success and the day has come when she is going to offer the blood from her breast. Jayadev could not tolerate it and he takes the favour of his wife and says:

> "Mohini must not insult herself" (18).

Mother does not like the behaviour of her son. Because in Indian society a mother cannot tolerate that her son takes the favour of his wife. Mohini suffers from this mental tension that she has no right to get the favour from her husband. Mother-in-law interferes in every way.

She is the unique creation of ideals. For the sake of her husband, she can sacrifice her life. In the novel the marriage symbolizes the union of the opposite traits while Jayadev is an incarnation of the aesthetic and emotional life. Mohini suffers in the Big House due to the superstitious temperament of her mother-in-law. If a lady cannot give birth to a child, it is not the fault of a girl only; her husband is also responsible for it. But society blames her because our society is a male dominated society. She is the victim of everybody's comment that she is a barren woman. She is considered the doom of the big house. She is very much disturbed in body and mind.

A married girl feels helpless because she cannot openly revolt against the family members as she is not the member of this family. She belongs to the other family. How can a lonely girl get success? Similarly, Mohini cannot go against her mother-in-law but has to adjust herself to the village life or traditional life. She accepts the challenges of adverse customs and superstitious beliefs by her practical common sense. Circumstances forced her to change herself from a naughty carefree and frolicsome girl to an understanding daughter-in-law.

For countless centuries women in India had been subordinated to men and are socially oppressed. The various religious practices in India as well as the personal laws based on them considered woman inferior to man. They do not have any individuality in their character. They could not find any other expression of their talents or desires except as housewives. This role suits to them most.

According to the Hindu mythology, woman is recognised in the society only by the name of her husband. Marriage is a very pious relationship between man and woman. Although we are called civilized, our orthodox thinking and behaviour are full of superstitions and false belief.

After marriage sex-relationship also plays a dominating role in the sweet relation between wife and husband. But in that field Mohini is unfortunate. She is disillusioned by Jayadev's ideologies. She believes in the warmth of love and compassion which she fails to get. But Jayadev assumes that love on the spiritual side is more prominent than love on the physical plain. So she faces the indifference of her husband and thinks that for the happy married life such compromise is essential. As S.C. Harrex points out, "this synthesis counts for the main social premise of the novel" (48).

Jayadev who is considered different from his wife Mohini, worked for the betterment of his traditional village, Behula. The novelist presents in Jayadev the character of a social reformer who dreams his wife to be his co-worker in the social field. But Mohini is helpless to co-operate him without the consent of her mother-in-law. Though she is dissatisfied she never shows her dissatisfaction.

Mohini always suffers because of sarcasting remarks of her mother-in-law like you are barren. It is unbearable to her. So she says in anger, "It is not what you are thinking mother. I am going to have a baby, I never will" (167).

> On hearing her words, mother bursts into anger again. "What will destiny, made me bring you into this home? Your barrenness will curse it for time. You will put an end to the Big House" (167).

Contemporary issues play dominant role in the writings of Bhattacharya. The author analyses the political, religious, social and economic problems of modern India in the perspective of his basic conflict in our ethos. The character of Jayadev embodies the best of the Indians and the western values. He has the sympathy for the poor. In the end of the novel he also feels sympathy for Mohini. He says:

> "There is no room in the Big House for crazy beliefs. The village looks to us for ideals and a way of living. The pattern we set is not our private affair".

Jayadev's main aim is to build his village a modern village. So he does not like the superstitions of his mother. Being a modern man he says to his mother:

> "Values mother? There are values beyond your grasp. Since you all always try to reach them with your reason, never with your feelings, life has punished you.... Blind belief shapes your thinking, and blind belief cannot make a sentiment" (30).

Bhattacharya seems to suggest the significance of the title when he writes "her life was music, the true quest for every woman. Her deepest need" (188). As long as she was in the company of the old mother and father and her affectionate brother, her life was quite musical. Her life was bed of roses. But she had to face a different type of music after marriage in the Big House. She is indeed the 'Goddess of Music' and music has established itself to be the food of love.

"If music be the food of love, play on/Give me excess of it" (Shakespeare, 274. Ultimately the music raises the harmony of the Big House).

The main aim of the novelist is to present the best ideal Indian woman. She is always ready to do the best for her family as well as to save the Indian culture. She is considered as a selfless woman. She doesn't neglect the old but whatever the good and relevant is there she accepts. Mohini in the novel struggles to establish herself against the unavoidable circumstances. The novelist shows that the woman as a wife or beloved is not only for entertainment but also a human being and equal companion of man. Equality does not mean sameness. Bhattacharya successfully blends the two opposite values, tradition and modernity in *Music for Mohini*. It is an intense desire of the novelist that fusion should be complete in every sphere of life. Bhattacharya is a utopian trying to create a better atmosphere for the people of his country. Mohini has extraordinary power to come out of the adverse circumstances. Literary critics have seen the best heroine in Mohini.

WORKS CITED

Bhattacharya, Bhabani. *Music for Mohini.* New Delhi: Orient Paperbacks, 1978 (All the reference are from this edition only).

Kaushik, Asha. *Politics, Aesthetics and Culture: A Study of Indo-Anglian Political Novels.* New Delhi: Manohar Publications, 1998.

Shakespeare, William. *The Comedies.* Bolton: Aurora Publishing, 1995.

Singh, Shashikala. "The Image of Modern Indian Woman in Bhattacharya's *Music for Mohini.*" *The Novels of Bhabani Bhattacharya* ed. Monika Gupta. New Delhi: Atlantic Publishers and Distributors (P) Ltd., 2002.

"Women in My Stories." *Journal of South Asian Literature*, Vol. 12, 1977.

27 An Exposition of Poetry in Girish Karnad's *Hayavadana*: An Application of Kuntaka's *Vakrokti Siddhantha*

Indu Arora

There has been a marked awareness of the language of poetry in the recent decades. Not only poets and critics but also linguists, philosophers and stylisticians have become conscious of the creative language in literature. Style is no more regarded as sugar-coating but a useful key to the total meaning of a work.

Criticism of literary/poetic language has taken several directions in almost every school of western criticism from Formalism to New Criticism. Formalism views literature as a specialised mode of language and proposes a fundamental opposition between the literary use of language and the ordinary or practical use of language. The writer by disrupting the mode of ordinary linguistic discourse makes strange the ordinary world of everyday perception and renews the reader's lost capacity for fresh sensation. The fundamentals of the New Criticism also make an emphasis on the use of language in literature by saying that a poem is an object, parts of a poem are organically related, a close analysis of the text enables a critic to understand and enjoy a poem. The stylistician also focuses on the study of the use of language in literature, involving the entire range of the general characteristic of language as a medium of literary expression. As applied to literary studies structuralism views literature as a second order system that uses the first order, structural system of language as its medium. According to it, a piece of literature should be analysed primarily on the basis of the language used in it.

As far as discourse analysis is concerned, it focuses its analysis of a piece of literature on the use of language in a running discourse, continued over a sequence of sentences and involving the interaction of the writer and the reader in a specific situational context.

In dialogic criticism a literary work is not only a social phenomenon but a text whose meanings are produced by the play of linguistic forces. It is a site for the dialogic interaction, multiple voices or modes of discourse. Each utterance owes its precise inflection and meaning to attendant factors.

It's remarkable that Indian Sanskrit *Acharyas* were really aware of some of the crucial problems pertaining to the language of literature, which they called *vakrokti*. They have made several exploratory but penetrating views, having a distinct bearing on literary expressions that still confront the modern scholars. Acharya Kuntaka elevated the concept of *vakrokti* to the full-fledged doctrine of analysing literature in his *Vakroktijivitam*.

The most exhaustive treatment of *vakrokti* was attempted in the 10th C and 11th C. Kuntaka, the greatest exponent of this theory, at the very outset of his *Vakroktijivitam*, states that his objective in writing fresh treaties on poetics is, "to establish the idea of strikingness which causes extraordinary charm in poetry." He, further, describes, *vakrokti* as a striking denotation *(vicitra abhidhā)*, and concieves of it as a striking mode of expression, depending on the peculiar turn given to it by the skill of the poet. Taking *vakrokti* in its broadest connotation, Kuntaka affirms again and again that it constitutes the only possible embellishment of poetry. He classifies *vakrokti* as six levels. In this study I am using obliquity, the translation of *vakrokti*, as given by other scholars like R.S. Tewari, M.S. Kushwaha, Kapil Kapoor, Shrawan K. Sharma in their works.

1. *Varna-vinyāsa-vakratā* or Phonetic Obliquity
2. *Padapurvārdha-vakratā* or Lexical Obliquity

3. *Pada-parardhā-vakratā* or Grammatical Obliquity
4. *Vākya-vakratā* or Sentential Obliquity
5. *Prakrana-vakratā* or Episodic Obliquity
6. *Prabandha-vakratā* or Compositional Obliquity

In this paper an attempt has been made to study Act-I of *Hayavadana* in the light of *Vakrokti-Siddhanta,* with a view to analysing the sub-variety of *vakrokti* as has been enumerated above. At the very outset let us define phonetic obliquity. The charming arrangement of phonemes is the foremost basis of poetry. Kuntaka calls this arrangement *varna-vinyasa-vakratā* or phonetic obliquity. In his *Vakroktijivitam,* he has mentioned all possible arrangement of phonemes or consonants.

The first kind of arrangement is the free and irregular repetition of similar or identical phonemes and consonants at varying intervals. Kuntaka further divides it into three sub-kinds—repetition of one phoneme, repetition of two phonemes and repetition of more than two phonemes. The second kind of *varna-vinyasa-vakratā* or phonetic obliquity too has three sub-kinds: (a) when stops are combined with their homorganic nasals, (b) when liquids are doubled and (c) when consonants become conjunct with 'ra' etc. Kuntaka also includes the arrangement of consonants or phonemes without any interval—as the third sub-variety of *varna-vinyasa-vakratā* or phonetic obliquity. The fourth sub-variety, according to Kuntaka, is the repetition of new consonants or phonemes. Kuntaka also regards chime as a sub-variety of *varna-vinyasa-vakratā.* In his view chime should be used without extra effort, adorned with syllables which are not harsh and in consonance with feelings conveyed. Now let us see how Girish Karnad uses this device in his play. The following example best demonstrates this obliquity:

> "But what a *forehead*! What a *forehead* if it was a *forehead* like yours, I would have accepted anything. But this! ....I have tried to accept my fate. My personal life has naturally been blameless.
> Magicians, mendicants, maharishis, fakirs, saints and sadhus—sadhus with short hair, sadhus with beards—sadhus in saffron, sadhus in the altogether, hanging,

> singing, rotating, gyrating—on the spikes, in the air under water under the ground—I've covered them all."

There is repetition of phonemes at varying intervals /f/, /r/, /h/, /d/, /i/ in the first stanza and repetition of phonemes /m/, /s/, /z/, /n/, /r/ in the second stanza. The skillful rhyme employed by the poet is not an ornament devoid of any emotions. Here, Hayavadana describes his miserable condition on being an incomplete personality. He can neither be called man nor animal. He has undertaken many journeys, sought the way out through many holy persons—but all in vain. This physical state is emphasised skilfully by using "piled alliteration" and "crossed alliteration"—a sub-variety of *varna-vinyasa-vakratā*. Repetition of 'forehead', 'sadhus' and repetition of /f/, /m/, /s/, /g/ brings out the pitiable state of Hayavadana more emphatically. Another example of this sub-variety of *varna-vinyasa-vakratā* is given as under:

> "Or was it some holy place of pillgrimage, a punyasthana, which you desecrated? Or could it be that you insulted a pativrata, dedicated to the service of her husband?"

Here, we see the repetition of phonemes, /p/, /t/, /d/ supports the meaning of the expression. The plosive bilabial phoneme /p/ suggests quickness, triviality and scorn coming to affricate palato alveolar /t/ and /d/ which suggests discomfort and harshness. Bhagvata inquires Hayavadana the reason for his sorry state and before listening to the answer, comes to a harsh opinion which generally people form for such a personality.

Again, an example of sub-variety of *varna vinyasa vakratā* is when Hayavadana gives a quick reply to Bhagvata:

> "What do you mean sir?
>
> Do you think just because you know the Puranas you can go about showering your Sanskrit on every one in sight?
>
> What temple did I desecrate? What woman did I insult? What?
>
> What else, What rishi? What sage"? What?
>
> Who have I wronged? What have I done to anyone?

Repetition of 'what' in last four lines emphasised the innocence of Hayavadana more forcibly. Karnad conveys more than the literal meaning, sometimes just by rhyming and interchanging the words, for example:

"What a good mix?
No more tricks.
In this one that,
Or that one this?
Ho! Ho!"

Samvrti-vakratā or obliquity of concealment, a sub-variety of *pada-purvārdha-vakratā* or lexical obliquity, operates when the subject of description is screened by the use of pronoun in order to achieve excellence. For example:

"Why should love stick to the sap
of a thick yearning of the many-
petalled, many flowered lantana,
Why should I be tied down to
the relationship of a single flower?"

Karnad here uses pronoun to convey the central theme of the play effectively. The female chorus in the play sing this song from the beginning, until the meaning becomes clear in the action of Padmini, at last.

The subject matter or content of the work may be *sahajā* (natural) or *ahārya* (imposed). Sometimes the poet, by his natural power of contemplating the natural objects, allured the heart of the sensitive reader *(Sahajā vakratā)*, while at other time he attains the expression of heightened beauty due to the use of skill *(Ahārya vakratā)*. Karnad suffuses his subject matter with figure of speech, when he describes the beauty of Padmini:

Her fore locks rival the bees, her face is a white lotus.
Her beauty is as magic lake. Her arms the lotus-creepers.
Her breasts are golden urns and her waist....

Any work of art as portrayed by the poet is not the true or faithful copy of life. The poet colours the picture with his own imagination according to his need.

In this way, we see that imagination plays an important role in transforming or changing the source material of the composition. The beauty caused by this imagination is *utapadya-lāvanya,* or appeal in modified source story. It is a sub-variety of *prakarna vakratā.* The writer also aims at introducing universal element in the source story. The plot of *Hayavadana* is derived from *Kathasaritsagara.* But Karnad has borrowed it from Thomas Mann's retelling of story in *The Transposed Heads.* The original story poses a moral problem, which Mann uses to ridicule mechanical conception of life which differentiates between body and soul. Karnad's play puts forth the problem of human identity in the world of tangled relationship. The sub-plot of *Hayavadana*, the Horseman, intensifies the importance of the core theme of incompleteness by treating it at different levels.

There is another variety, i.e. *Bhāvapurnasthiti ki udabhāvanā* or creation of emotional state, of *prakarna vakratā.* Here the poet is in frenzy of creation and thus his work is suffused with charm and strikingness. This variety can be seen in *Hayavadana* when Padmini is overwhelmed with grief, on seeing the dead bodies of her husband—Devadutta and of Kapila. Before the statue of Goddess Kali, she breaks down:

> Oh God! What this? Both! Both gone! And didn't even think of me before they went? What shall I do? Oh, Devadutta, what did I do that you left me alone in this state? Was that how much you loved me? And you Kapila, who looked at me with dog's eye—you two? How selfish you are—how unkind? What shall I do now—where shall I go? How can I go home? Home? And what shall I say when I get there ? What shall I say happened?

The repetition of phonemes /w/, /h/, broken short sentences, repetition of questionings brings forth the intensity of the emotional state very effectively.

Anothor sub-variety of *Prakarna vakratā, Prakarana-ka-upakārya-upakāraka-bhava* or mutual relationship in episodes, is valued most by Kuntaka. In his view, the organic unity which binds all the incidents towards the intended end, shows the creative originality of the poet. The organic unity is maintained very skilfully by Girish Karnad in *Hayavadana*, The reader's suspense is gripped and he goes on reading impatiently to know what lies ahead? What is going to happen when Padmini, who wants a man of steel, is married to a weak-minded, weak-bodied Devadutta? Will the interchanging of heads solve the problem or entangle it more than ever? Will Hayavadana, who has gone to Chitrakoot, to the temple of Goddess Kali, be able to attain completeness? What next, is the curiosity of the reader that is very artistically maintained in episode after episode, thus imparting them a unity.

Angirasa nisyandanikasa or consumption of principal emotion, sub-variety of *Prakarna vakratā* takes place in epic poem, or a poem of equivalent scale and compass. *Hayavadana* bears *adbhuta rasa* in Act-I, when the heads of Kapila and Devadutta are interchanged.

Devadutta — Mixed up heads!

Kapila — Heads mixed up!

Devadutta — Exchanged heads?

Kapila — Heads exchanged?

Devadutta — How fantastic, all these years we were only friends.

Kapila — Now we are blood relations. Body relation, what a gift!

The latter part of the drama bears *karuna rasa;* putting forth a big question mark as Bhagvata, the protagonist, says, "What indeed is the solution to this problem," which holds the entire future of these three unfortunate beings in balance? Must their fate remain a mystery?"

The mystery drags on, making condition miserable for Devadutta, Kapila and Padmini. Ultimately the two men die fighting with each other and Padmini commits *sati*, leaving behind her a small son. The play starts with *adbhuta rasa,* there by giving way to *bhayanaka rasa* and finally *karuna rasa.* This provision for other friendly rasas along with the principal emotion makes the work more delightful. Kuntaka calls this device *rasāntra vakratā* or obliquity of changing the *rasa* which is again a sub-variety of *Prabandha vakratā* or compositional obliquity.

According to Acharya Kuntaka, the title of the work is also replete with a kind of obliquity. The title of the story is sometimes symbolic and sometimes suggestive which unfolds the meaning of the work. According to Kuntaka, a good title should convey the central theme. It is the soul of the work. Kuntaka calls it *nāmakarana vakratā* or obliquity of title. The title of the play under review is impregnated with oblique meaning. The title of Karnad's plays convey the very intention of the work. Hayavadana, i.e. the horseman, treated in the sub-plot, deepens the significance of the main theme of incompleteness by treating it on a different plane.

WORK CITED

Karnad, Girish. *Three Plays: 'Hayavadana.'* New Delhi: O.U.P., 1994.

28 Gita Mehta's *Karma Cola*: A Vituperative Satire on Indian Spirituality

Hemlatha K.

The two Wars, the Korean crisis, the Vietnam debacle, the Cuban fracas, the Cold War—all these upheavals seemed to have disoriented the western youth. With the Beatles belting out their blues, the flower children on a high, gravitate towards peace and freedom and seek solace adopting questionable means. Some of them turn towards seeking freedom from the consumerist society by looking eastwards especially India—the land of spiritualism guaranteed to wash away one's karma.

The British, on leaving India, left Indians oscillating between Eastern and Western culture. The literature of this period also reveals the cultural conflict in the minds of the people. So the need for gurus, arose, to guide the seekers and bring about clarity, clearing away the cobwebs of ignorance and delusion.

Gita Mehta's *Karma Cola* is an eye-opener of the exploitation of the people in the name of spiritualism. A fascinating encounter of the surreal, spiritual world of gurus is exposed surgically layer by layer by the incisive observation of Gita Mehta, a product of post-independence liberal India. Satirical, and at the same time bringing out the crude lustful exploitation of the unwary lamb—the seeker from the West, *Karma Cola* is sprinkled with nuggets of anecdotes, bringing out the various liberal views of God and salvation and the multiple paths leading to the universal soul. Gita Mehta, an Indian writer, who has also lived in England and the U.S., was ideally placed to observe the spectacle of European and American "pilgrims" interacting with their hosts, and she has elucidated what happens when the traditions of an ancient and long-lived society are turned into commodities and sold to those who do not understand them. Mehta's eloquence and wit lightens the burden of acceptance of having thrown logic to the wind.

As in any field of human endeavour, the institution of the Guru has also been misused for self-promotion, power and money. The veneration and unconditional surrender that is integral to the relationship opens up the possibility of exploitation by unscrupulous individuals who use their position to milk their followers for money or for sexual abuse.

In the book *Karma Cola* various ashrams have been described. Feeling God's aura, getting a hit off the energy are the various processes taking place in the ashram, worshipping the guru as God himself, and listening to his lectures on revolution, Jesus, Marx and so on, and with declaring himself to be an intellectual are the various initiation techniques taking place in these ashrams.

In the past, the curious had to sweat it out for years before the wisdom of the Upanishads was revealed to them. Moreover, the wisdom was transferred verbally and not written down so as to prevent mishandling. Modern age gurus just barge into gurudom and use their knowledge indiscriminately and unwisely thereby leading to more damage than good.

For instance, in an attempt to get over anger and violence one of the neo-gurus conducts a special session of meditation where his followers beat each other black and blue trying to vent their anger. These people were not supposed to be indulging in violence but were supposed to be exorcising demons and ghosts so that the next day they could look at themselves in the mirror and not be afraid of themselves. The guru allows the followers to beat each other, make love, do whatever comes to their mind in a barbaric manner, subtle gift wrapped in the spiritual lingo.

Another form of meditation practiced in an ashram, which can prove dangerous, is when a person stares at a mirror for a long time, without blinking and without even noticing tears that start streaming down the cheeks. In case one survives half an hour of staring without fainting, then one can relive one's past; but that could also be dangerous—as, a newly wed girl suddenly realized that she was her husband's mother in the past and that made her feel guilty of incest and thereby made her go crazy.

Contrary to the age-old belief that the guru is one who guides one through the ups and downs of life and helps one to emerge from ignorance into the sunlight of self realization, in the marketplace of gurus today, there seems to be too much of a good thing. There is almost a surfeit of godmen, saints, mahatmas, yogis, mahants, healers, avatars and jnanis, who are actually making spirituality a commodity. In the West, this commodification has become an accepted fact with hourly payments in dollars.

A guru who has an ashram in western India with a large number of foreign followers, confided to a correspondent from *Time* magazine:

> "My followers have no time. So I give them instant salvation. I turn them into neo-sanyasis" (102).

Even though the neo-sanyasis are supposed to have renounced the world socially as well as physically to seek truth and are vowed to remain dedicated to poverty and chastity, when one sees them sharing a chillum of hashish, and fondling each other, one cannot help wondering whether the whole institution of spirituality and gurudom is all humbug and the act of renunciation an "aggressive mockery" (103).

Indian philosophy and spirituality attracts foreigners. Beginning in the late 60s hundreds of thousands of Westerners descended upon India, proclaiming that the magic and mystery missing in their lives was to be found in the East. Aldous Huxley and William Butler Yeats were impressed by the

Upanishads. Later on the Beatles discovered India on the banks of the river Ganga at Rishikesh. For the Westerners, eliciting and comprehending information from Indians, be it spiritual, physical or just the fastest way to get to the next town was very difficult. Moreover, the experience of the East is simply not accessible to the Western mind as the East is simply not concerned with so-called intellectual aggrandizement. So much so, Yung testily called the Eastern mind childish, a mind that did not even ask questions, but simply perceived them.

Foreigners from Germany and Switzerland tinned up because they were tired of dollars, dinars, telephones, telex and they came to India to get a holistic picture of life. India gives a picture of "noisy, dirty, silence" (75). What impressed the tourists was that in India so many millions were being born, live and die without any fuss. Contrary to Switzerland where people were only concerned with money and banking, in India people were continuously reminded of the significance and insignificance of life.

Kabir, a saint of yore, has described a guru thus:

"My Guru is a great wasp;
He takes other insects and
Suffuses them with his own Hue,
Making them as he is."[2]

Ironically, modern age Gurus waste no time fooling gullible people. There is a reference to a village in Andhra Pradesh where it was rumoured that the Guru's urine changed into scented rose water. An Englishman who happened to arrive to view this miracle was applauded and encouraged, "In a gesture of unprecedented magnanimity to drink the entire content of the vessel" (82) The aristocrat who drank it, observed with typical British humour later, "it tasted remarkably like ordinary urine" (82).

Contrary to the age old statement by Kabir, that Guru suffuses others with his own Hue, this guru seems to be suggesting to his followers to cleanse themselves with his micturition. Also gurus were able to materialize rings, watches and holy ash from nowhere. Diplomats of foreign nations wearing Dior sunglasses, Hermes Alligator skin handbags and wearing Saville Row suits waited anxiously for gurus to perform miracles. The guru produced a fistful of ash, gave it to the American ambassador and insisted that he eat it.

There are rumours of gurus performing such unbelievable miracles as reviving a dead man back to life. The guru went into the morgue and revived a dead man from his toes upwards that he sat up like a Frankenstein monster, to the awe of everyone, around him. Also such gurus were able to relieve all physical and spiritual distress by making disciples roll their eye balls which they claim is the focal point of all distress. After performing this eye rolling exercise for an hour, one guru could not read the speech which he had written to be read out to the audience. If he had read it would definitely have been an optical miracle. Gita Mehta's comment here is that "The guru's powers were sometimes limited to controlling the bodies of others, but not his own" (55).

An air-conditioned ashram was run by an Indian woman considered an embodiment of a guru. The pious exhibited their piety in a number of ways. Some were performing manicure, others pedicure, someone else was massaging her shoulders, an another would pluck at the hem of her garment and go out; except plucking her eyebrows, everything else was being attended to. As for Ma herself she was attending various calls—as an "uneducated Hindu woman with one caller, the arrogant spiritual leader with another, and the flirtatious woman of the world with the third" (145).

Associating with the Sadhus at a tender age can bring about ridiculous behaviour in children. Aboard a plane which took off from Tehran airport, a drugged boy, who claimed to be a sadhu in his past life, stripped off all his clothes and proceeded to streak up and down the economy section. The case was dismissed as a young man seeking reassurance and Gita Mehta's comment is: "If you run up and down a locked airplane, you will get this reassurance" (87).

In the name of spirituality people can disturb the normal growth and life of children. According to certain traditions, a female child of 5 or 6 years is declared as the incarnation of the Goddess and people offer prayers to her. This girl on reaching puberty is declared to be unholy and "her descent to humanity is softened by a lifetime pension for herself and her family" (151) This little girl cannot procreate and has to remain a virgin throughout life.

There is a story of a two-year-old boy who saw the photograph of God and fell in front of it telling his father that he was not his father but that the man in the photograph was his father. When this was reported to the guru in the ashram, he immediately declared the boy to be, Buddha, the enlightened one. Since then, he was treated as God and worshipped by one and all. The irony is that the poor little baby asked the next visitor who met him whether he could get him some guns and soldiers to play with.

There are other instances of mendicants flaying children pierced with iron rods on either cheeks, in front of large crowds and inducing viewers to fling money at them in recognition of their asceticism. Once an American and his French girlfriend tried to rescue one such girl child, but she proved a difficult girl, mistaking their goodness for weakness and tried to please the American sexually. The basic instincts of sex and survival seem to be well developed in her. When the American reported this to his guru, the guru convinced him that the world and Good and Evil were merely illusions and that it is useless trying to impose a morality in a world where it was no longer applicable.

Miracles are like the first sip of Divine Nectar that ultimately can lead to transformation of the heart. Most gurus perform miracles to help their disciples see the limited nature of their visions, and the need for expansion of consciousness. There are references to miracles in Gita Mehta's *Karma Cola*. In the Bom Jesus Cathedral at Goa the mortal remains of the great Jesuit saint and missionary Francis Xavier, kept miraculously intact since eighteenth century, used to be displayed for the congregation once every year. It is reported that about

80 years ago a lady who filed past the body overcome with doubts, bent over the body and bit off the big toe of the Saint. The body turned out to be flesh and blood, and so struck with fear, she ran as fast as her legs could carry her, but to her amazement, a miraculous trail of blood followed her, wherever she went, until she spat out the toe and asked for forgiveness for her profanity. The humorous remark of Gita Mehta is that, "in the land of sages it is probably politic to keep the mouth free of foreign objects" (92)

The trouble with miracles is that confusion prevents discrimination. Difficulty is encountered in separating the chaff from the gross. One school of archeologist has traced the presence of Jesus in India when Jesus was between 12 and 30 years of age. It is stated that Jesus learnt mysticism, fasting and levitation and that was how he was able to spend 40 days in the wilderness without food and drink and also could remain in the tomb meditating for 3 days and nights alter his crucifixion and be able to levitate on Easter Sunday.

In a humorous manner Gita Mehta has also explained how in India travel can be educative and help one to gain philosophical knowledge.

"Our streets and our stations are thronged with people from a thousand different backgrounds with whom it is practically impossible to avoid conversation. During the conversation you may find that your money has been stolen or that you have been speaking to a sage. Both experiences are considered educational" (86).

There is an unusual collocation here—speaking to a sage is equated with finding that your money has been stolen. Both are equally deceptive and hazardous.

Gurus were also supposed to have a predisposition to supernatural insight into logic and semantics. When once the people waited with bated breath to hear a guru's speech, the guru began his speech informing the people that God exists because if you look in the *Oxford English Dictionary* under the letter 'G' you will eventually find the word God and added: "It is in the dictionary. Let those who doubt the existence of the divine look for proof in the dictionary. How could what does not exist, then exist in the dictionary?" (104). Such ample proof for the existence of God!

The despicable state of widows at Banaras and the ruthless manner in which priests ask for money at the crematoriums in Banaras whenever a body is to be cremated have been vividly elucidated in Gita Mehta's *Karma Cola*:

> "Priests bargain with bereaved families over the price and the quantity of sandalwood and clarified butter to be used for the funeral pyre, to help ignition and salvation. Battles are fought over the price of each verse of the holy Sanskrit scriptures to be recited while the body burns" (136).

A man has to be paid to take care of the body until it gets reduced to ashes so that it does not fall into the hands of 'Sadhus' who are used to eating human flesh. Hippies spent their time smoking joints sitting on the burning ghats, watching the smoke rising from the dead bodies. Gita Mehta's comment is that:

> "India prides herself on having the best record on controlling illegal drug traffic in the world. While the bureaucrats congratulate themselves on the efficacy of their controls, the drug traffic grows and grows and Banaras looks set on replacing Bangkok as Needle City, Asia" (138).

In the modern-day world the very word 'karma' has conveniently acquired multifarious meanings, suiting the needs of people using them. The word was first used by Krishna to initiate Arjuna to act, stating that only action will save him from the bondage of action. But now coincidence, chance, Déjà vu, anything goes as karma. Once a tourist enquired of another as to what he was doing in India, the tourist replied:

"I am being."

"Pardon?"

"Being."

"Ah I catch on . Being. Yes we all be. We definitely are, no doubt. But what are you *doing?*" (34).

With this there was an irretrievable breakdown in communications. The conversation was mutually unintelligible as one of them could not understand how the other could just

"Be", waiting for things to happen. The solution to all problems seems to be to just sit and Be, and that by joining in the meditations and learning to be silent one could reach a terrific height without bothering about what is in store for the future.

Karma Cola took a sardonic look at the Western belief that instant spiritual enlightenment can be acquired by hopping a jet to India and finding the nearest Guru. In it Gita Mehta displays her extraordinary talent at interweaving bizarre anecdotes, history and current events into a humorous and witty documentary satire. Gita Mehta has very effectively demystified the intricacies of achieving salvation offered by the holy men of India in the "saffron robes of renunciation" (ix). *Karma Cola* is a book of Revelation for the uninitiated, of what not to get initiated into, on the path of Karmic liberation.

WORKS CITED

Chopra, Parveen. *Life Positive*. New Delhi: Magnus Media Pvt. Ltd., Oct. 2004, 110.

Mehta, Gita, *Karma Cola*. New Delhi: Penguin Books India (P) Ltd., 1979, 102. All subsequent references to the book have been indicated by page numbers within parentheses in the text.

29

Immigrancy as Cause and Effect: The Protagonists of Indira Ganesan's *The Journey* and *Inheritance*

N. Poovalingam

Indira Ganesan, herself a Srirangam Tamilian, moved to the United States as a young girl "to enter elementary school in Rockland County, New York" much like her own protagonist Renu Krishnan in *The Journey*. And as a writer, Indira Ganesan sees herself as a "part of the immigrant tradition and as a woman of color writing in a culture not entirely her own" (Wright, 115). In view of her two novels and their thematic preoccupations, which is undeniably about the intersectional realm between India and America, it may not be wholly unwarranted to presume autobiographical strains in these two novels. This paper, hence, attempts to study the two novels of Indira Ganesan—*The Journey* and *Inheritance*, in order to deduce her stance with regard to immigrancy.

Interestingly, the central character of *The Journey* longs, during her brief sojourn in India, to recapture her Indian life despite her present, cultural hybridity. Renu Krishnan realizes the impossibility of such a return and forges reconciliation at the end. On the other hand, Sonil in *Inheritance*, finding herself displaced in India by her half-American-half-Indian birth, seeks refuge in the US.

Both the novels *The Journey* and *Inheritance* have the imaginary island of Pi for their setting. "Imagine a chunk of

India that is not quite India torn free to float in the Bay of Bengal—this is Pi." And this is an Indian island which has derived its name from "Prosperous Island" shortened to be P.I. or Pi (*The Journey,* 17). Moreover, both the novels have a woman protagonist as their central character, and both novels are open-ended.

While Renu Krishnan in the first novel finds her return to Pi from the US to be a painful experience, Sonil in the second novel is increasingly depressed by the conservatism and uneventful life of Pi and escapes to the US. If life in Pi brings memories of the irretrievable past and therefore is unbearably haunting and nostalgic to Renu, the island life feels oppressive and suffocating for Sonil. Thus, both the protagonists of Indira Ganesan seem to indicate that immigrancy by itself does not inhere any insurmountable problem. And, in an imaginative writing like a novel, the dilemma of the immigrant who straddles two or more cultures is nonetheless an individual's dilemma and, therefore, must be addressed more introversively, self-searchingly than through any partial and cultural or social generalization. Indira Ganesan is, perhaps, afraid that an overtly politicized theme like immigrancy may result in her novel becoming propagandistic.

Taken as a ten-year-old to the US, Renu Krishnan in *The Journey,* has spent almost all the years of her adolescence there until her return to Pi on hearing the death of Rajesh, her "twin" cousin. The novel begins with her journey towards Pi and evokes in Renu memories of the childhood spent with Rajesh. Remembering that lost state of careless independence, Renu cannot help seeing her present life in the US that is quite the opposite. For, with the death of her father, for the fifteen-year-old Renu life had turned repressive. Ironically, the American lifestyle that is normally envied by Indians at home becomes doubly burdensome for Renu. The "Americanization and Westernization with which he'd tried so hard to shape their lives began to fall away." And the mother, Rukmani, having had to bring up her two daughters single-handedly in a foreign country, slowly fell into a puritanic excess and moral righteousness in bringing her daughters up. Thus, Indira Ganesan writes that the

> "early rebellions were reined in by their father's death, and Renu reacted by throwing herself to the task of preserving the family.... Losing contact with friends, letting the phone alone, it was easy to reduce the circumference of her world. But nothing could stop the slow flush creeping up her throat in high school, inventing excuses...saying no to excursions and dances. Island girls do not date, her mother had said, crisply, severely, no more nonsense" (44).

And it is further stated by the narrator that letters from home reintroduced the myth and stories 'banished' by the father. The "holy ash and *kimgamum* blessed by the priests" started coming from Pi. And Renu's mother, Rukmani Krishnan, despite being a scientist herself, "put away her coordinated pant-suits and wore saris from Lexington Avenue under her lab coats." She "curtailed the girls' activities, refusing to allow them dances and late nights" (21). Such regression to a set of Victorian values had made Renu yearn for the company of Rajesh; for Renu believed that while the strict moral codes of her mother would not permit "a squeaky-clean, blue-tuxedoed, corsage-carrying" American to take her out for dances, Rajesh being her cousin "would have automatic approval from her family" (132).

At Pi, Rajesh's death and the resultant sense of loss overpower Renu too personally to relate to anyone her anguish. Her intense sorrow drives her once "deep into the garden, past the mimosa tree, past the lemon trees, where only the monkeys could hear her...and she let out scream after scream" (127).

Renu and Rajesh had once killed a monkey accidentally in their grandfather's garden while they were playing. Though Rajesh had forgotten it, Renu was frightened that they had killed Lord Hanuman's messenger and would be punished severely for it. Fearing the indefinitely deferred punishment, Renu starts developing a guilty conscience. Indira Ganesan writes:

> "whenever [Renu] slipped into the American way of life, when she stopped wearing the red tikka on her forehead, when she stopped going to temple, she could not free herself of the idea that the gods were still hunting her, that they were waiting to seek retribution" (14).

Having waited long for divine retribution in vain, Renu gradually loses her faith in religion itself. While her disillusionment leads her to an existential angst, the death of Rajesh drives her to a greater hopelessness.

Though Indira Ganesan does not overtly state that Renu has developed a love for Rajesh and she yearns to be with him forever, the intensity with which she mourns his death betrays her. And her inability to seek solace or to speak her mind is perhaps because of the unnaturalness of her love. For Renu and Rajesh are not marriageable cousins—their mothers being sisters, they are supposed to be brother and sister. Thus, Renu's sense of guilt now has its source in her almost incestuous love and not in the childhood accident of killing a monkey.

Renu accompanies her younger sister Manx (Meenakshi shortened and Americanized!) to Trippi, "a town famed for its population of psychics and near-magicians," a place of "all-day, all-night carnival" (97). But whatever she does, or wherever she goes, Renu gets no respite from the memory of Rajesh and his death. On their way to Trippi, Renu becomes aware of her sister's affair with an itinerant American Freddie Flat. Manx met Freddie in the marketplace sometime ago and had befriended him. Having been drawn towards Freddie, Manx is found sleeping with him during this trip and Renu being aware of it, wonders at her younger sister's *sangfroid* and guilt-free attitude. Indira Ganesan writes that Renu

> "envied their naturalness, their ease, disquieted on seeing embodied before her what she herself longed for, the unself-conscious movement, the beauty of the casual" (91).

The unthinking physicality of Freddie and Manx is what Renu longs for. But she feels quite incapable of achieving it for herself owing to her introversion. And further this same longing in Renu is reiterated by Indira Ganesan while she writes the following:

> "a beautiful man drinking from a coconut whose bare back made Renu's heart ache even more" (104).

Rajesh died traveling in a train from Madhupur to Coimbatore. A rainstorm had hit the train while it was crossing bridge and the carriages were thrown off the track into the river below. That Rajesh died in water in itself portends, for Renu, her own death by fire. For, she remembering a superstitious belief that if one of the twins dies by water the other will die by fire, she starts expecting her own death. With the death of Rajesh, her repressed sexuality torments her and she feels doomed and has no hope of release. Becoming obsessed with death, believing it to be her only way out, Renu tends to romanticize death and vaguely considers *sati,* too, for herself.

Thus, towards the end of the novel, Renu's increasing desperation drives her momentarily to choose death as the only alternative. She gets drawn, in a moment of hallucinatory trauma, towards a smouldering drum of fire on the road to kill herself, but somehow escapes. After this "token" death, she decides to return to the US. Renu's rejection of the marriage proposals brought by her mother and her decision to leave for the US undermine the otherwise open-endedness of the novel.

While expressing her dissatisfaction with some of the younger generation of Indian writers for failing to make "authentic presentation of the social reality in India," Shyamala A. Narayan includes Indira Ganesan, with particular reference to this novel (134). And Annie-Marie Conway, reviewing this novel in the *TLS*, has been quite perceptive with her following observation:

> "[the novel] seems to be trying to do too much at once: at different points Ganesan looks at culture clash, the nature of heroism, rites of passage, loyalty between friends and lovers, adolescent sexuality, political activism, fate, genocide, dream symbolism, national identity, the thin dividing line between the spiritual and the superstitious."

Indira Ganesan's second novel, *Inheritance,* seems to be an off-shoot and an extension of her first in that, it seems to be an elaboration of the affair between Renu Krishnan's younger sister Manx and Freddie Flat. Manx is transformed into Sonil the central character of *Inheritance.* While Manx is Americanized due to her upbringing in the US, Sonil is half-American by blood as her father happens to be a white-American. And similarly, the same purposefully created Freddie Flat of *The Journey,* becomes Richard here. Interestingly, the United States that intensified and aggravated a repressive adolescence for Renu Krishnan is reversed here to represent liberation for Sonil.

Sonil is the third and last daughter of Lakshmi. Lakshmi's first marriage comes to an end with her widowhood as her husband was old enough to be her father. Her second marriage never materializes because the film producer who courted her deceives her after sexually exploiting her and fathering her second daughter. Disillusioned with marriage, Lakshmi does not accept to marry the American freelance photographer who is her third daughter Sonil's father.

At a very young age itself, Sonil is made to be aware of the strangeness of her complexion and suffers an uneasy conspicuousness. Furthermore, Sonil's mother, having had enough of her share of sufferings perhaps, disregards the half-white daughter. Sonil's two half-sisters are married and they shy away from their disreputed mother.

Deserted by her mother thus, Sonil is deprived of even the single parent love that she might have hoped for. The peculiar outcast-status of Sonil drives her to seek love and protection from an American, Richard. The fifteen-year-old Sonil is unmindful of the vast difference between them in age. Much like Manx, in *The Journey,* getting attracted towards a much older man Freddie, Sonil falls in love with Richard. On her return to home after her first meeting with Richard, Sonil describes her elation thus:

> "...I realized how starved I had been for a real conversation, that the person I knew most was myself. Talking with Richard made my heart light, and even the flowers around

> me seemed more potent. I was heady with excitement at the time I'd just had" (56).

And one cannot help remembering the remark that Renu Krishnan makes, as if explaining to herself the incongruous affair of her younger sister with a man nearly double her age: "perhaps she misses her father." While the father's absence in novels could thus be an explanation, in the case of Sonil, in *Inheritance*, her love for an American becomes symbolic in that it foreshadows the escape that she later makes to the US. And while Richard deserts her in Pi, making his mother's arrival on the island an excuse, Sonil's escape to America also does not bring her the peace that she seeks. She becomes an aimlessly drifting person there.

Her visit with her father in the US helps her to understand her mother better. She grows sympathetic towards both her parents. However, even in the US, Sonil is unable to forget her first love. In the gestures of a stranger, or the movement of a passer-by, Sonil is often reminded of Richard. Indira Ganesan presents Sonil's understanding of her parents and the maturity of her perception of life that are the result of her visit to the US in the following lines:

> "He was talented, my father, but not famous. Perhaps he still loved my mother, in the way I loved Richard, maybe even more. I had to stop trying to figure them out; they were changeable and in motion. I had thought inheritance was inescapable. It is, but not in ways I imagined. My family is ingrained in my actions, they are uppermost in my mind. Yet there are parts of me that are nothing like them, a random mix of genes and attributes" (151).

With a philosophical endurance, Sonil has learnt to bear with the pain of memory. The loss of faith that caused so much conflict in Renu Krishnan in *The Journey* paves the way for Sonil in *Inheritance* to go with drift that life offers and not to have anything as presumptuous as an ambition.

Kavery Nambisan, an Indian woman novelist herself, finds the story to be "vapid and totally without depth" and all the characters in the novel uni-dimensional (43). And concluding her review she attacks the novel further as follows:

> "The *Sunday Times* has extolled this novel as 'a book that glows with the magic of Indian childhood...a quiet, intelligent novel.' It appears that the *Sunday Times* reviewer knows precious little about Indian childhood, and the author not much more" (44).

Whatever the artistic failings of Indira Ganesan might be, these two novels of hers do depict the immigrant Indian writer's dilemma through immigrant Indian protagonists. Having been written in the late eighties and early nineties, these two novels seem to evade the issue of diasporic dislocation and postcolonial politics. And though Indira Ganesan might have evaded for other reasons these issues, it still holds good that the preoccupation of a literary work is much more than such short-sighted issues.

Immigrant writers are often charged with the accusation that they write for the Western readers and not necessarily for the Indian readers. But these two novels of Indira Ganesan—by evading the issue of immigrancy and through an existentialist portrayal of her protagonists—seem, on the one hand, to suggest how particular issues are subsumed by the wholeness of a literary text and, on the other, to point out the risk of rendering a work dated by making it explicitly issue-based.

WORKS CITED

Ganesan, Indira. *The Journey.* New York: Alfred A. Knopf, 1990.

——. *Inheritance.* New York: Alfred A. Knopf, 1998.

——. "Of Genius and Human Foibles." *Indian Review of Books,* 4:1 Oct.-Dec. 1994.

Conway, Annie-Marie. "Review of Indira Ganesan's *The Journey.*" *Times Literary Supplement,* 1991, 18.

Curtis, Sarah. "Review of Indira Ganesan's *Inheritance.*" *Times Literary Supplement*, July 18, 1997, 22.

Nambisan, Kavery. "'Disinherited,' Review of Indira Ganesan's *Inheritance.*" *Indian Review of Books,* 6:11, 1997, 43-44.

Narayan, Shyamala A. "Voyage as Motif in Indian English Fiction." *New Perspectives in Indian Literature in English* (Essays in Honour of Prof. M.K. Naik), eds. C.R. Yaravinlelimath *et al.* New Delhi: Sterling Publishers, 1995, 126-136.

Sanga, Juina C. (Ed.), *South Asian Literature in English: An Encyclopedia.*

Thillainayagam, S. and N. Poovalingam. "From Introversion to Decadence: Women Characters in Indira Ganesan's *The Journey.*" *Contemporary Indian Women Writers in English: A Feminist Perspective,* ed. S.N. Pandey. New Delhi: Atlantic Publishers and Distributors (P) Ltd., 1999, 97-107.

Wright, Marilou Briggs. "Indira Ganesan (1960-)." *Writers of the Indian Diaspora: A Bio-Bibliographical Critical Sourcebook,* ed. Emmanuel S. Nelson. Connecticut: Greenwood Press, 1993, 115-121.

30

Self and Society in Nissim Ezekiel's Poetry

Reema Varshney

Nissim Ezekiel, one of the major poets in Indian English tradition, looks at literature in relation to society. In all his writings Ezekiel stresses the centrality of man in the universe and prefers poetry of statement and purpose. The poetry is the most complex art which passes through the most subtle ways before it attains its final exquisite form—the highest achievement which invites an interplay between head and heart, inner and outer self of man.

The poetic self of Ezekiel has two divergent poles—the existential enigma on the one hand and the poetic enigma, i.e. the need for a correspondence between art and life, on the other. He has the sensibility of a modern poet whose 'self' confronts the fallen world and stands in an ironic contrast to the ideal world. The title of the poem in the first collection *A Time to Change* is suggestive of the dilemma of Nissim Ezekiel. The poet's self is in quest of an ideal which is neither found in the past nor in the present, the hope lies only in the future.

"But who can say
there shall be no more
Discovery of cities fresh as brides
Bright legends of a recent birth
New orchids and unimagined seas?"

(*A Time to Change,* 48)

Poetry or poetic truth helps him to sympathize with the inconsistencies between his compulsive urge for redemption and his intense passion for the world. Ezekiel's quest for such identification is a sort of cyclical journey from oneself through the world of realities to one's ownself.

In fact the poetic self of Ezekiel moves between the two extremes of "Introspection-contemplation" and "the outward active." His poetry is the record of self's confrontation with the tension between the opposites, an emotional involvement in life and a desire for detachment from it. He tries to juxtapose poetry, art and life with a view to bringing about harmony between the inner life and the outer world. He tries to use poetic art as a means to get most of the sense of alienation. In his poem, 'Poetry' he writes:

"It is why
The how, the what, the flow
From which a poem comes,
In which the savage and the singulars
The gentle, familiar
Are all dissolved, the residue
Is what you read, as a poem..." (236).

The self of the poet is desirous of associating itself with whatever is pure in the lives of the great, and evolving a right idiom. He yearns to have an inward eye by establishing kinship with the elemental symbols of life in order to work into reality of things.

Self-exploration is very much evident in 'London'. It seems that the persona is searching and probing the innermost recesses of his self. His personal quest goes on relentlessly. Linda Hess finds that Ezekiel is "an endless explorer of the labyrinths of the mind, the devious delving and twisting of the ego, the ceaseless attempt of man and poet to define to find, through all the myth and maze, a way to honesty and love...."(31). The tension between the self and the poet's other self provides the inspiration, as in 'Advise to a Painter' the self urges the other self towards creation of its world,

"Do not be satisfied with the world that
God created create your own
Be voracious with your eyes and appetites
The will to see, the passion in the act of love
Or learning lead to brighter prospects
In landscape, still life nude, abstracts
And also higher prices" (205).

Self is a mystery for him which he tries to unravel to come face to face with. He shifts his thoughts and emotions, dissects them and looks at his experience from various angles. He tries to find a path in the conflicting maze of emotions and desires in order to understand his self.

In fact his poetic self struggles for the recovery of the vision. But he also believes that ignorance of ordinary existence or the lower world will not help a man to understand the higher world. He, therefore, stresses the need of commitment, sincerity and integrity as essential conditions for the completeness of a poet. Ezekiel exemplifies this in his poem 'Enterprise' in which the pilgrims face the paradox due to the want of commitment, sincerity and integrity. The pilgrims, towards the end of their pilgrimage, discover to their dismay their destination. The center of vision is as unacceptable as the city from which they try to run away. In the last line of the poem Ezekiel points out with conviction that the grace of fulfillment consists in the identification of the self with the object of the world and transmutation of "the passion of the blood" into human good. This is the evolution of Ezekiel's poetic self. He develops a belief that the commitment of poetic self to the 'script of universal theatre' will result in the right interpretation of 'the sense of transparent existence.' The central metaphor of his poems pertains to journey, departure and sea voyage. His poetry embodies the experience of a man who travels widely to unknown lands to bring back primal knowledge.

In his poems Ezekiel 'exposes' people's, especially his countrymen's, follies, foibles, weaknesses and deficiencies. The weaknesses he exposes include their sticking to superstitions, not being able to tackle problems efficiently. In his poem *India* he writes:

"Always is the sun's eye
Here among the beggars
Hawkers, pavement sleepers,
Hutmen dwellers, slums
Dead souls of men and gods.
Burnt out mothers, frightened
Virgins, wasted child
And tortured animal
All in noisy silence
Suffering the place and time...."(31)

When he talks of 'burnt out mothers', he may be referring to the cruel incident of burning widows or brides for not having brought with themselves from their parents as much dowry as the in-laws expected, when he talks of frightened virgins he may be referring to the incident of eve-teasing and outraging the modesty of girls.

He has also exposed the altruism. He exposes in his poem 'the truth about the floods' in which he ridicules some students for their pretending to be engaged in providing relief in a flood-affected area and highlights the fact that they are interested in propagating that they are doing relief-work rather than in actually providing relief. The poet shows all this in the following stanza of the poem:

"Don't make a noise
Said the student
Sit down in a circle.
The villagers sat down in a circle.
They did not say another word.
The transistor was on,
The biscuits were distributed,
The camera clicked
Then the student left
Humming the tune
Of a popular Hindi film song...."(20)

Ezekiel also attacks government officials and shows them to be totally alienated from the masses of the country. He does this too in the poem 'The Truth about the Floods' in which he shows that the flood affected people are so disgusted with the government officials that they do not want even to talk to them. He does so while narrating the personal experiences in a flood affected area where people do not talk to him until they are told that he is not a government official as he says:

"I arrived at Arde
But the villagers would not talk to me
Till I told them I was not government official...." (21)

The attitude of Ezekiel is that of a highly educated, cultured and polished man not belonging to any extreme of society, but as part of the social milieu, as a whole. From the fallen out subhuman level of individual and social set-up, the poetic self of Ezekiel takes flight in order to achieve balance and harmony. The central metaphor of his poems pertains to journey, departure and sea voyage. His poetry embodies the experience of a man who travels widely to unknown lands to bring back primal knowledge.

In Ezekiel's poetry life is gloomy but not hopeless. In fact he is a sensitive man, overwhelmed by the innumerable contradictions in life. But Ezekiel does not lose his faith in mankind. Ezekiel sings in "A Psalms of David":

"Deliver me, o my god, out of the hands of the wicked,
out of the hands of the unrighteous and cruel men" (28).

He suggested to the people that they should go back to the wisdom, enshrined in their own cultural heritage rather than run after modern European ideologies. He wants to bring about radical changes in people's views and ways. He says in "Subject of Change":

"Not a stone in the edifice
Well loved, is likely to suffice
Everything calls for a new place
A different rage behind my face...."

Like P.B. Shelley, Ezekiel's self is desirous of associating itself with whatever is pure in the lives of the great. He yearns to have an inward eye by establishing kinship with the elemental symbols of life in order to look into the reality of things. For this he aspires to dissolve his microcosmic self in the macrocosmic universe. He is of the view that the development of individual consciousness, moral and spiritual motivation of all human action can alone salvage the "fallen world" as in the poem *The Patriot* he says, "One day Ram Rajya is surely coming..." (237).

WORKS CITED

Ezekiel, Nissim. *Collected Poems*. New Delhi: Oxford University Press, 1989.

Hess, Linda. "Post Independence Indian Poetry." *Quest*, No. 49, 1960.

31

Cross-Cultural Dilemma in Bharati Mukherjee's *Desirable Daughters*

Beena Agarwal

Bharati Mukherjee with her peculiar sensibility for the cross-cultural crisis in the era of globalisation, endeavoured to dive deep into the distorted psyche of those immigrants who had been surviving in the conflict of traditional Indian values, inherent in their personality and their fascination for Western mode of living that they had chosen out of their professional compulsions or for their urge to achieve a greater freedom in liberal and dynamic society of America. In her personal life Bharati Mukherjee witnessed the anguish of Indians both as expatriates and immigrants but in both the conditions, Indian life, Indian values, dignity of rituals, the fidelity to traditions, the grace of human relations, social and religious mode of human existence constantly stirred her imagination and moulded her creative sensibility. The defence of Indian cultural ethos is neither a sentimental quest in her life nor it is a photographic representation made by an "outsider." It is endowed with deep emotional and psychological significance. It renders her vision a rare humanitarian quality and universal appeal. In one of the interviews to Alison B. Crab, she categorically points out:

> "I was born into a Hindu Bengali Brahamin family which means, I have a different sense of self of existence and of mortality than do writers like Malamud. I believe that our souls can be reborn in another body, so the perspective I

have about a single character's life is different from that of an American writer who believes that he has only one life" (Interview Crab).

The affinity to Indian soil and culture is rooted in the mental map of Bharati Mukherjee. Hence her approach to life and its problems is moored in her Indian upbringing. To quote Maya Manju Sharma:

> "In her fiction Mukherjee handles western themes and settings as well as characters who are westernised or bicultural. Yet she is forced to admit that the very structure of her imagination is essentially Hindu and essentially moral" (18).

However, the critics like Mala Shree Lal still express their aversion to the Indian sensibility scattered in the novels of Bharati Mukherjee and consider her only an "outsider", over-reacting to her native Indian tradition of typical Bengali origin. Mala Shree Lal's argument is:

> "Mukherjee has deliberately problematised her identity perhaps overreacting to the likelihood of being enclosed in a coterie culturally, geographically and ideologically separate from her chosen home and citizenship. One must allege here that her sense of Indianness is narrow, restrictive, somewhat bigoted for no writer is characterised by his or her passport details what is the literary material to which imagination is super-imposed" (57-58).

Bharati Mukherjee through her female protagonists expresses her concern for the problem of assimilation, the assimilation of traditional Indian mode of living with new materialistic values encouraged by American society. Fear, constant anxiety, the obsession of 'not belonging', the panic of crime world and the final retreat to Indian spiritualism is the recurrent motif in the novels like *Jasmine, The Tiger's Daughter, Wife* and *Desirable Daughters.* Commenting on this aspect in the novels of Bharati Mukherjee, Pushpa N. Parekh comments:

> "Fear, anger, pain, bitterness, confusion, silence, irony, humour as well as pathos underline her observations as she discovers for herself the undefined median between the

preservation of old world and the assimilation into the new one" (197-211).

The novel *Desirable Daughters* (2000) is a novel with complex ideologies revolving round the life of three sisters—Padma, Parvati and Tara. All of them maintain distinctive individuality in their attitude and approach to life. The novel begins with the description of bridal procession of Tara Lata, an ancestor whose life history becomes a focal point of Tara Chatterjee's family chronicle. Tara Lata, a child bride, faced the greatest misfortune because on her wedding day the groom had died from snakebite. Tara Lata's father, Jaikrishna Gangooly decided to marry his daughter to a tree to avoid the social curse and social humiliation of being a widow. Married to a tree, she will at least "remain a wife, a wearer of vermilion powder in her hair part and not a widow" (15).

Tara Chatterjee, the narrator, had always treated the story with a distant dread and it is after divorce from her husband, Bishwapriya Chatterjee, she became curious to know about the trauma of tree bride.

The progress of the narrative in the novel is not linear but circular. Tara, through the life of her other two sisters Parvati and Padama, her husband Bish, her illegitimate nephew Mr. Christopher Dey, introspects on her own crisis of identity as an immigrant and she continually expresses her desire to seek a consolation in her native traditions. Tara and her sisters spent their childhood in Calcutta—their affluent background of Calcutta *Bhadralok* that was a privilege to "share a tradition of leadership, of sensitivity, of achievement, refinement, and beauty that was the envy of the world" (22). The three sisters for their exceptional accomplishments were featured on the annual "Miss Brains and Beauty" cover of Eve's Weekly (22). Padma, the eldest, was a lady of progressive vision and charming personality. Parvati, the second, preferred to live in Bombay with her husband. Tara and Padma moved to modernist society of America. Tara at the age of nineteen was married to a software engineer from an outstanding Bengali family. After her marriage Tara was shifted to American society, viz. Atherton California where her husband Bish tried to carve out a semblance of Indian traditionalism. The traditional upbringing of Tara was absolutely unpalatable and unamusing to westernised American society. Through the introspection and interactions of Tara, Bharati Mukherjee constantly juxtaposes the images of Tara's adolescent life with her impressions of a liberated society. The nostalgia of Tara for her past, her protective existence in India, her helplessness to assimilate in the glamorous life of USA has become a voice of all those immigrants who lead a life of 'subaltern' in the highly mechanical, progressive and prosperous society of America. In his review of *Desirable Daughters,* Jopi Nyman comments:

> "Bharati Mukherjee's fictions rewrite the traditional immigrant story, imagining new spaces and forms of identity as a result of travel and dislocation" (53-56).

In the beginning of the novel, we get the impression of Tara's arrogance in her revelation of her own legacy of "Calcutta high society." However, her life changes after her shift to California. She was expected to make remarkable changes in her habits and manners. As a good housewife, she could not utter the name of her husband but she was compelled to call him "Bishu." In spite of the fascination of Upper Height in San Franscisco, she is reminded of mountain resorts in India, "I almost expect the chattering of monkeys, corn and peanuts, smoking on open braziers, the tinkling of women's bangles and Buddhist prayer wheels" (24). In her parental home in Calcutta, inspite of higher education and refined manners, Tara observed all the norms of social order postulated by women of typical Bengali origin. Tara expresses her aversion for the westernized manners of her elder sister who used to have uncertain liaisons with one of the Christians, known as Ronald Dey. The sudden appearance of Christopher Dey and his claim of relationship with her elder sister Padma compels her to evaluate the situation. Bharati Mukherjee in order to expose sanctity of family relationships in India refers to typical Indian titles. Christopher Dey addresses to Tara as "Auntie." To make it more precise, Tara asks, "I mean to your pishi, not mashi." Tara is all the time conscious about the distinction between Indian values and American traditions. Tara retrospects to evaluate the life of Padma who used to maintain a living that might have been relevant to American society but not conducive to India:

> "In India, we didn't have outside influences like the media, or lax schooling, or cars and dating and drugs. We didn't know family breakdown. Our families existed inside an impenetrable bubble. Anyone entering or existing was carefully monitored. We honoured the proprieties. There was no rebellion, no seeking after individual identity" (43-44).

With the appearance of Chris, doubt grips the mind of Tara regarding the identity of Chris and the real relationship of Chris and Padma didi. Tara's over sensitiveness to the suffering of Chris is suggestive of the sympathy for human relationship. In order to discover the real secret of Chris' birth, she rings to Parvati who lives in Bombay with her husband Aurbindo Basu. Tara feels that Parvati maintains harmony in her relations living in India. In making a reference to Aurbindo's eating habits, Tara makes a reference to Indian dishes like "Mishti doi," "raabri," "rasamalai" and "chom-chom" from Calcutta. She pays tribute to the village deity, "Shitala", the goddess of small pox and malaria. She prefers that Rabi should call her "Ma." To her "Ma" and "Babu" sound better than "Mummy" and "Daddy". Tara has divorced Bish but she fears that this rumour should not be spread in India otherwise it might bring disgrace to the family. Besides, inspite of her separation from Bish, she never detains Rabi to meet Bish because she is still confident that marriage is certainly an unbreakable tie. Tara fails to assimilate the American society and Calcutta with its distinctive culture and the nostalgia of Bengali tradition constantly haunts her. When Tara comes to India, stays with Parvati, Auro criticises their savagery as being westernised Americans. To Auro Rabi seemed a savage "a trust fund American savage" and he advises Tara to come back to India and to look after old parents, "Our parents are getting old and weak and your child isn't American or Indian and if you stay there any longer, you won't be either" (66). Bharati Mukherjee asserts that in the process of assimilation, man seems to lose his meaning and purpose in life. In the process of migration, the immigrants can neither adopt alien culture nor can leave their culture of 'home' and finally a new hybrid culture comes to flourish. To quote Bil Ashcroft:

> "Post colonial culture is inevitably a hybrid phenomenon involving a dialectical relationship between the grafted European cultural systems and an indigenous ontology with its impulse to create or recreate an independent local identity. Such construction or reconstruction occurs as a dynamic interaction between European hegemonic and 'peripheral' subversion of them" (195).

In America Tara could imagine any number of Atherton families, Bish's friends, coming here for weekend, flooding the courts and riding paths but Tara could never imagine Bish enjoying these situations. Tara always feels herself guilty of lavish spending and conspicuous luxury, "I'm feeling just a little alien and uncomfortable, a tinge of not belonging, in the midst of such welcoming comfort and I think it must be the way Bish feels" (75). This loneliness brings a greater isolation in the life of Tara and she feels herself alienated in American society. In India the details of religion, caste, subcaste, mother tongue, place of birth are all integral part of man's personality and one can't dare to go beyond them. Tara confesses:

> "Nobody pays attention to me other than to ask for spare change or press a handbill into my closed fist. I am not the only blue-jeaned woman with a Pashmina shawl around my shoulders and broken-down running shoes on my feet. I am not the only Indian on the block. All the same, I stand out, I'm convinced. I don't belong here, despite my political learnings; worse, I don't want to belong" (79).

She terribly suffers for her separation from Bish because the concept of divorce is not acceptable, according to Indian code of matrimony. She left Bish because the promise of life as an American wife was not being fulfilled. When the relationship between Bish and Tara becomes intolerable, she comes to a bitter realisation, "In America, it seemed to us, every woman was expected to create her own scandal, be the centre of her own tangled love nest" (83).

Bharati Mukherjee seems to establish that India is a land of spiritual values, stability, variety of languages and tradition that American society would never be able to appreciate. When someone refers to Nafisa's mother who also speaks Hindustani, though in a different dialect, Tara is irritated, "Nafisa's mother and I don't speak the same dialect. We don't even speak the same language. I am tired of explaining India to Americans. I am sick of feeling an alien" (87). In personal life, Tara is torn between two extremes. On the one hand Padma took it as a shame to reveal her divorce in India but now she (Padma) is disowning her own child (Christopher). She advises Tara to model her life on the pattern of Sita, Savitri, the virtuous wives of Hindu myths.

Bharati Mukherjee through the nostalgia of Tara, significantly exposes the loss of spiritual values in the materialistic glamour of the west. Tara is anxious regarding the proper education of her son Rabi that may be close to typical Bengali tradition. The concept of American education was all illusion to her. She has a firm conviction:

> "Existence was too easy in Atherton, they agreed, America made children soft in the brain as well as the body; it weakened the moral fiber. They grew up without respect for family and tradition" (154).

Padma, inspite of her immigration and dynamic attitude to life, only devotes herself to the popularity of Bengali life and culture. Padma, digging the layers of her past, concludes that a true Bengali family can't even be fully westernised, "Our family's 'Westernisation' was superficial, confined to convent school, Metro Cinema and movie magazines which overlaid a profound and orthodox Hinduism" (178). No doubt Padma poured out her bitterness of the situation when she was given the offer of acting in the movie of Satyajit Ray. However Padma, whose utterance was couched in hatred for those times and for the family and for the city, was still trying to lead a traditional Bengali life in New Jersey. Now she has joined Saturday Morning Bengali telecast. Bharati Mukherjee not only highlights the longing of immigrants for Indian cultural heritage but also expresses her disgust at the changing scenario within India itself. In both the situations, the sense of loss is intense. Tara during her conversation with Padma expresses her sense of loss at westernised India and all pervasive cultural pollution. If she is disgusted with materialism of the West, equally disgusting is the scene in India:

> "I don't want to be a perfectly preserved bug trapped in amber, Didi. I can't deal with modern India, it's changed too much and too fast, and I don't want to live in a half-India kept on life support" (184).

Tara feels a consolation at Jackson Heights that is the commercial centre of Indian life in America. She appreciates life at Jackson Heights because, "side-walks full of Indians, every face is Indian, every shop and storefront features Indian jewelry, Indian clothing, Indian travel, Indian food and spices, Indian sweets and restaurants. The smells and the noises are familiar" (199) and she finds everything intoxicating. The anguish is conspicuous that in an immigration one has to make a choice between one's own culture and the temptation of money. She admits that most of the "Immigrant Community" comes with a zeal for money. She admits, "Jackson Height is a landscape of potentialities that had been denied in India" (200). Against the filth of materialistic passion, Bharati Mukherjee glorifies Indian moral values, dress codes, jewelry, religious books and stable human relations. Tara quotes the words of Brother Anthony, a Goan, "Bengalis understand the soul" (216). She considers high tech craze of Indians a profane activity that encourages migration along with the passion for drug smuggling and cyber crimes. In lieu of money, people are leading life in insecurity and dissatisfaction. "I know that money makes an enormous difference. But right now, all the money in the world isn't buying me even simple security" (233). Tara finds that Bish's complete identification with American style is better option than her uncompromising longing for her cultural roots. Though Bish fails to maintain his fidelity to his household, there is no doubt in his convictions and finally he emerges as an image of perfection, "He had failed in his *dharma*, the basic duty of a man in the householder phase of his life, to support and sustain his marriage" (265). In fact the separation between Bish and Tara was also the result of the failure of cultural assimilation. When there was discussion between Bish and Tara towards their attempt to reconcile, to reunite family, Bish argues that they share the same values, they have come from the same place, share the same food, same language, there can't be a question of loneliness. Tara confesses, "He would not permit collective guilt. Marriage is man's manifest dharma, his test, his duty, the outer sign of his inner strength and harmony" (266). As soon as the news spreads that Tara's house has been attacked by powerful explosive, the nervousness and anxiety of Bish is beyond measures. Between the early morning bombing and the beginning of Rabi's Christmas vacation, Tara stayed with Bish. In her personal touch the intimacy becomes closer between the two. Tara retreats into past and intends to build her present on the foundation of past but Bish has no willingness to spoil the beauty of present on the grounds of past. Finally, Tara decides to come back to India to reinvestigate the story of Tara Lata (Tree Bride). She visits her sister Parvati, enquires about friends and relatives and expresses her longing to support her parents in their old age. She confesses:

> "I've come back to India this time for something more than rest and shopping and these gin-and-lime filled evenings with my mirror-self. I'm like a pilgrim following the course of the Ganges all the way to its source" (289).

In the later part of the novel, Bharati Mukherjee presents an elaborate account of the pious atmosphere of Rishikesh and the banks of the Ganges. She supports her parents and finds an exceptional peace of mind in those mountain ranges. The teachings of Swami Radhakrishnan, Vivekananda, the glory of Goddess Kali seem to transport her in a world where life is pious and pure beyond all fears and doubts. In contrast to the spiritual satisfaction in the company of her parents, she finds materialistic passion waste and futile. She evaluates the meaning of the word Bish, "...the harsh poison of the bomb is not, in the eye of God, any more tragic than the poisonous maya of attachment to making money. Bish's nickname is cosmic pun waiting for a punch line (304).

WORKS CITED

Ashcroft, Bill, Gureth Griffiths and Helen Tiffin. *The Empire Writes Back*. London: Routledge, 1989.

Crab, Alison B. "An Interview with Bharati Mukherjee." *The Massachusetts Review*, Winter 1988-89.

Lal, Mala Shree and Bharati Mukherjee. "The Maximalist Credo." K.N. Awasthi (ed.), *Contemporary Indian English Fiction* : *Anthology of Essays*. New Delhi: ABS Publications, 1993.

Mukherjee, Bharati. *Desirable Daughters*. New Delhi: Rupa & Co., 2003. All subsequent references in the text are cited from the same edition.

Nyman, Jopi. "Transitional Travel in Bharati Mukherjee's *Desirable Daughters*." *The Atlantic Literary Review*, Vol. 3, No. 4, Oct.-Dec., 2004.

Parekh, Pushpa N. "Telling Her Tale: Narrative Voice and Gender Roles in Bharati Mukherjee's *Jasmine*." Emmanuel S. Nelson, *Bharati Mukherjee: Critical Perspectives*. New York: Garland Publishing.

Sharma, Maya Manju. "The Inner World of Bharati Mukherjee from Expatriate to Immigrant." Emmauel S. Nelson, *Bharati Mukerjee: Critical Perspectives*. New York: Garland Publishing.

32

Social Realism in Arun Joshi's *The Foreigner*

B.C. Pandey

Arun Joshi (1939-93), whose oeuvre consists of five novels and one collection of short stories, was educated in the West like many other Indian English writers. His American sojourn laid the foundation of the search for roots and identity as well as the existential vision which dominates his writings. One can witness in his writings influences such as of the *Upanishads*, *Vedanta* and the *Bhagvad Gita*, on the one hand; and Albert Camus, Sartre, Kierkegaard, Karl Jesper etc. on the other. Joshi himself acknowledges the influence of Sartre and Camus, whereas he could not understand Kierkegaard "anything except odd statements." Joshi's existential outlook has resulted in the dominant theme of alienation and search for identity in his novels. No doubt, the novels of Arun Joshi do not belong to the realistic tradition proper. However, the fact remains that Joshi covers the bare bones of his stories with details of historical and social setting. The agonised identity quest of the protagonist finds expression through realistic details.

Arun Joshi made his debut as a novelist with his seminal novel *The Foreigner* in 1968. The novel has cross-cultural setting as it is partly based on his experiences in America. Joshi himself admits that some parts of the novel "were written when I was a student in America. I gave it up then and completed it later in 1966." Thus the novel has two countries, viz. India and America in the background. Similarly, there are mainly two classes of the Indian society—the upper business class and the lower worker class—that dominate the story. The attempt to study historical and social realism in no way runs counter to the study of the mental recesses of Sindi Oberoi, the narrator hero, rather it aims at having a better glimpse of his quest.

The existential issues got limelighted against the backdrop of the two World Wars. Joshi reflects this historical reality through the reaction of Karl, a European student friend of Sindi. Karl is so deeply oppressed by the agonies of war that he bitterly criticises the Gandhian philosophy of non-violence and non-cooperation as well as the Indian faith in religion. He reacts:

> "The trouble with you is you have never known war. If you were bombed every night for a year, why, even a month, I would like to see how many of you would still go around, preaching the Bhagwad Gita" (67).

Sindi, as an uprooted young man, does not represent any particular class, culture, country or ethnicity. He is born in Kenya, educated in London and America and ultimately returns to India where he finally settles down. His father was a rationalist Hindu and mother a Christian. Both of them died in an accident when Sindi was just an infant and left him with a deep sense of parental void. He is never at ease when he is asked to introduce himself. He does not like June's queries about his roots: "That just about spoiled everything. I wished she hadn't asked that question. Everybody always asked the same silly question" (22). Joshi deliberately gives this cosmopolitan look to Sindi who defines himself as an "uprooted young-man living in the latter half of the twentieth century who had become detached from everything except himself" (164). Hence he feels a foreigner everywhere.

Joshi shows meticulous craftsmanship of a poet whenever he finds an opportunity of describing nature. His fascination for beauty of nature of America can be seen in descriptions like: "The roads were covered with ankle-deep snow and it was still falling in thick heavy flakes like a horde of parachuting angles" (80), or through scenes depicting the mental state of the narrator hero, Sindi, "The pathlessness of the bone-white road was sad and beautiful. Huge trucks passed us periodically, looking like bright-eyed ghosts" (81). Narrating the bewitching beauties of New England Beach, Sindi tells that he forgets his loneliness and detachment whenever he visits the beach. He is filled with a sense of fulfilment and admits that "The sea struck me with humility" (66). Sindi finds even the autumns in America very beautiful as compared to Indian autumns which are quite unpleasant. Sindi becomes highly poetical when totally absorbed in the beauties of nature:

> "But far beyond all this, far beyond the reach of man's greed, the autumn sun went down in majestic splendour. A gigantic golden fleece stretched across the horizon from one end to the other. Mauve tufts of cloud crowded along its middle, and beneath it the sky was green. For a long while we stood there watching the blazing ball and its surrounding brightness fall from the air" (57).

Apart from the poetic beauties what shows Joshi's craftsmanship here is the skill with which he contrasts the beauty of nature with man's greed and materialism. Joshi is particularly nostalgic about the spring season in America with all its vigour and festivity. There is great enthusiasm all around to welcome the season. People discard inter clothes and enjoy the pleasant weather: "Everybody wanted you to be gay and happy. Whatever griefs you may have had in your private universe, spring in America ruthlessly extracted its toll of gaiety" (109).

Joshi's imagination is arrested not only by the beauty of nature but also by human activities. He often surveys the lore of humanity in its multiple colours. The novel presents the typical scenes in private and public places, which is one of the interesting features of realism. Sindi recalls how once on his way to his apartment he took the subway where the air is generally dirty in the dark cavern, but it being spring season, there was fresh and fragrant air all around as the herald of the season. Similarly, Joshi often gives descriptions of public places like Radio City Hall, where children can often be seen enjoying a film:

> "It was a Walt Disney movie and the hall was full of children. The movie was about a boy and his dog. The dog could read and play an accordion. He was a great delight for the children, stirring up lively little melodies every five minutes. I sat ensconced between two little girls who sat sedately, dangling their legs below them. Each had a huge box of popcorn in her lap as if she expected to be locked up in Radio City Hall for the rest of her life. They smiled self-consciously at me and occasionally passed objects to each other" (155).

Similarly, we come across a live description of the roadside hotels in America. Sindi describes roadside America as—"bright, clear, and lonely as a heap of stainless steel" (81) where the "waitress ambled up leisurely to take our order. She was a plump little girl with pitch black hair and hands like two pink fish in the pockets of her waterproof apron" (81). Joshi refers to the typical American style of parting with strangers "promising to meet again, knowing full well they didn't mean it" (23). Similarly, he also mentions the liberty and freedom allowed to women in American society. Their dress and hair style being like boys made it very difficult for foreigners, specially Indians, to differentiate them from boys.

During his stay in America, Joshi not only pursued his studies but also had an in-depth study of the American social, cultural and educational system. His experiences as a foreign student there gave him a clear idea about the problems and prospects of foreign students. The novel shows two categories of foreign students: one, who adjust themselves to the educational and social system of America and are quiet successful there. Sindi Oberoi represents this class. The second category consists of students like Babu who live in the world of their own illusions and fail to understand the harsh realities of life which results in both academic and mental disaster as happens with Babu also. Through Babu we get a clear picture of the American education system which is quite different from the Indian system. Many Indian students fail to cope with the changed situation as the American system has a periodical assessment and grading system requiring the students to pass all the tests failing which they have to go. Babu, who is used to the Indian system, fails to acclematize with the new situation. Sindi bails him out in the first instance but when he fails to clear the examination the second time, Babu is expelled by the university. The problem of Babu is not his personal one but common to many foreign students as well. So reacts Sindi: "It is especially difficult when you are not used to the system. I have seen a lot of foreign students have the same trouble" (94). For such students there are many government and social organizations working in America as to make them feel at home. Sindi himself hosts such parties as a part-time agent of one such government agency. Ironically, he is quite critical of such parties because he finds them failing in their purpose:

> "Yet, something about it—a feeling that it was a bit of a charity or something—rubbed people the wrong way. It is one thing to be invited to somebody's house for a party, quite another to go to a public hall, buy a ticket and then search the place for a girl you can dance with. I hated it. I never went to those things except as an ex-officio host" (21-22).

However, such parties do not mean that the Americans are free from any prejudice or ill-feeling for the foreigners. Mrs. Blyth, June's mother, is a typical American who leaves no chance of highlighting Indian poverty and laughing at them. The collection of slides of her package trip around the world includes some slides portraying the poverty and squalour of Indians which she shows to each visitor. She dislikes Hindus for their idol worship. She tells her daughter that Indians being very poor need good diet: "You wouldn't believe, June, how small they are, she said. About the size of sixth-grader. And they die at about thirty-two" (88). Sindi has quite an objective view about apartheid and he accepts it as a reality: "I was born an Indian and had been spat upon; had I been a European, I would have done the spitting. What difference did it make?" (26).

Joshi very carefully charts the social system of America through various anecdotes. As compared to Indians the Americans are very busy people and they do not encourage unnecessary discussion. Babu is at a loss to understand this particular habit of Americans. He complains that "the people on the street" are "damn uninterested. The moment they find out you have nothing particular in mind they excuse themselves and get away" (19). Joshi links the progress and prosperity of the Americans with their perseverance. He demonstrates how a menial worker like a truck driver wants to contribute to the economic progress of the country. Sindi narrates how in a dark snowy night near Boston a truck driver, who has not slept for two days, is determined to reach New York in time lest his contractor should lose his contract. However, Joshi does not forget to suggest that the Americans have been trapped by a blind chase for money. Sindi laments: "I wanted to take his hand and tell him to hell with the Christmas goodies. New York could live without them" (82). He further adds:

> "There was something wrong about a man having to drive hundreds of miles in blinding snow when he hadn't seen a bed for two days. He probably made a lot of money in the process, but still it didn't seem right" (83).

Joshi often draws our attention towards the hollowness of the American life and shows how the Americans who feel proud of the Statue of Liberty are enslaved by materialism, always searching for "wrong things in wrong places" (83). It all leads to Prufrock like mental sterility. Sindi tells June that Americans find mental disorder behind every illness like every song in rock'n roll.

In their reckless chase for money Joshi does not find the upper class Indians different from the Americans. Through the character of Mr. Khemka, an unscrupulous tax evader, Joshi expresses his disapproval of this hunt for money. So we find Sindi voicing his gloom: "In truth it had only been a change of theatre from America: the show had remained unchanged" (174). Sindi finds himself totally alienated and uprooted for two reasons: first, because he personally does not belong to any particular culture or country; and secondly, because he has been brought up in the western culture which he finds rootless. He tells Mr. Khemka that he does not mind being called immoral because:

> "You had a clear-cut system of morality, a caste system that laid down all you had to do. You had a God; you had roots in the soil you lived upon. Look at me. I have no system of morality. What does it mean to me if you call me an immoral man. I have no reason to be one thing or another. You ask me why I am not ambitious: well, I have no reason to be. Come to of it I don't even have a reason to live!" (118).

Joshi had very close relations with the business tycoons in India. After getting Master's degree in Industrial Management from Massachussets Institute of Technology, U.S.A. in 1960, he joined. D.C.M. in 1962 in managerial capacity. On the basis of his first hand experience of the working of the industrial houses he gives his readers a glimpse of the untold stories behind their success. We find a very grim picture of our industry as represented by Mr. Khemka. Sindi is shocked to see the servility of Mr. Khemka's employees. They cringed before Mr. Khemka and his daughter as if they "were malevolent spirits whose curse would be all-consuming" (15). Sindi, who never before did have any such experience, feels quite disgusted with this sort of relationship.

Joshi gives a very minute and detailed description of Mr. Khemka's house. The second chapter of the novel is all about Mr. Khemka's house and his office. The house has a magnificent lawn contrasting beautifully with the red gravel of the drive. The single storeyed palatial house has air-conditioned rooms, plush Persian carpets, rosewood furniture and every luxury available worldwide:

> "I looked at the empty glass in my hand and then at the richness of Mr. Khemka's drawing room. This was no doubt India's affluent society. Plush carpets, low streamlined divans, invisible lighting, bell buttons in every corner, and sculpture. That is where Babu must have played as a child.

> The rich Persian carpets, those sculpture-ridden walls must have concocted the innocence that destroyed him and very nearly buried me" (12).

Sindi is welcomed in the house by Shiela with whiskey though Sindi wants water. What one should remember here is that the novel portrays India not of today but about forty years ago when the standard of living was cooperatively quite low. Joshi highlights the pomp and show with which these rich people arrange social parties. During the drinks and gorgeous dinners they only talk about making more money without any concern for the poor. They always want to suggest that they can buy the whole world. Sindi is disgusted to find that despite all legislative efforts towards socialism, only the rich are prospering:

> "They left the impression that they could buy up anybody they wanted. Perhaps they could, but it all sounded meaningless to me. I had read much of inequality in India; now I could see it masquerade as company law and the amendments of Parliament" (16).

In contrast to his house the office of Mr. Khemka is quite ordinary. It is a "cramped little place, much too small for his growing empire" (15). Actually the small size and ordinary look of the office is part of Mr. Khemka's gimmick to evade tax. There are detailed descriptions of this corrupt practice of the rich but the readers are consoled to find that Mr. Khemka's empire ultimately crumbles down as a result of this fraud. However, Joshi very intelligently detracts the efficiency of the Income Tax Department by suggesting that the action against Mr. Khemka is partly because of Mr. Ghosh who was Mr. Khemka's employee and who after being sacked joined the Income Tax Department. Sindi initially being kept in dark about the fictitious accounts and later shamelessly being expected to shoulder the responsibility of the crime when finally proved, clearly vindicates how unscrupulous these business tycoons are. Sindi rightly calls Mr. Khemka a jackal. Utterly disgusted, he thinks that all old men of Mr. Khemka's age "kept two books like Mr. Khemka" (175). To his dismay, Sindi is told by Mr. Khemka that what he did was not wrong "because everybody does it. You can't run a business these days without doing these things" (178). Khemka is so confident of his money power that he tells Sindi that it is not possible to get him. Ironically, it is these upper class people who look down at the poor. Mr. Khemka warns Sindi against mixing up with the lower class people who he believes are not trustworthy. Sindi, on the contrary, believes that it is the rich like Mr. Khemka "who have swindled those miserable wretches in rags" (180), who push carts on their streets and die at twenty-five. Joshi shows a deep concern for the plight of the poor in India. He is greatly moved by the failure of the measures taken towards their upliftment by the government and other agencies. Mr. Ghosh, who himself is a victim of the whims of the rich, is quite optimistic about the process of socialism initiated on Gandhi's appeal after independence. He feels that despite obstacles, like Mr. Khemka, India is heading towards radical changes. But Joshi is aware of the lack of political will-power towards materialization of the Gandhian dream. Sindi tells Mr. Ghosh that "there is no end to suffering, no end to the struggle between good and evil" (39). Socialism, thus, is an illusion, a dream.

The advocates of socialism often use strikes and agitations as tools for turning their dreams into reality. Joshi gives a vivid picture of one such agitation under the banner of "All India Scavengers Union". He emphasises how the union leaders exploit such situations for their own good "searching endlessly for the road to Parliament and then to the Cabinet" (47). The crowds know that they are not going to get jobs yet they enjoy listening to the leaders just for fun.

Joshi's concern for the unprivileged suffering class is discernible also through the sketches he draws of the poor and their surroundings. Babu tells Sindi and June that they have only poor people as their servants. When Sindi personally visits Mr. Khemka's house and office he is shocked to see the plight of the poor. The gardner's child is "hungry looking," and another servant who brings Sindi a glass of water has very thin wrists. Sindi, before he really visits India, fails to digest the slide show at Mrs. Blyth's portraying the poverty, dirt and squalor in the slums near Sealdah. At another place, Joshi gives a live description of activities in one such slum in Delhi:

> "In the slums across the street, bundles of soggy humanity shuffled out of their huts and spread their miserable rags to dry. Full-breasted women, their thighs naked under wet saris, scurried back and forth like animals quarrelling over small bits of tin. Naked children rolled in filthy pools, squealing with delight" (40).

To add, the quality of foodstuff these slum-dwellers cannot but relish is "rotting fruit and gluey sweetmeats" (40). Even the government constructed one-room tenements for low-income group are not different. It goes beyond one's imagination how two families with more than one dozen members can live comfortably in one such room but it really happens with Muthu who finds it "no trouble at all living with so many" (186).

Joshi candidly portrays various aspects of the Indian life. As Sindi welcomes Babu in America his attention is drawn by the non-western look of his otherwise rich suit due to Indian stitching. We are told about Indian gardens with people sitting in groups but no lovers as one can find in the West. Sindi feels that Indians keep on discussing things more than any other people. Mr. Khemka tells Sindi about social contacts being very essential for moving up in India. Also, we are told about how in India every thing ended in seeking money.

Our attention is also drawn towards the population explosion in India. Apart from Muthu's house, we are told about the overcrowded buses and poor condition of roads in Delhi:

> "Bright red buses of the Delhi Transport Undertaking sloshed through the mud splattering pedestrians with grime. In spite of the rain they were full; in India things are always full whatever the circumstances" (40).

One of the interesting features of realistic writing is the description of stock characters. We have several examples of this kind of amusing characters in the novel. The income tax clerk Mr. Ghosh is one such character with his own typical clerical traits, eccentricities and romantic views about socialism. He wants the office of Mr. Khemka to be wound up and given to the proletariat. Sindi feels pity upon his plump figure and describes how easily irritable and short-tempered he is. Then, we have a sketch of a typical *tonga* driver who languidly lingers around passers-by appealing them to hire his *tonga*. Sindi wants to get rid of one such *tonga* driver by offering him a cigarette which he accepts but still tries to persuade him by discussing the problems of the *tonga* drivers unless a policeman intervenes. In Chapter 3, Sindi tells about the old men in the Y.M.C.A. lounge smiling at passers-by and just waiting for death. We have yet another stock character Mrs. Blyth who would seize every opportunity of giving vent to her pride as an American and showing the slides of shots taken during her package trip around the world. We also learn from the novel about the callous neglect and discouraging attitude of the Indian consulate officials in granting visas. Again, we get a picture of the functioning of the income tax department. Mr. Ghosh tells Sindi that there should be no courtesy week because:

> "Election stunt, this courtesy stuff, if you ask-me! All year we kick people's bottoms and then we give them a week of courtesy. Mind you, I am not saying that they don't deserve the kicking, but still I would rather kick them all year than make a fool of them with this courtesy stuff" (37).

Joshi displays a remarkable skill in sketching reality through contrasts. He puts together two diametrically opposite situations or scenes so meticulously that they become a part of the same design as well as limelight the contrast. To cite a few examples, Sindi and Shiela are sitting in a luxurious restaurant Wengers and view through the window a crowd of poor scavengers on the other side of the road waiting for their union leaders. Similarly, the window of Mr. Khemka's office gives a full view of the slum where half-naked humanity lives in a miserable plight. Again, the magnificent lawn of Mr. Khemka has a gardener with a hungry looking child by his side; and the luxurious drawing room of Mr. Khemka has a servant with very thin wrists. Likewise, the hardworking sweating labourers at Khemka's factory earn only two to three rupees a day as compared to Mr. Khemka's earning of rupees three thousand a day. The beautiful description of New England Beach where even Sindi forgets his strangeness and loneliness is disrupted as a "bomber formation flew into the empty spaces" (66) as trouble was brewing in Berlin. Such instances of contrastive reality can be seen at philosophical level as well. Karl does not accept the Gandhian philosophy of non-violence because he has seen war very closely. Similarly, reality for June is possession whereas for Sindi it is detachment. Sindi who has continued his search for meaning in life, fails to get it through his experiences in the abundance of England and America or even in Mr. Khemka's society, but gets it from a pauper. It is Muthu, a poor worker, who has the treasure of knowledge. He as a real *karmayogi* can tell Sindi, "We won't mind working twenty hours a day to keep ourselves in bread" (187). It is Muthu's suffering that causes the sudden illumination dawn upon Sindi that real detachment is action without desire—the message of *Gita*. Now Sindi develops a sense of togetherness with those of Muthu's class. So, Sindi whom we find a foreigner all through the novel, searching for roots and meaning in life, gets a full and final solution from none other than Muthu. He cancels his ticket for Bombay and finds a purpose and meaning in his life which he was altogether missing so far. Thus we find that Joshi's purpose is not only to limelight the alienation and existential problems of the individual but much more than that.

WORK CITED

Joshi, Arun. *The Foreigner*. Delhi: Orient Paperbacks, 1993. All references to the text are from this edition.

33

Nana Saheb in Manohar Malgonkar's Novel *The Devil's Wind*

Vikas Sharma

Manohar Malgonkar's novel *The Devil's Wind* presents a detailed account of the life, rise and fall of Nana Saheb without taking any liberties with verifiable facts or probabilities. It is a serious and sincere effort to tell the story of Nana Saheb, "The heir apparent to the late Peshwa"—from an Indian point of view.

Nana Saheb headed and guided the upsurge at Kanpur. Malgonkar's *The Devil's Wind* depicts in an absorbing way the first Indian struggle for freedom of 1857. The novel narrates in the first person, the story of Nana Saheb, the heir to the late Peshwa Baji Rao II. It concentrates, especially, on the rebellion in Kanpur. It blends beautifully the artist and historian. It is a conscious work of historical documents. As a part of fiction, it is also a painstaking literary work of art. It presents the course of events of the upsurge of 1857. The novel presents the other side of Nana Saheb, completely and carefully distorted by the Britishers, and shows him as one of the able leaders of the revolt. The first two sections of the novel, Bithoor and Kanpur deal exclusively and intensively, with a documented history.

The Britishers, naturally and instinctively, created Nana Saheb to be a monster, ruthless, reckless, violent and inhuman being. They Painted him very subjectively in dark colour distorting his fine character. The black painting of Nana Saheb by the contemporary and the later English historians is the consequence of the failure of the revolution. In every political revolution, the organizers of the revolt are unmistakably dubbed as the conspirators. They are dealt with as the traitors. It is a well-known and commonly accepted fact that nothing succeeds like success. These very "traitors" and "conspirators" would have become liberators and heroes if the revolt they engage themselves had been successful. Obviously, the failure in political revolution is the greatest crime. The mutiny of 1857 failed. Therefore, its heroes ceased the claim to greatness. They did not earn the epithets like the "liberators of the country" or "the heroes of Indian War of Independence." On the same score, the great upheaval remained a mutiny. It could neither be a national movement nor the war of independence. On the contrary, the heroes of this movement were condemned as savages, brutes, barbarians and inhuman. Nana Saheb made visits to the principal centers of revolt in order to give it a definite and proper direction. He visited these centers before the actual outburst of the rebellion. There were well-designed plans to start the Mutiny on May 31, 1857. Nana led the revolutionaries in Kanpur. There is a little wonder that this active and energetic man fell a victim to the ire of the foreign historians. Manohar Malgonkar in *The Devil's Wind* tries to present Nana Saheb from proper perspective. A British Review shows Nana Saheb to be a hard line criminal:

> "Few names are more conspicuous in the annals of crime than that of Nana Saheb who achieved an immortality of infamy by his perfidy and cruelty at Cawnpore" (Author's Note).

Assessing the estimates of Nana's character, Malgonkar shows a French view:

> "A scented Sybarite, who read Balzac, played Chopin on the piano and lolling on a diwan, fanned by exquisite odalisques from cashmere, had a roasted English child brought in occasionally on a pike for him to examine with his pince-nez" (Author's Note).

Manohar Malgonkar takes pains to spotlight the true character of this grievously wronged man in a scholarly way. The foreigners made him emerge as:

> "The arch villain from the so-called Indian Mutiny of 1857-1858" (Author's Note).

He was made "a monster to frighten children with" (Author's Note) Every book written, in anger, in the second part of the preceding century shows the principal villain to be the same:

"Nana Saheb—infamous, dastardly, despicable, crafty demon, barbarous butcher, and arch assassin, Nana. In England he replaced Napoleon Bonaparte as the hate object of a nation" (Author's Note). The Indians did not share this view. In the villages, the ballads extolled Nana Saheb "as a patriot and parents privately warned their children not to believe the history taught in schools. What the British had tried to pass off as a mutiny was, to most Indians, a national uprising for achieving independences" (Author's Note). After independence, "India acclaimed Nana Saheb as a hero and raised a memorial to him, at Bithoor" (Author's Note). Malgonkar tells the story of Nana Saheb from an Indian point of view, yet he never deviates from the facts of history. He claims truth to facts and states:

> "It is fiction; but it takes no liberties with verifiable facts or even with probabilities" (Author's Note).

Nana inherited two major obsessions of Baji Rao—sex and religion. Baji Rao revealed in sex in the hours of darkness. He remained engaged in religion in the hours of light. A Benares priest taught Nana Saheb Sanskrit. He was taught the art of fencing and riding. Tantya Tope, a great name in history, was Nana's fencing master. Tantya was a popular figure. In fencing, he had no rival. He had joined the company's cavalry for six months: "to see for himself what it was that made the British invincible in war, and had come back with the conviction that the British were not invincible" (*The Devil's Wind*, 14). Nana came in contact with a girl named Mani. She, too, went to the riding school and the fencing school. She was Baji Rao's

God-daughter, brought up by the Peshwa to be wedded to Nana Saheb. Mani, later, was given away in marriage to the old and ailing ruler of Jhansi. All these details of the childhood of Nana Saheb are furnished substantially by Malgonkar in *The Devil's Wind.*

Manohar Malgonkar in his novel, *The Devil's Wind*, shows the calculating and well-planned exploitation by the Britishers. The fabulously wealthy kings and the rich landlords were reduced to the impoverished men with no land holding during the company's rule. Nana was forced to live after the death of Baji Rao in 1851, the life of a commoner. All the facial assurances made by the East India Company to Baji Rao proved abortive. The policy of confiscation effected forcefully and meaningfully by Lord Dalhousie had turned India into misery and turmoil. Dalhousie's avarice for annexing states and swelling the treasury is spotlighted in Malgonkar's novel. The Governor General refused to recognise any person as Maharaja Dhondu Pant Nana Saheb. Nana's persistent requests to Dalhousie to grant him titles and privileges were turned down. Dalhousie stated that Nana had no claim to company's charity. Nana's special emissary to England to seek justice, Azini, only found humiliation. He realised to his disgust that: "In England the Parliament was even more powerful than the Monarch and the East India Company far more powerful than the Parliament" (56).

The Britishers justified the annexation on the ground of corruption and misrule by the Indian princes. They also sided with the terrible misery and oppression of the down-trodden masses. Whatever may be their justification, the given statements of Disraeli, Dalhousie and others make it evidently clear that the design behind these annexations was unmistakably imperialistic. Naturally, the Indian princes detested Dalhousie. In the words of Nana Saheb:

> "He had taken the form of an enormous giant who spat fire and gave out blood-curdling honks as he went about swallowing kingdom after kingdom as though they were his natural food" (54).

The annexation of Oudh in early 1856 shocked Nana, as it did every Indian. Nana took it to be a neighbour's house set on fire. Oudh was very close to Kanpur. To Nana, the Dalhousies' of the company were the terrible moon that enters at the time of the lunar eclipse. They were far more dangerous than that of the demons Rahu and Ketu, for they never spared their victim.

Malgonkar's Nana is certainly different from what the Britishers have painted him. He has all the human instincts—love, fears, hopes and desires. He shrank and shuddered at the thought of brutalities. He was brought up as a vegetarian and Brahmin. He respected learning and culture. He "taught to believe that all life—human, animal and even insect life—was part of a great single divinity and therefore sacrosanct" (75).

Thus Nana appears to be a true patriot. He is human and kind. The novel insists on Nana's clarification of his own point of view. Nana at his best in the midst of the crisis of 1857 had appropriated for himself the role of a mediator and a negotiator. He was highly esteemed on both the sides. He felt confident of his voice of reason. He promised to Hillersdon that he would give an advance warning to Wheeler in case of an attack by his men. Malgonkar, through these events, shows the real feelings and emotions of Nana and his times. Nana's offer to Hillersdon bears ample proof of his aspiration. He says, "The three of us—you, Wheeler and I can bring it off, if we make that our principal aim; to Kanpur unaffected" (136). Nana's offer perplexed the Collector. He stated: "I don't understand, you mean just go on pretending nothing is happening in Meerut and Delhi and Fyzabad? How can we?" (136). Nana was sincere in his efforts for surmounting the crisis. Very sincerely, he served as a link between the Indians and the English. Showing the truth that Nana kept his promise given to Wheeler of intimating him beforehand the plan of the Sepoy to attack British colony, the noted historian states: "On June 6th Wheeler received a letter from Nana Saheb telling him that he was to be attacked" (Edward, 54-55).

Malgonkar in *The Devil's Wind* tries persistently and vigorously to give a true picture of Nana Saheb whom the English took to be their arch rival and painted black. The Britishers accused Nana of cruel killings in entrenchment, on the river Ganges in the boats and at other important places. Napoleon Bonaparte was replaced by Dhondu Pant Nana Saheb of Bithoor as the hate object of a large section of the world. The British historians and their stooges recorded the atrocities committed by Nana's men in an amazingly hyperbolic proportion. The barbaric and heinous act perpetuated by the British were widely extenuated in or eliminated from the historical documents. The cruel and monstrous acts committed in Delhi, Lucknow, Kanpur, Bithoor were cunningly and convincingly defended. The English, practically and successfully, banned all mention of evil deeds done by them from the history-books. Malgonkar studies the motivated and highly distorted history from the true Indian perspective. He offers arguments to show the compulsions of the British for making Nana a monster. He holds the view that the common people in their heart of hearts did not believe the history taught in schools and universities.

Malgonkar, thus, rows against the current in a bid to present, what he firmly believes, true facts of history. He absolves Nana of all charges of barbarity, infidelity, unreliability, cruelty and ferocity leveled purposely by the British. To make his points clear, Malgonkar presents convincing arguments. There is no doubt that against the prejudiced and biased history written by the English, Malgonkar offers the Indian point of view. He shows how the British created monster to be kind and sympathetic. Yet, Malgonkar does not deviate from the facts of history. He does not trust and turn historical events to his conveyance and advantage. He claims rightly, truth to all events—even "to their probabilities".

Thus, Malgonkar not only follows history, he also contributes to it positively. History fails to trace Nana after the revolt. Malgonkar, in the third part of the novel, engages in imaginative speculation. But, truly, he presents the historical events with accuracy.

WORKS CITED

Edward, Michel. *Battles of the Indian Mutiny*. London: Pan Books Ltd., 1963.

Malgonkar, Manohar. *The Devil's Wind*. New Delhi: Orient Paper Backs, 1972.

34 The Glimpses of Hindustani Ancient Literature and its Impact on Indian English Literature

Vinay Kumar Pandey

In ancient times the fluorescent Indian Sanatan philosophy was so pervasive that inquisitive Greeks dispatched Megasthenes as ambassador to India during Chandra Gupta Maurya's reign (well before 306 B.C.) to know the hidden treasure of Indian philosophy which had brought peace and prosperity to the Indians. Significantly Megasthenes stayed for a long period at Patliputra (now Patna, the Capital of Bihar). He recorded his reminiscences in the book as under.

> "That the Indians are robust, long-lived, and healthy and they do not take intoxication. They are simple and high intellectuals, Indians never tell a lie. They believe extremely on each other. Indians never lock their houses because there was no occurrence of theft in India."

Following the growth of world civilization, over centuries, intellectuals from other parts of the world continued to evince keen interest in Indian philosophy as evident from the fact that Americans, Europeans and others are even today flocking around Indian *Gurus* in search of peace for their lives which have become highly materialistic and self-centred due to their skewed civilization. Indian philosophers (*Rishis*) perfected the technique of concentration (Meditation) to know the material world (*Ehlok*) and the other world (*Parlok*). They perceived the presence of almighty (*Parmatma*) everywhere and maintained that soul (*Atma*) exists in all the living beings and thus depicted a universal linkage in the nature. This formed the core of Indian wisdom that inspired Sanatan literature for centuries in an uninterrupted manner.

The almighty has bestowed India with wonderful gifts. Nature has been benevolent to India as it has got varied climates, forests, landscapes, rivers, species (including birds and animals), conducive to spiritual growth of human beings.

The Indian philosophers have extrapolated the philosophy of universal linkage for the welfare and love of the entire living beings with the special emphasis on symbiotic relationships with Nature. Significantly, Sanatan prayers are for the goodness of the entire world and welfare of the mankind as well as for the world peace.

Social Approach

For an individual, Sanatan literature stipulated four tight compartmentalized systems for the proper growth of a human being. As per the system one should maintain strict celibacy for twenty-five years to prepare himself for the challenges of life. Thereafter, it stipulated twenty-five years for family life to rear one's offsprings. *Banprastha* is casting away of entire worldly pleasure to attain the ultimate peace and truth that is the almighty.

Indian culture is the oldest culture of the world. It is the combination of many cultures. Sanatan literature talks about the old Indian culture where can be seen the four missions of human beings. India was absolutely developed in *Dharmashastra* (book of theology), economics, *Kamshastra* (art of love-making), *Vyavhar Shastra* (sociology) and *Kalashastra* (fine art). Through this literature, we get the message that human beings should accomplish their spiritual progress in four areas—*Dharma* (religious progress), *Artha* (economical progress), *Kam* (social progress), and *Moksha* (salvation). These are known as four *Purushartha* (total accomplishment of perfection in this life).

Scientific Approach

Sanatan literature is full of scientific background. Strangely, modern scientific discoveries had been well documented in our ancient scriptures which need deciphering a competent scientist having a deep knowledge of our ancient scripture. In the domain of medieval sciences, Sanatan literature has treasure of *Ayurveda* which was a separate *Veda* (Holy Book) devoted to medicinal longevity through its practice.

Human beings have been granted with the key to unlock many of the secrets of life, that key is meditation. Through meditation we can attain eternal bliss and immortality. We should try to get self- confidence, develop independent judgment, cultivate the indomitable will and to practice self-control and mastery overself. One cannot attain freedom of mind or peace without self-control. The individual should try to expel the worldly intoxication of pride, delusion, pain and grief. We should make our mind disciplined, stand adamant under all conditions and at all times, keep a cool and balanced mind to serve the world with redoubled force and energy for human prosperity. May human beings prosper gloriously!

The importance of *Pipal* tree is matchless. *Pipal* is the only tree which exhales oxygen continually. *Pipal* tree helps and protects the society more than a hospital. The air of the *Pipal* tree destroys countless bacteria.

In the same way leaves of *Tulsi* keep the human beings free from diseases. The sound of *Sankh* kills the bacteria. Sun bath is extremely beneficial for human health.

In Indian philosophy maintenance of an individual healthy life over a long period was useful for one's over all spiritual growth. In Indian system one's life was considered with hundred years for this purpose. *Ayurveda* had enough measures and medicines to keep an individual fit and alert for hundred years. Surprisingly, it was more based on ethics, food and daily routine, supported by medicines which Nature yields.

In Indian life philosophy, a sense of harmonious uniformity is found everywhere, the chief reason behind this good feeling is the religious attitude of the Indian *Rishis*. Religious attitude, linked with the welfare and love for living beings, was the main motto of this sacred soil, which gave a complete and continuous uniformity to this country. Our *Rishis* had performed *sadhana* and *prayer* for the well being of the human beings.

Indian Sanatan literature is the writings by Indians since time immemorial, depicting a particular school of thought, covering vast areas—healthy human lifestyle, politics, social norms, economics, religion etc. It has been written after long, sincere, dedicated and scientific researches by Indian *Saints* and *Rishis*. India is based on the principles of *Vedas* and the *Upanishads*. Tolerance, generosity, universal brotherhood were the main motto of Indians since time immemorial. The message of the *Vedas* is:

> "My dear follow, none is higher and none is lower among you. All the people of the world are brothers. Try all together to get the name and fame."

This was the sacred message of Sanatan literature. This literature always talks about progressive, peaceful, healthy, concentrated, cooperative, scientific and intellectual human society. It propagates the idea that the whole human race, birds, beasts and plants, have been made by the one potter, who is almighty. There are on the whole 84 lakhs of creatures as germs, insects, reptiles, birds, quadrupeds, bipeds and human beings. Human birth is attained only after passing through all these lower births. Proper understanding of *Vedanta* and its principles and practice of *Vedanta* in daily life is sure to bring peace, solace and happiness to a world, distracted by war, communal strife, petty quarrels and religious fights. *Atma* or the self is the ultimate reality. It is the ultimate philosophical principle, it is the substratum for everything, and it is the only living truth.

Sanatan literature reflects the cultural heritage of India in which we get that there is a sense of honour and gratitude for even soil, medicine, herbs, plants and trees.

We should feel pride of Indian saints, *rishis*, scholars and thinkers who have established a social tie among the whole human race, keeping in mind the benefits of the globe. Their attitude was conceived with the ideas of integration of human race. They had welcomed and embraced the good views from every corners of the world.

"*Aano Bhadra Kartava Jantu Vishvah*"

[Let noble thoughts come from all sides of the globe].

The esteemed Indian philosopher, Adi Shankaracharya, has established the four *pithas* in the four corners of India namely *Dwarika, Badrinath, Jagganathpuri and Rameshwaram* to establish the cultural unity of India, which reflects high cultural entity of India.

Hidden Treasure

Sanatan literature throws light on the hidden treasure within human beings:

> "Within you is the hidden god. Within you is the immortal soul. Within you is the inexhaustible spiritual treasure, within you is the fountain of joy and happiness. Look within for this happiness, which you have sought in vain in the imperishable sensual objects. Rest peacefully in your own *Atma* and drink the nectar of immortality."

Indian Rishis have announced the worldly brotherhood feeling among the inhabitants on the earth:

"*Udar Charitanamtu Vashudeva Kutambakam*"

This literature says that each man and woman is like god. The first learning of the *Vedas* is:

"*Matri Devo Bhava, Pitri Devo Bhava,*
Acharya Devo Bhava, Atithi Devo Bhava"
(Mother, Father, Teacher and Guest are equivalent to God).

Further, this literature talks about the top position of female community. Manu has said:

"*Yatra Nariyastu Poojyante Ramante Tatra Devata*"

(Manu, 3, 56)

(Where ladies receive honour and respect, God arrives there).

T.S. Eliot, the greatest modern American-British poet has admitted, "My own poetry shows the influences of Indian thought and sensibility." To find and examine explicit references to and examples from Vedic scriptures like *Upanishads* and *Bhagwat Gita* one may turn to Eliot's poetry: *The Waste Land* (1922), *Four Quarters* (1935-42) and *The Indian Who Died in Africa* (1943).

Like W.B. Yeats, Eliot was highly influenced by the Indian spirit and tenets of *Srimad-Bhagvadgita, Upanishads,* Patanjali's *Yoga Darshan.*

T.S. Eliot recapitulates the wasteland, which is devoid of real love, fertility, virtue and life, by establishing an analogy between this rocky dry and barren life in the wasteland of the western world and the barren country. But he does not become disappointed or frustrated rather he looks forward for the sunshine of life and expects a lot that the modern world can be liberated from the curse of wasteland only by seeking shelter in the shrine of oriental philosophy of *Upanishads*. In that Eliot has intensively exerted to survey the world literature to great extent for seeking the hope for peace and salvation of the modern society; but in the last resort he had no choice except fishing the deep waters of *Vedas* to set the wasteland in order. The poet tries to consult several resources going back to the earlier origin in the Sanskrit *Upanishads*. And he draws the formula of three keys for the triple peace of mankind in the eternal truth of *Vrihadaranyako Upanishad* 5, 2, 1-3.

"Give," "Sympathy" and "Self-control" are the three keys with which triple peace and salvation—the birth of higher self—are possible. The closing lines are the core of the poem. This three-fold message *Da, Da, Da,* which signifies give, sympathy and self-control, is given thunder by *Prajapati* to his three kinds of disciplines—men, gods and demons. Man himself is the microcosm of the three peculiar properties, human, angelic and demonic. This formula should be taken together to form the three-fold path of deliverance of humanity from the darkness and sterility of spirit. Also this formula can be a path for social salvation which will make the blessings of Heaven descend on the tormented humanity like the refreshing gentle rain—shantih, shantih, shantih—and lead to state of peace which is beyond the finite key of human understanding.

Again, to examine and understand how much Eliot was influenced by Indian philosophy one may turn to the *Four Quarters* which takes recourse to the Upanishadic knowledge presented by the *Bhagwat Gita.*

Bhagwat Gita was so dear to Eliot that he called it, "the next greatest philosophical poem to the *Divine Comedy* within my experience."

Indian English writers, poets, philosophers, novelists, and dramatists were very much influenced by Indian Sanatan Literature and they have used this literature as a vehicle in their writings. Raja Rao, the well-known novelist, has focused the effect of myth in his first novel of high repute *Kanthapura.* The use of the mythical technique is seen at its best as the strange kind of *Harikatha* as recited by Jayaramachar, the *Harikatha* man. In his *Harikatha,* the past and the present are juxtaposed and contemporary events and personalities are constantly linked up with Puranic gods and epic-heroes and heroines. The use of the mythical technique makes *Gandhi* the visible god, and *Moorthy* the invisible *Avtar.*

Myths play a significant part in Indian life. It is common for Indian preachers to give a mythological or spiritual significance to physical presence.

On his return to India in 1946 he went to Banaras. He met Swami Atmanand, the great Vedantic scholar, whom the novelist accepted as his Guru, Guide and Mentor. Hence, as he attached such great importance to the role of a *Guru* that the quest for a *guru* is a recurring theme in his novels.

In the early thirties, before leaving for France for higher studies *Raja Rao* had written couple of essays to express his love for his motherland and his fascination for Indian culture and Vedantic philosophy. And this love of Indian culture and philosophy colours *The Serpent and the Rope.* He founded a new genre—the philosophical novel—and has vividly and forcefully realised the confrontation of eastern and western culture. This novel is also regarded as the spiritual autobiography of the novelist.

Aurobindo's poems *Urvasie, Love and Death, Savitri* are Hindu in setting, sentiment, and expression. These poems are full of sensuous images and sweet music. He is a great metrical artist who tried to adapt a number of classical metres to English. His mystic poetry has a metric quality very close to the Vedic *mantras*. His achievement lies in the fact that his poetry carries an aroma of the spirituality of India and achieves a rare fusion of personal vision and the spiritual personality of India.

B.G. Tilak by introducing the Ganapati Festival in Maharastra, instilled the Indians with courage, patriotism, discipline and unity. Students were also persuaded to take part in these celebrations. The festival was used as a suitable instrument for educating the masses and making them politically conscious. Tilak also started the Shivaji Festival in 1895 to encourage Marathas to emulate their beloved leader. A new longing for freedom and a firm resolution for a united national Govt. were fostered by festivals like these. Sanatan literature has played an important role in Indian freedom struggle and so it does in the novel.

Reaction Against the Western Influences

Due to western influences there was much free thinking which was rather negative in its religious conclusions, and thus the result was a reaction. There was a movement for the revival of Hinduism. Nalin Sen, the poet, has a prominent place in this reaction against western influences. Bankim Chandra Banerjee's *The Scot of Bengal* also lent his support to this neo-Hindu movement. This movement was also taken up by Ramkrishna Paramhansa and his famous disciple Vivekananda. Swami Dayanand founded the Arya Samaj.

The influences of Vaishnav poetry is indeed great on Tagore. His mythopic imagination transforms old legends and makes them vehicle of his ideas of peace, joy, beauty, love and harmony. Tagore is no preacher but still his poems do have an underlying message or preachings. And when message is in the form of a beautiful myth, it is more effective. Here is a mythical fable:

> "Masters are many in your hall and songs are sung there at all hours. But the simple Carol of this novice struck at your love one plaintive little strain mingled with the great music of the world, and with a flower for a prize you came down and stopped at my cottage door" (Poem-49).

This poem preaches that the power of love is great. The simplicity and honesty are the great virtues to win over the almighty. He comes to you because of your true love and devotion rather than scholarship or austere practices.

Humanism is the dominating theme of Tagore's poem. Man is his recurrent theme and Tagore is concerned with man's glorification, welfare and his salvation.

Mahatma Gandhi has admired Sanatan literature in his Autobiography which made a deep impression on his mind. He has expressed feelings about the *Bhagwad Gita,* the book struck him as one of priceless worth, "The impression has ever since been growing on me with the result that I regard it today as the book for excellence for the knowledge of truth." It has afforded me invaluable help in my moments of gloom.

The feeling of globalization was thousand of years ago in the mind of our great saints and *rishis* and Sanatan literature always throws light on achieving pleasure, peace and prosperity. The heart of Sanatan literature lies in the following lines:

(a) "*Bahujan Hitaya, Bahujan Sukhayae*"

(b) "*Serve Vantu Sukhinah*
Serve Santu Niramaya
Serve Bhadrani Pashyantu
Maa Kashchit Dukh Bhag Bhavet"

(Everyone to be happy, everyone to be disease free, everyone to be cheerful and no sorrow to anyone).

The modern world has became deserted, sick, unhappy, selfish, restless on receiving power, money and sexual pleasure. It is the sacred duty of the elite group to come forward to awake the society to restore lost harmony, prosperity, wisdom, love, mercy, contentment and peace in the society.

This paper may be the lifeblood for establishing the super human society in which the eastern thought is fused in western language.

WORKS CITED

Kyon-Madhavacharg. Delhi Publication.

Mahamahopadhyaya Giridhar Sharma Chaturvedi. *Vaidika Vigyan and Bhartiya Sanskriti.*

Mahatama Gandhi. *My Experiment with Truth.*

Rabindra Nath Tagore. *Gitanjali.*

Raja Rao, *Kanthapura.*

Shri Mad Bhagwat Gita. Gita Press, Gorakhpur.

"Vedic Themes in T.S. Eliot's *Wasteland* and *Four Quarters.*" Ramesa Chandra Tungaria, *The Indian Journal of English Studies.*

35 Application of *Vakrokti* in Maha Nand Sharma's Poetry

Mamta Sharma

"Interestingly enough," says Dr. Prema Nanda Kumar, "a few academics kept faith with their Milton and Tennyson. Nor did they turn away from their own Valmiki, Vyasa and Kalidasa. Among them is Maha Nand Sharma, author of *A Rudraksha Rosary* and *A Spiritual Warrior*."[1] Remarkably proficient in Western approach, Sharma, a poet of Sanskrit also, imbibed his Indian aesthetic approach from the aforesaid three Indian poets among others and many others. It is the object of this paper to trace in Sharma's poetry the application of *vakrokti*, an important ingredient of Indian aesthetics.

Maha Nand Sharma has to his credit nine works of poetry and one of criticism. His works of poetry are: *The Pageant of Seasons* (1956), *Flowers and Buds* (1984), *A Rudraksha Rosary and Other Poems* (1987), *A Spiritual Warrior* (1991), *Scattered Leaves* (1991), *Divine Glimpses* (1996), *Gushing Streams* (1996), *Flowering of a Lotus* (1998) and *Autumn Strains* (2004). *Wodehouse, the Fictionist* is his work of criticism.

Kuntaka established the *vakrokti* school of criticism. The direct meaning of the word *vakrokti* is 'round about way of speaking.' Abhinava Gupta says:

शब्दस्य हि वक्रता, अभिधेयस्य हि वक्रता लोकोत्तरेण रूपेणावस्थानम्।[2]

(*Vakrokti* is the arrangement or placement of circumlocutory words and meaning in a novei in striking way).

Vakrokti was accepted by Bhamaha as the basic element of *alankaar*.

It was considered by Vaman to be *arthalankaar* or meaning-based figure in the form of a *lakshan* or symptom having similarity as its root. Rudrat treated it as a figure of words. Kuntaka valued it as the basic element of poetry. Of these four views about *vakrokti,* some of Kuntaka's approaches to *vakrokti* are applicable to Sharma's poetry. In the subsequent paragraphs, Sharma's poetry is tested according to the comprehensive views of Kuntaka.

Kuntaka classifies *vakrokti* into six categories: (i) *varna-vakrata,* i.e. circumlocution in a letter; (ii) *pada-poorvardh vakrata,* i.e. circumlocution in the first half of a word or compound; (iii) *pada-parardh vakrata,* i.e. circumlocution in the latter half of a word or compound; (iv) *vakya vakrata,* i.e. circumlocution in a sentence; (v) *prakaran vakrata,* i.e. circumlocution in the narration of subject, topic, occasion or their context; (vi) *prabandh vakrata,* i.e. circumlocution in the arrangement of material and the novelty, consequent upon that, in a whole work.

The use of the word 'circumlocution' in the portions quoted above has to be understood in the light of two words in Sanskrit—*vakra* and *vaidagdhi* used by Rudrat in his following explanation of *vakrokti:*

वैदग्धी भंङ्गी भणिति:।[3]

Vaidagdhya means cleverness. The explanation thus implies that *vakrokti* is a clever statement. The word *vakra* means 'clever'. While the word clever is used in its pejorative sense, 'cunning', also, it has its non-pejorative meanings such as 'skilful, talented' as well. It is in this non-pejorative sense that the word *vakrokti* or 'circumlocution' should be understood.

Of the six categories of *vakrokti* given above, the first three are related to linguistic aspects. They do not apply to English since the structure of English language is different from that of Sanskrit language. The remaining three categories, traceable in his poetry, are illustrated below:

(i) *Vakya Vakrata:* Circumlocutions which go by the name of *vakya vakrata* in Sanskrit, are found in Sharma's sentences. "Shalv will kill all his rivals with his scimitar"—this is expressed through *vakrokti* in the following lines:

"The single scimitar-wielding hand of shalv
Could put to sleep eternal, all his rivals."[4]

(ii) *Prakarana Vakrata* (*Circumlocution in the narration of a subject, topic, occasion or their context*): *Prakarana* means 'context, subject, topic, occasion'. An instance of this circumlocution occurs in "Light versus Fire". Kartikeya insists upon his marriage to his sweetheart forthwith, prior to the marriage of his elder brother, Ganesh. Since the elder brother should be married first according to the tradition, Lord Shiva is perplexed at the insistence of his younger son Kartikeya. He, therefore, prescribes a test in order to treat both his sons alike:

To treat you both alike, to give you both
An equal chance, is all that I can do.
You both shall take a round of her that gives
The food essential and the boon of life
And whosoever will first stand shall be
The first to wed.[5]

Here, in the context of Kartikeya's insistence, Lord Shiva uses a *vakrokti* in which he does not specify what he means by 'her that gives the food essential and the boon of life'. Ganesh rightly takes 'her' to be his mother, Parvati, and takes a round of her and gets married first. As against this, Kartikeya mistakes 'her' to be mother Earth and takes a round of the whole earth. He gets delayed and is married afterwards. Thus, the crucial part of the story revolves round a *prakarana vakrata*.

(iii) *Prabandh Vakrata (Circumlocution in the arrangement of material and the novelty, consequent upon that, in a whole work):* The poet uses *vakrata* or cleverness in the management of the plots of all his three works—*A Rudraksha Rosary, A Spiritual Warrior* and *Flowering of a Lotus*—which have epic strain. Lord Shiva is the hero of *A Rudraksha Rosary.* He is eternal—birthless and deathless. He cannot be shown as taking birth and dying. But his heroic deeds upon this earth are to be presented. The poet cleverly selects an incident from *Shiva Purana* in which Lord Shiva comes down to earth to mediate between Brahma and Vishnu in their quarrel. This is an ingenious substitute for the birth of Lord Shiva on the earth. Then showing Lord Shiva's career upon earth—His marriage, the birth of His sons, His fight against Andhak etc., the poet brings Him from the period of myths to the partly historical period in *Mahabharata* in which He fights as Kiraat with Arjuna. This sequence of time from the mythical to the historical is cleverly maintained by the poet in *A Spiritual Warrior* in which the hero, Bhisma, and the other characters are historical figures. However, the myths such as the rising of the child Bhisma from the Ganga, and the boon of Lord Shiva in person to Amba intervene. Then the poet shifts ingeniously to the predominantly historical period of Bhartrahari, in *Flowering of a Lotus* in which there is only one myth, namely, the myth of the fruit of immortality. The poet's *vakrata* or ingenuity is mirrored in this organisation of as many as three works with epic strain from the point of view of the sequence of mythological and historical periods with a marked decline in the mythological element.

The poet's skill in marshalling the plot of a single work is observed in his suitable inventions in *Flowering of a Lotus.* The account of Bhartrahari's career has been handed down in folklore from generation to generation. The poet makes inventions either without changing the substance of the incidents in the folklore or if he modifies the substance of some incident, he takes care to see that the modification lends more propriety and poetic merit to the incident given in the folklore. The folklore merely mentions that Bhartrahari fell in love with Pingla and married her. The details of his falling in love are not given in the folklore. The poet invents the details in keeping with the traditions and ways of old times. According to the traditions of those times, Bhartrahari goes on hunting in the forest near Ujjayini on receiving information that his subjects were often attacked by wild beasts and robbers. While returning from the hunt, he finds in the woods on the outskirts of Ujjayini, the beautiful girl Pingla in moonlit night, and falls in love with her. Needless to say, these inventions suit the old times as well as the situation of love demanding privacy.

No less skilful is the poet's invention in Cantos vi, vii and viii of this work. The poet makes a departure from the folklore in inventing places for Bhartrahari's *tapas* and writing the three *shataks*. According to folklore, Bhartrahari is supposed to have performed *tapas* either near Ujjayini itself or near Gorakhpur or near Ajmer. Discarding all these places, the poet makes Bhartrahari perform his *tapas* on the Himalayas—first on the foothills, then in the higher-middle regions and then in the highest regions. Appropriately enough, he gets *Shrangar Shatak* written on the foothills called *Tarai* region, where the hiss of the serpents coincide with the bitter disturbance in his heart which is caused by the disappointment in his love with faithless Pingla who has been separated from him just a little before. Still more appropriately, the poet, at this time and place, makes Bhartrahari write *Shrangar Shatak* which reflects Bhartrahari's disappointment caused by his physical separation but emotional attachment to faithless Pingla.

The poet then takes Bhartrahari to the middle heights of the Himalayas which, with the absence of hissing serpents, are relatively calm. The outward tranquility there synchronizes with the inner tranquility which Bhartrahari begins to feel when his disappointment has ended with the passage of time. It is in this suitable environment of outer and inner calm on the relatively high altitudes that Bhartrahari writes his *Neeti*

Shatak which deals with the affairs of the world which are higher in importance than those of sensual love.

In keeping with his ingenuity in the management of plot, the poet puts Bhartrahari on the highest altitudes of the Himalayas where the utmost peace outside matches the utmost peace within him who has been fed up with writing on worldly affairs too. It is in this environment of complete calm that the poet makes Bhartrahari write *Vairagya Shatak,* a work of very great spiritual significance. All this testifies to the poet's *prabandh vakrata,* his cleverness in marshalling the plot.

To conclude, the application of *vakrokti* and such other aesthetic devices in his poetry has rightly entitled Maha Nand Sharma to the comments of Dr. A.P.J. Abdul Kalam on his poems, "For the first time I was really moved by the poems... when I finished the books I felt the effect of the poems. Tears were flowing."[6]

WORKS CITED

1. Manuscript of the review sent to the writer by Dr. Prema Nanda Kumar. The review is to be published in *Journal of Indian Writing in English,* published from Gulbarga.
2. Dr. Vijay Pal Singh. *Bhartiya Kavya Shastra.* Allahabad: Jai Bharti Prakashan, 1999, 109.
3. *Ibid.*
4. Maha Nand Sharma. *A Spiritual Warrior.* Meerut: Ashutosh Prakashan, 1991, 69.
5. ——. *A Rudraksha Rosary and Other Poems.* Meerut: Ashutosh Prakashan, 1987, 99.
6. Kalam's letter dated April 16, 2004 [Unpublished].

36 Indian Woman Torn between Tradition and Modernity as Depicted in the Short Stories of Ruth Prawer Jhabvala

Vibha Goyal

As a short-story writer Ruth Prawer Jhabvala's talent is aesthetically distinctive and technically effective. Her art excels in various spheres of the short story such as modes of narration, method of description, and delineation of character. She uses Indian English, typical Indian modes of behaviour and ways of feeling to put across her sense of life in a particular cultural context. Being a writer of domestic life preeminently, Jhabvala presents the joys and sorrows, harmony and friction, fulfilment and frustration of domestic life. Marital dissonance with its clash of wills, personalities, temperaments and values is widely presented in her fictional world. The conflict between a growing sense of individualism and the orthodox tradition of a man-ridden Indian society is genuinely representative of the post-war phase of Indian society. In fact she presents a panoramic view of modern developing, changing, conflict torn Indian urban society and in that too especially the position, the role and the status of modern Indian urban woman who is struggling hard to realise her own identity. Jhabvala's keen insight into Indian woman's heart enables her to explore the miserably confused psyche of this woman, who is trying to establish a harmony between the traditional values and modern revolutionary ideas. At one point she is notable to discard the age-long familial values and emotional and mental responses and wants to fulfil her responsibilities as a wife, as a mother, as a daughter-in-law, at the other point she wants to enjoy complete freedom—freedom of speech, freedom of movement, freedom of decision. She does not want anyone to overpower her and at the same time she does not want to hurt the fabric of the family. In fact modern woman has become a very complex person who wants to accomplish contrasting tasks, bear contrasting responsibilities and live two contrasting worlds and this intricate personality of her has been effectively depicted by Ruth Jhabvala in many of her short stories.

In her story *The Housewife*, Shakuntala is a matronly housewife, married to a prosaic, sensible man, and supervising a middle-class household. Her daughter Manju is already married and has a small baby Baba. In this ordinary humdrum household an extraordinary poetic motif is inducted in the shape of a music teacher and as a consequence, there is Shakuntala's intense passion for music. She has her music lessons from the teacher and the experience opens out new vistas for her soul:

> "But it was true that with her music she lived in a region where she felt most truly, most deeply herself. No, not herself, something more and higher than that. By contrast with her singing, the rest of her day, indeed of her life, seemed insignificant" (*How I Became a Holy Mother and Other Stories*, 88).

However, Shakuntala is struggling between her sense of duty towards her family and her own passion for music. Her husband, though a caring man, has no interest in her music. Her Phuphiji and her daughter also have no interest in her music. She is required by everyone in her traditional role as a dutiful wife, caring mother and responsible daughter-in-law. Nobody would like her to go beyond this familial atmosphere and start her career as a singer. Nobody wants even to accompany her to attend a musical concert.

This indifference of the family towards her passion for music is painful and frustrating for her. However, she does not get annoyed with anyone for this indifference. In fact she accepts it as something natural and does not expect anything from her family members. On the contrary she is conscious of her own duty as a housewife. She does not want her passion for music to come in the way of her domestic life. She wants to make her husband happy and comfortable and that is the foremost aim of her-life:

> "She wanted him to be always entirely comfortable and recognized it to be her mission in life to see that he was" (90).

Thus she is torn between two things—her role as a traditional housewife and her desire to fulfil her craving for music and thus have her own individual identity:

> "It was because of him, who said nothing that Shakuntala sometimes felt guilty. And because of her daughter and her little grandson. She loved all of them, but she could not deny to herself that her singing meant even more to her than her feelings as wife, and mother and grandmother" (88).

It is this intense involvement in music which finally leads her to surrender herself, body and soul, to the teacher. Shakuntala is deeply touched by the teacher's suggestion that she may give a public performance, and this kindles a sensitive chord in her being. The death of the teacher's wife and his subsequent visits to cheap restaurants and low women compel Shakuntala to save his soul. Then she cannot be contained by the conventions of a middle-class home, her husband, daughter or Phuphiji. She involuntarily follows the dictates of her spirit, her longing for music and her involvement with the teacher's soul. She goes to the restaurant and finds him drumming his hand on the table. He leads her to his poor house and she surrenders herself to him, to music and the musician.

> "He was about the same age as her husband but lean, hard and eager, as he came on top of her, she saw his drugged eyes so full of bliss and he was still smiling at the tune he was playing to himself. And this tune continued to play in her too. He entered her at the moment when, the structure of the raga having been expounded, the combination of

> notes was being played up and down, backwards and forwards, very fast. There was no going back from there, she knew, but who would want to go back" (102).

In this key passage the theme, the characters, the event in the story find their highest consummation. Shakuntala's whole being is merged in music and the man who embodies it. The housewife in her transcends her convention bound self and is united in body and spirit with art, life and the person who embodies this harmony.

In her story *Rose Petals*, Jhabvala brings out this predicament of woman in the higher class of the society. The main character as well as the narrator of the story is the wife of a cabinet minister. There is a sharp contrast between the husband and the wife. The minister is a great activist but his wife likes to lead a quiet, secluded, slow life. But being the wife of a minister she is forced to get involved in public life in spite of her not liking it. Like any Indian woman she also finds it to be her moral duty to maintain the dignity and honour of her husband and behave accordingly, though in the depth of her heart she does not relish it at all. She is compelled to attend all sorts of functions, preside over them, deliver speeches and mingle with all sorts of people, she says:

> "It is not easy to be a Minister's wife. People ask me to do all sorts of things that I don't like to do. They ask me to sit on welfare committees and give away prizes at cultural shows. I want to say no but the Minister says it's my duty. So I go" (57).

Her daughter, who has inherited the dynamism of her father, also wants her to attend parties and functions and participate in all activities enthusiastically. But she has no interest in the hectic life of the Minister and his social engagements. Though morally and emotionally she is associated with her husband and is deeply concerned about his well-being, she finds no temperamental affinity with him. She finds her life to be meaningless and hollow in the midst of all the hustle and bustle. Her husband though loving and caring does not understand her inner self. He is not bothered about her likings and dislikings. Even before he became the minister he was fond of leading a busy, hectic life and without caring for his wife's requirement, he wanted her also to actively participate in all his busy schedule:

> "Wherever we went, he drew up a heavy programme for us which I found very tiring, but since he himself never needed any rest, he couldn't understand why I should" (57).

She finds herself lonely and her life purposeless. Her husband is not able to give her a sense of inner satisfaction. However, she finds a temperamental affinity with her husband's brother Biju who wants to lead a dull, slow and inactive life like her. She says:

> "Fortunately just at that time Biju came back from abroad and he began to spend a lot of time with me, so I did not feel too lonely" (57).

She loves to sit with him for hours idly, discussing something or cracking childish jokes. She enjoys his company so much that she becomes forgetful even of her regular duties when he is around. It is only when he is away that she pays more attention to the Minister and the house :

> "On those days when Biju is not there, I seem to see more of the Minister. If he is late, I wait up for him to come" (65).

However, she cannot endure Biju's absence for long because it is he who understands her loneliness and gives her real company:

> "...if there is no sign of him by afternoon, I get restless" (65).

When she is not well it is only Biju who has time to sit with her for long. The Minister and Meena are concerned about her but do not have much time to spend with her. She finds nothing great and charming in her life to give her a healthy feeling and to create a zest for life in her. She sometimes thinks:

> "Is life only a game for Biju and me?" (59).

She feels that she is leading a withering life like the rose petals that are fallen, "from the rose and lie soft and withering by the side of the vase" (68).

Thus she represents the dilemma of the higher class Indian woman whose inner-self and external-self are two separate identities having no harmony between them.

In *Bombay* Jhabvala portrays a Parsi household in the cosmopolitan city with the uncle and Nargis, his niece, as the two main characters. It was a strange house in which the two brothers live, both lovers of Persian poetry and Victorian literature and very fond of music. They were once married but the wives were no more, so for all practical purposes, they lead the lives of bachelors. Their main aim is to educate and entertain Nargis whom they love. Nargis becomes the sole motif of their life and her every requirement is fulfilled, every desire taken care of. When she reaches the marriageable age, she is married to a man of business, of pale yellow complexion, who ran the firm of Panivala and Sons. He is a very rich and kind man and finds jobs in his firm for her father as well as for the uncle. Meanwhile, Nargis' father dies and her uncle moves back to his small house in the suburb though he keeps visiting Nargis frequently. The story is mainly concerned with the sufferings of Nargis' uncle—a sensitive and helpless soul thrown against the hard realities of life, but it brings out the hollowness of the life of Nargis also. Nargis, who was the most important figure in the life of her father and her uncle, becomes secondary in the house of her husband. Though she has no apparent problems but her life becomes prosaic and dull. She leads a mechanical life, where there is no enthusiasm, no great aims, no opportunities to prove one's identity. She becomes a typical Indian housewife lost in her household duties, forgetting her own individuality completely.

In the Mountains is again a story of the predicament of a middle-aged, middle-class woman who is suffering in life because of her rebellious attitude towards life and because of not clinging to the traditional code of conduct prescribed for an Indian woman. It is the story of Pritam, who lives in a secluded part of hills all alone and tries to absorb the spirit of the hills and valleys and thus seeks the fulfilment of herself. Her mother arrives from Delhi to stay with her in her lovely resort in the hills. The old woman is initially shocked to know that her daughter has found a spiritual companion for herself in an infirm old doctor, though later on she accepts their relationship. Her arrival is followed by the arrival of her other relations in three cars who come to stay for lunch.

Pritam takes all pains to cook delicious food for all of them, for Sarla her cousin and her husband Bobby. Bobby and Pritam had met in the past on many occasions and had discussed free love. Now they are meeting after a long time. They get an opportunity to meet on a lovely path in the hill where Bobby confesses his great feeling for Pritam. He drinks whisky and she too has a few sips which send her blood rushing in her veins. She begins to experience new sensations. However, soon Bobby has to leave as all her guests are departing for Shimla.

In the end Pritam is shown throwing three stones at the three cars, which symbolises her rebellion against the common, sickening traditions and customs. Jhabvala shows how Pritam suffers because of her modern independent outlook. Even her own mother does not approve of her relationship with the old doctor when she invites him to stay with her in her house all winter, when the roof of his hut falls because of snow and Pritam does not hesitate in making a fun of her mother:

> "Oh yes, all winter, Pritam said, mocking her, And all alone, just the two of us. Why did you have to tell her ? She reproached Doctor Sahib. Now she is shocked. Just look at her face. She is thinking we are two guilty lovers" (156).

However, Pritam herself is least bothered about what others would say. She has her own independent life, independent views. Seeing the selfishness and the materialistic approach of the people Pritam is so fed up with them that she is not bothered about any of them. She says about her relatives:

> "What's so special about any of them? They may come, they may eat, they may go away again, and good bye.

> Why should I care for any one ? I don't care. And also you! you may also go, right now, this minute, if you like —and I will stand here and wave to you and laugh!" (158).

She does not find any emotional, mental or spiritual relationship between herself and her relatives, that she finds in Doctor Sahib and so she cares for him.

Jhabvala's another story *The Suffering Women* also brings out the predicament of modern urbanized Indian woman. It is the story of Anjana and Sultana, two film actresses (Anjana retired and Sultana still working) who are trying to establish a harmony between the old and the new. Anjana has taken retirement from film line and is living with her daughter Kiku in a comfortable flat. Sultana is still working to meet her expenditure as she is extravagant by nature and needs more and more money to spend. In their youth Anjana and Sultana both were friends as well as rivals and both loved one and the same person. Finally Anjana got married to him which made Sultana very furious. However, later on, she reconciled to the fact because the marriage of Anjana did not prove to be a happy one as her husband could never accept her, as he belonged to "an old Lucknow family claiming descent from courtiers, while Anjana's mother and grandmother (like Sultana's) had been dancing girls" (109).

This is the irony of the life of Anjana that she is sexually exploited, made pregnant and yet never accepted emotionally by her husband. Though he marries her but never accepts her in spite of all her love and devotion:

> "He could not forget his fall, and she too had become deeply imbued with feelings of guilt. She did all she could to make it up to him, keeping him in the luxury that he loved and pampering him in all his desires and manifold tastes. Nothing did any good..." (109).

After the death of her husband, Anjana tries to seek a feeling of security and belongingness in Thakur Sahib, a married man though again she has ideological differences with him too. Anjana learns to accept the free attitude of her daughter Kiku who loves to roam around with her boyfriend Rahul, but Thakur Sahib does not approve of this freedom, given to Kiku. He is very strict towards his own daughters. Though Anjana tries to explain the healthy relationship of Kiku and Rahul; Thakur Sahib does not agree with her. When she says that Kiku and Rahul are "just two children, a little boy and girl playing together," (104) Thakur Sahib says in a calm voice "there was only one game little boys and girls played together" (104).

Thus even in Thakur Sahib Anjana does not find a true companion, though she is confused and insecure without him.

Sultana is also a torn soul. She does not find anyone giving her real joy or happiness. Though she has many young friends and she patronises them, cares for them and spends a lot of money on them, but none really bothers about her. She finds herself lonely in the midst of so many friends. It is only her rival friend Anjana who bothers for her and takes care of her whenever she is depressed or tense. Thus through both Anjana and Sultana, Jhabvala brings out the confusion, instability, insecurity and bewilderment of the modern Indian woman in the modern society.

It is evident from the above discussion that Jhabvala has deep insight into the psyche of modern Indian woman. She is able to move in the labyrinths of the head and heart of middle- and upper-class woman of modern times who is torn between old and new, tradition and modernity, restrictions and freedom, responsibility towards the family and responsibility towards her own identity, ideology and individuality.

WORK CITED

Jhabvala, Ruth Prawer. *How I Became a Holy Mother and Other Stories*. New Delhi: Penguin Books.

37

Simrit's Quest for Identity in Nayantara Sahgal's *The Day in Shadow*

Archana Trivedi

Nayantara Sahgal, the daughter of late Vijay Lakshmi Pandit, entered the literary scene in the second half of the fifties. Though admittedly a minor writer she has lately been placed on a high pedestal with eight novels, published by her so far. Her literary background, associated with her "fecund imagination' and 'susceptible sensibility' has inspired most of her novels in which she shows a perfect command over her medium. Most of the novels by Nayantara Sahgal explore and highlight the attitudes of women. She presents women's quest for identity, real life conflicts, marital tensions, the lack of communication between people, especially husband and wife. All this results in unhappiness and prevents human fulfillments.

Nayantara Sahgal advocates women's struggle for freedom and self-realization in her fiction. Her heroines always try to realize their selfhood, happiness and fight against injustice. In fact fighting against injustice is a recurrent idea in Sahgal's novels. The women all over the world have remained under the male force. They have to face the sense of insecurity, the sexual harassment and violence which are similar in the advanced as well as in the developing countries. In this male dominated society a woman has been the victim of male-hypocrisy, violence and exploitation since the earliest times. Indian woman is the victim of her husband's subtle and inhuman form of exploitation, a sort of beating where "blood and bruises don't show" but she could not freely narrate or openly discuss these experiences.

Sahgal's women characters—Maya Shivpal, Rashmi, Saroj and Simrit in *The Day in Shadow* are highly individualistic but are still bound by traditions of Indian society. In "husband centered" society, they have no standing. They are portrayed as passive creatures in the beginning, to whom only things happen. Her women are a typical example of qualities one would look for in a traditional Indian woman; qualities such as patience, forbearance, adherence to family.

Indian woman who is an object of silent suffering and who is an upholder of Indian culture now could seek personal gratification and self-fulfillment. Women are certainly more aware of the injustice done to them by men, but habit makes them a willing prisoner in this world of exploitation and injustice. It may not be entirely irrelevant here to repeat Beckett, "Habit is the ballast that chains the dog to his vomit" (19).

In this male dominated world where men pass orders and women carry them out, where men create situations and women live them, women accept the order of life created for them by men without any protest.

Sahgal expresses her views that Indian woman is a victim of her husband's subtle and inhuman form of exploitation. But the woman, in the novels of Sahgal, fights with both suffering and anguish. She presents women's quest for identity. Women, striving to achieve individual fulfillment, deal with eternal search for freedom, freedom to express themselves, freedom to be their own selves.

They show their personal courage, though short-lived, to revolt against conventions. Nayantara Sahgal favours women's freedom, identity, self-satisfaction and happiness and fight against injustice.

In *The Day in Shadow* Nayantara Sahgal shows how an Indian woman attempts to liberate herself from the moral and social pressures. Here she presents her personal experience of conventional reaction.

Through the character of Simrit, Sahgal exposes the suffering and position of a woman in Indian society. While the *Sita-Pativrata* tradition tells her to suffer in silence, her modern educated mind asks, what if her husband is not like Ram? Is she still to remain a faithful wife? She is unable to bow silently like a *pativrata* and neither can she be on her own. When Simrit wishes to break a seventeen year old marriage she has problems not only in coping with her own irrational fears and tensions but also with society which does not recognize a woman's identity apart from her husband. A divorced woman is curiously watched by other as if "divorce were a disease that left pock marks" (*The Day in Shadow*, 4). The mere habit of living with someone for many years makes it difficult for Simrit to accept the idea of living alone, all by herself. The frightening dream that she has gives us an idea of her inner conflict where pain follows her like a shadow never leaving her even for a moment.

Sahgal's Simrit looks like "liberated" woman who has the courage to break a long relationship which has become meaningless with no sense of companionship or partnership between husband and wife.

The heroine, Simrit, is the wife of a Punjab industrialist, Som who gives an outwardly generous divorce settlement to her. In the meantime she falls in love with Raj, an M.L.A., who is kind and considerate to her. Simrit's mood of depression that overtakes her after separation from her husband is revealed fairly in the story. Som and Simrit seem to get on well during the first few years of marriage. But Som's inability to understand her, except as an object of physical attraction, fit only for physical pleasure and enjoyment, compels her to seek human communication outside the marital bonds.

Som treats her not as a person but as possession. She is not only the victim of Som's inhuman attitude but also of a system: "The Hindu dharma which maintained that a wife is her husband's property and has no individuality outside of that system" (Sharma, 171). Som depresses Simrit and she finds herself unable to respond to her husband's physical needs and remains "separate, excluded and rebellious" (*The Day in Shadow*, 62), Simrit withdraws from him emotionally which naturally impairs their physical relationship too. He feels insulted at Simrit's physical withdrawal, reacts wildly and walks out of her life. Simrit has no other wayout except divorce, "Simrit fell on the verge of a fatal realization. She was no longer able to follow the goals which Som had set for himself, and the inability seemed to be spreading through her veins, affecting the very womb of her desire, drying up the fount within her" (*The Day in Shadow*, 90).

Nayantara Sahgal wanted to do more in this novel than convey this emotional holocaust. She wanted to show how even in a free country like ours where women are equal citizens, a woman can be criminally exploited. The condition of Simrit "'may be she had been an animal, only a nice, obedient domestic one, sitting on a cushion, doing as she was told. And in return, she had been fed and sheltered" (*The Day in Shadow,* 57). Simrit remains a victim all through her life and part of it is due to the social conditioning which perpetuates around the woman. First, she falls a prey to Som's charms, she gets married to Som, a businessman, against the will of her Brahmin parents, then becomes a victim of his whims. She remains unhappy with this marriage and ultimately takes divorce from her husband. But "the divorce results in a disorganized life and her innocent signing on the dotted line of the 'consent terms' finds herself in the midst of economic problems. Her divorce places Simrit not in the world of freedom but in the unenviable position of a trapped animal" (Dhawan, 3). Simrit encounters difficulties on building a new life for herself as a writer and for her children. She has so many daughters and only one son, Brij. Som shows no affection for his daughters and is considerate only to his son. Even after the divorce he cares only for Brij. Her children are against their mother's attitude. The daughters do not bother much for her, they have their own life to lead, the son has been fascinated by his father's world and likes to spend more time with him than with his mother. She was like "An overloaded donkey" (*The Day in Shadow*, 56). A heavy tax liability is imposed by Som on Simrit in the form of a corpus of six lakhs which his son, Brij, would inherit at the age of twenty-five. But his financial settlement enslaves her with taxes and makes it impossible for her to make a decent living.

In one of her articles "Of Divorce and Hindu Women", Nayantara Sahgal states in this book (*The Day in Shadow*) "I tried to figure out something that has happened to me—the shattering experience of divorce. I wanted to show how even in a free country like ours, where women are equal citizens, a woman can be criminally exploited without creating a ripple." The crux of the problem, says Sahgal, is that nobody bothers about it, neither the lawyer who drafts the settlement nor the court that approves it. Although Simrit herself has signed it, she has done it without understanding, what it is all about. Sahgal states that "divorce for woman nature is like a sin, and in exploitation of her share of guilt she stays mute and acquiescent over the settlement, willing to accept it as part of her *Karma*. Simrit is symbolic of the Hindu race."

In Indian society where men hesitate to marry a widow and a divorcee, it is unbelievable to find a man like Raj Garg, the socialist-minded Member of Parliament who embraces a middle-aged woman with huge economic liabilities and a host of children to look after. Pankaj K. Singh gives relevant comment, "Raj's total behaviour merely reinforces the patriarchal myth of man's superiority over woman. He seems to respect her independence and her individuality." "She didn't need a man for identity or status" (*The Day in Shadow*, 139). One wonders that a person like Raj can understand or share her agony and tensions. Standing on the high pedestal he has chosen for himself, a partner or companion to Simrit. But she, oppressed by her immediate problems, says "I feel so disorganized" (*The Day in Shadow,* 14). The point of suffering is blown aside by the wind of words, in her fight against injustice the woman finds herself helpless.

There is need to receive help and cooperation from right thinking and enlightened individuals. The only way to fight against the injustice to create public opinion against it, Simrit "as a freelance journalist she could make it an issue in the papers and meanwhile, regards herself as free from any binding obligation to honour the documents terms. Clearly the change had to be brought about by democratic means."

In several ways Sahgal's *The Day in Shadow* shows interesting parallels to Ruth Jhabvala's *Getting Ready for Battle*. At last Simrit feels freed after a lot of suffering and struggle. She is placed at "a high spot" where "an immense valley of choices spread out before her gaze and she felt free at last to choose what her life would be" (*The Day in Shadow*, 236). Having understood the message, she throws away the shackles of man's slavery. As a result of her struggle she has gladly retained the link with her children. A new world of real liberty, freedom and horizon has now opened out to her. Thus *The Day in Shadow* is basically a study of the 'new woman'. Simrit is able to project the image of the new woman who maintained herself economically independent and is initiated into a search to discover her deeper identity. Sahgal's pioneering quest for woman emancipation will, no doubt, be momentous literary document of the present era.

WORKS CITED

Beckett, Samuel. "Proust." *Proust and Three Dialogues with George Duthuit*. London: Colderce Boyars, 1965, 1970.

Dhawan, R.K. (Ed.), *Indian Woman Novelist*, Set II., Vol. IV. New Delhi: Prestige Books.

Sahgal, Nayantara. *The Day in Shadow*. Delhi: Vikas Publishing, 1971.

——. "Divorce and Hindu Woman." *The Hindustan Times*, 13 Dec. 1971.

Sharma, Krishna. *Positive Living: A Brief Examination of some Features of Nayantara Sahgal's 'Strom in Chandigarh'* and *'The Day in Shadow'*.

Singh, Pankaj K. "Feminism and Nayantara Saghal's *The Day in Shadow*." *Feminism and Recent Fiction in English*, ed. Sushila Singh. New Delhi: Prestige Books, 1991.

38 'Give Me a Break' Leila Seth's *On Balance*: A Study of a Woman Who Fights Against Self-Pity

Malti Sharma

Reading of *On Balance* by Leila Seth left me wondering whether woman still remains to be a question? Hasn't woman empowerment really started? I would say—yes, it has. Notwithstanding the fact that crime against women shows that she is paying a higher price for this. But this is not her problem as her will to snatch her fair share gets her in daily news for joining military services, taxi driving and other hitherto exclusively male areas. So, what does this new woman need? Not the stories of surrender and confinement to her inevitable fate of a poor thing. I feel highlighting her problems (which may be a part of life, not whole of it), her human insufficiency would be a damage coming to her from the world of literature. In a crowd of feministic protests *On Balance* comes with a fresh breeze for here is a woman, who is speaking for woman but not against man, who isn't trying to win our sympathy by telling her tale of exclusive miseries. And, if there are any troubles in life, she doesn't curse anybody for this, she doesn't even hesitate in taking her share of miseries. For a change, we come across a woman purchasing her success at a fair price and also admiring the fact.

On Balance is an autobiography of Leila Seth, mother of fictional Ace Vikram Seth, in which she narrates the story of a small girl who grows up in the twisting lanes of Darjeeling, following equally twisting ways of destiny. Fatherless, shelterless child who dares to look straight into the eyes of life. *On Balance* spontaneously becomes a clue to the treasure-house wherefrom Vikram Seth has perhaps borrowed the spirit, the attitude and the talent that he is. By the way, story of *A Suitable Boy* moves around marriages and match-making in the family. Again *Two Lives* is the story of his mother's uncle who had gone to England to study dentistry, joined army, later became a dentist, and married a German Jew.

On Balance is an interesting work narrating the unusual story of a simple but intelligent girl whose father, a railway engineer, quite boldly declares at the time of her birth that he would give no dowry for her marriage and that which is more important, she would have to stand on her feet when she grows up. At the age of nineteen she is already being marginalized, as in her world also there seems to be no life without marriage. Passing through a period of transition, tradition has not been lost. Her mother's views on marriage are honoured and finally she marries a boy approved by her mother. The family holds tradition wherever it stands for contributing to universal meanings of life. Their home reminds us of Wordsworth's skylark who soars, roams and their harmony comes out of the blending of heaven and home. She, mother of two children, was studying law in England, as her husband was posted there. In spite of variety of responsibilities, she topped the Bar Final Examination and the newspaper said:

Star, 5 Nov. 1957

Mother-in-Law

"Here is a mother who knows all about the law—28 year-old, Lucknow born, Mrs. Leila Seth. She has come top over all men candidates, in the latest Bar Final Examination" (Qtd. in *On Balance,* 115). Back from England she started working for law practice which was quite a difficult task in 1950s. The clients used to say that they wanted to see a lawyer and not a woman. Hard times always made them wiser and stronger. During a CBI inquiry against her husband, her son wrote in a letter to his father: "What's happening to you is terrible, but remember what Dr. Johnson said: A fly, sir, may sting a stately horse and make him wince; but one is but an insect, and the other is a horse still" (239). At the age of 48 she became a judge at Delhi High Court. Authority gave her a clear sense of responsibility. Moving confidently on the challenging road of legal profession, she became first Lady Chief Justice of a High Court (H.P.). There she explored every possibility of relating with true sense of service to society. After retirement, she no more in official power, had to go through the disheartening by-lanes of a corrupt system, but she was in no mood to idealize or moralize. She did her best to correct the system, but she didn't fuss with others for not doing it.

A composed mother, she feels blessed with her children's achievements as Vikram's Magnum Opus has been dedicated to Papa, Mama, and the memory of Amma. Marriage of her children was time for enjoying the feel of a deep-rooted institution. She says about relevance of marriage: "It's about finding someone who helps you become the best person you can be" (454). Retirement didn't take her away from her responsibility towards society. Her enthusiastic moves have been showing while working as a member and head of many boards and commissions. Now she looked into complications of legal profession which she could not do earlier. Well, in the end of the book she reflects that it has been almost finding the best of both worlds. But she feels that the balancing act hasn't been easy, no self-pity for doing a double role. It is rather finding an opportunity to explore your efficiency with a perfect and bright sense of achievement, she falls in self-love and admiration as she concludes: "In a sense, the little fatherless girl, with no connections, has come a long way" (469). And all I feel is about doing justice to oneself (taking no injustice and rejecting the blame-game). This is important because a happily productive citizen only can make a strong pillar to support the everlasting structure of society.

Autobiographies are generally the sum-total of achievements against challenges and one's desire to share them for the purpose of imparting inspiration. *On Balance* is a gender-neutral case study of an individual whose journey from zero promises to 100 per cent realization, has been followed. A life account of gains and losses, success and failure, that too without a sense of complaint or bitterness against anybody. One by one, people are appreciated because she knows how to leave the underserved and undesirable aside.

The world Ms. Seth creates in her book is a world with no grudges, pain or fatigue and this has been possible because justice has been guarded at every step. Giving or taking of injustice is sinful to her. She has been appreciative of everything because underserved condemnation she would never take. Neither would she bow to underserved humiliation. On demand of occasion she wrote to Chief Justice of India without bothering about the consequences whatsoever: "I am not used to being shouted at or spoken to in an offensive tone...further, I expect both to give and to receive a modicum of courtesy" (312).

We meet here a happy woman who was always capable of outshining her male counterpart but she makes her career without disturbing the family. But she also suggests that no progress can be seen in isolation. Leila Seth is among the pioneers who have moved a step ahead in the world of woman's tales. It can be weaker versus powerful but not woman versus man. This book can be easily taken as the new woman's guide for giving the best of her to surroundings without sacrificing her ambitions. Story of her professional success reveals the fact that no system is keen on taking you until and unless you are hardworking and sincere. Understanding of this came to her as she moved forward with intellectual advancement. In a state of indecision her son would come to help her when he said "Mama, I am so glad that you work and use your mind and don't talk to me only about the price of onions and the stupidity of servants" (153).

Simplicity in form and content both is the essence of the book. There is nothing that would establish the distorted world of complex psyche of modern man. Problems of life are deciphered and the simplicity of life is admired. Narrative is quite interesting and engaging. The book is almost a song of wisdom pouring down with soothing touches. Ms. Seth coming from a senior generation does not write in a lesser interesting manner. While describing nature she has the precision and sensuousness of romantics. She can confidently discuss normal-abnormal, heroic-unheroic, romantic-unromantic, beautiful and ugly side of life. Her style speaks of a spontaneous maturity which can be attributed to her wide experience and keen observation. Her character portrayal is so powerful that we almost know everyone personally. Ms. Seth's simplicity has worked wonders when she has talked of philosophy. As head of the inquiry commission she says about Rajan Pillai (the biscuit king's death in prison): "Who could have guessed that a man who lived in a fabulous house in Ridout Road in Singapore and possessed beautiful homes and cashew plantations should have his permanent address shown in the post-mortem report as Jail No. 4, Tihar, New Delhi" (385). Comparing the contribution of Vikram Seth and Leila Seth we feel that Vikram Seth leaves a style and technique as service to literary world and some attitude, whereas Leila Seth leaves all attitude in no bad style. In a materialistic age nobody wastes his time on reading a writer until and unless he promises a personal gain and the book serves this in more than one way. A present to her husband on his 80th birthday this book offers intelligent ideas for harmony in marriage. Any bonds for that matter, once started are forever and they suggest assurance of the order, restore our faith in institutions. In spite of any amount of problems, a mother is a mother, a brother is a brother and a friend is always a friend. This book is no thrill of incidents, no excitement of luxury or unusual things but every small incident is celebrated and so it becomes a thanksgiving occasion for the author, that too when she in on a forced bed-rest due to fracture. For a strangely behaving generation who is selling real-life bonds for pennies and buying the same in fictional world for pounds, *On Balance* is a vital clue to solve the puzzle. Literature needs to focus on the in-built strength of woman which boosts her moral. Already with courage and hard work, she is all set to create a gender-neutral world. Moral of the story says that instead of making propaganda through selling her world fixed in eternal miseries, literature needs to strengthen a fighters spirit in woman. So please don't disturb her, for she is following her dreams honestly and courageously. *On Balance* is one such example to inspire all who are of this sort.

WORK CITED

Seth, Leila. *On Balance*. New Delhi: Penguin Viking India, 2003. All references in the text are from this edition.

Contributors

Maha Nand Sharma. Formerly Reader, Department of English, C.C.S. University, Meerut, Uttar Pradesh.

Shrawan K. Sharma. Professor & Head, Department of English, Gurukul Kangri University, Haridwar, Uttaranchal.

Ramesh K. Srivastava. Formerly Professor of English, G.N.D. University, Amritsar; Currently UGC Emeritus Fellow Institute of Languages, Bundelkhand University, Jhansi, Uttar Pradesh.

Sunita Agarwal. Asstt. Professor of English, University of Rajasthan, Jaipur, Rajasthan.

Anju Bhatt. Lecturer, Department of English, Govt. Degree College, Tihri, Uttaranchal.

Sudarshan Sharma. Formerly Reader of English, Kamla Nehru College, Delhi.

Anuradha Verma. Research Scholar, N.A.S. (P.G.) College, Meerut, Uttar Pradesh.

Krushna Chandra Mishra. Lecturer, Department of English, Govt. College, Bomdilla, Arunachal Pradesh.

Abha Shukla Kaushik. Reader, Department of English, A.K.P.G. College, Hapur, Ghaziabad, Uttar Pradesh.

Monika Bhatnagar. Reader, Department of English, Meerut College, Meerut, Uttar Pradesh.

K.A. Agrawal. Reader, Department of English, Gurukul Kangri University, Haridwar, Uttaranchal.

Sangeeta Das. Reader, Department of English, D.G. College, Kanpur, Uttar Pradesh.

M.L. Garg. Reader & Head, Department of English, Meerut College, Meerut, Uttar Pradesh.

Ram Sharma. Senior Lecturer, Department of English, J.V. College, Baraut, Baghpat, Uttar Pradesh.

Malti Agrawal. Reader & Head, Department of English, N.A.S. (P.G) College, Meerut, Uttar Pradesh.

V.K. Singhal. Formerly Reader of English, K.R. College, Mathura, Uttar Pradesh.

Sharda Jain. Reader & Head, Department of English, D.J. College, Baraut, Baghpat, Uttar Pradesh.

Alka Rani. Reader & Head, Department of English, S.G. (P.G.) College, Sarurpur Khurd, Meerut, Uttar Pradesh.

Gunjan Chaturvedi. Reader of English, B.D.K. College, Agra, Uttar Pradesh.

Ranjana Mehrotra. Reader of English, B.D.K. College, Agra, Uttar Pradesh.

Arun K. Mishra. Reader & Head, Department of English J.V. College, Baraut, Baghpat, Uttar Pradesh.

Shilpi Saxena. Research Scholar, Dr. B.R. Ambedkar University, Agra, Uttar Pradesh.

Sunanda Mukesh. Reader & Head, Department of English, Kanohar Lal Girls (P.G.) College, Meerut, Uttar Pradesh.

Ajai Sharma. Reader & Head, Department of English, M.M. College, Modinagar, Ghaziabad, Uttar Pradesh.

Kshama Gupta. Lecturer of English, C.S.S.S. (P.G.) College, Machhra, Meerut, Uttar Pradesh.

Gunjan Mittal. Research Scholar, N.A.S. (P.G.) College, Meerut, Uttar Pradesh.

Manjusha Kaushik. Lecturer, Department of English, Kanya Gurukul Mahavidyalaya, Haridwar, Uttaranchal.

Indu Arora. Reader, Department of English, B.S.M. (P.G.) College, Roorkee, Haridwar, Uttaranchal.

Hemlatha K. Reader, Department of English, Kanya Gurukul Mahavidyalaya, Dehradun, Uttaranchal.

N. Poovalingam. Reader, Department of English, Manonmaniam Sundaranra University Abishekapatti, Tirannelveli, Tamil Nadu.

Reema Varshney. Sr. Lecturer, Department of English, MIET College, Meerut, Uttar Pradesh.

Beena Agarwal. Reader, Department of English, D.S. College, Aligarh, Uttar Pradesh.

B.C. Pandey. Reader, Department of English, M.M. (P.G.) College, Modinagar, C.C.S. University, Meerut, Uttar Pradesh.

Vikas Sharma. Sr. Lecturer, Department of English, D.A.V. (P.G.) College, Bulandshahar, Uttar Pradesh.

Vinay Kumar Pandey. Sr. Lecturer, Department of English, Govt. College, Bomdilla, Arunachal Pradesh.

Mamta Sharma. Sr. Lecturer, Department of English, D.N. (P.G.) College, Gulaothi (Bulandshahar), C.C.S. University, Meerut, Uttar Pradesh.

Vibha Goyal. Reader, Department of English, Meerut College, Meerut, Uttar Pradesh.

Archana Trivedi. Teacher, Department of English, N.A.S. (P.G.) College, Meerut, Uttar Pradesh.

Malti Sharma. Reader, Department of English, N.A.S. (P.G.) College, Meerut, Uttar Pradesh.